ANCIENT ANTIOCH

ANCIENT ANTIOCH

By GLANVILLE DOWNEY

PRINCETON, NEW JERSEY

PRINCETON UNIVERSITY PRESS

MCMLXIII

GLANVILLE DOWNEY is Professor of Byzantine Literature at the Dumbarton Oaks Research Library and
Collection of Harvard University and author of *A History of Antioch in Syria from Seleucus to the Arab
Conquest* (Princeton, 1961), of which this book is a
condensation. His particular qualifications for writing
on Antioch are summarized in a review that appeared
in the *Middle East Journal*: "Professor Downey par-
ticipated in the excavations at Antioch (1932-1939),
which are the sources of our newest information; he
is an acknowledged expert on Libanius, who is a prime
literary source; he is master of the ancient literature
and modern scholarship on the subject; and of particular importance for the study of Antioch, he is
thoroughly at home in the field of Church history."

IN MEMORY OF

E. BALDWIN SMITH

PREFACE

THIS book has been written to provide, for the nonspecialist reader, a condensed version of my larger *History of Antioch in Syria from Seleucus to the Arab Conquest*, published by the Princeton University Press in 1961. The larger work, being intended primarily for the use of scholars, necessarily contained technical discussions and detailed examinations of uncertain or disputed points which are not of moment to readers without a professional interest in the subject. In the present volume this learned apparatus has been eliminated and only the conclusions of the scholarly discussions have been retained; but when the evidence or the conclusions are uncertain, I have always taken care to indicate this. The reader who wishes further information may consult the larger work. At the same time, all the important citations of the sources and of the essential bibliography have been retained in the present volume, so that the book is complete in itself. The bibliography represents a selection of the items listed in the bibliography of the large history.

There are, however, several respects in which this work differs from the large history. The Prologue and the Epilogue are both new. Chapter IX, "Pagan and Christian Traditions," contains material on the educational and cultural traditions of the city in the period of the early Christian Empire which was not included in the earlier volume because I have already treated this material in some detail elsewhere; and Chapter X, "Fair Crown of the Orient," is wholly new, and brings together material that lay beyond the scope of the large history. This chapter is an account of the mosaics and other artistic products of the city, and it includes a study of the famous topographical mosaic that represents an imaginary tour of the city in the fifth century of our era. This unique floor, one of the most precious documents of antiquity recovered by archaeologists, gives us a vivid picture of the city and its inhabitants.

The illustrations represent an attempt to reproduce some of the most characteristic and significant specimens of the mosaics found in the excavations, and examples of other artistic products of Antioch or its vicinity. The wealth of the material available has made it difficult to choose samples for this volume, and the reader who wishes to know more of the art of Antioch and its neighborhood will discover an abundance of material in the books listed in the selected bibliography.

Like every other city of the Graeco-Roman world, Antioch lived its own special life and made its unique contribution to Hellenic Christian civilization, and thus to our own cultural and religious heritage. The present work is an attempt to show, in small compass, how the life of such a city developed and what it handed on to future times. The modern American and European city as the focus of culture is at least in some respects like the classical city. Antioch is one of the classical centers of life and civilization in which the function of the city, the *polis* of the Greeks, can most instructively be studied.

The preface to the larger history records my thanks to the institutions and the individuals to whom I was indebted for support and assistance in the preparation of that volume. Among the institutions which assisted the writing and publication of the larger history, the Dumbarton Oaks Research Library and Collection of Harvard University of course takes first place as the work could not have been done without the facilities and freedom I have enjoyed as a member of the faculty there. I am also under obligations to the Institute for Advanced Study, the John Simon Guggenheim Memorial Foundation, Princeton University, the Ford Foundation, Yale University, and the Princeton Theological Seminary. I gratefully recall the names of the friends who helped in various ways in the preparation of the larger history: Alfred R. Bellinger, Sterling Dow, G. W. Elderkin, the late A. C. Johnson, Carl H. Kraeling, the late David Magie, R. P. René Mouterde, S.J., W. J. Oates, Albert C. Outler, W. K. Prentice, Marvin C. Ross, Henri Seyrig, Richard Stillwell, the late D. R. Stuart, C. Bradford Welles, Donald N. Wilber. Other friends have generously assisted the preparation of the present volume, and to these I am indebted for procuring photographs or for other kinds of help: J. Audiat, E. T. DeWald, J. Charbonneaux, S. Abdul Hak, Edward S. King, Jean Lassus, Sherman E. Lee, Doro Levi, Arif Müfid Mansel, Sawyer McA. Mosser, D. C. Rich, Miss Gisela M. A. Richter, J. J. Rorimer, and John S. Thacher.

As before, I am grateful to the Princeton University Press for undertaking the publication of this volume, and I am once more indebted to Herbert S. Bailey, Jr., Director and Editor of the Press, and to Miss Harriet Anderson of the staff of the Press.

The earlier volume was dedicated to the memory of Charles Rufus Morey, who organized the excavations at Antioch and was responsible for my own participation in the expedition and for my studies of the history of the city. The present work is offered as a token of my gratitude to another teacher whose generous encouragement helped shape my interests in the early stages of my studies.

G. D.

Dumbarton Oaks,
Washington, D.C.
March, 1962

CONTENTS

ILLUSTRATIONS

SOURCES AND ACKNOWLEDGMENTS

ANCIENT ANTIOCH

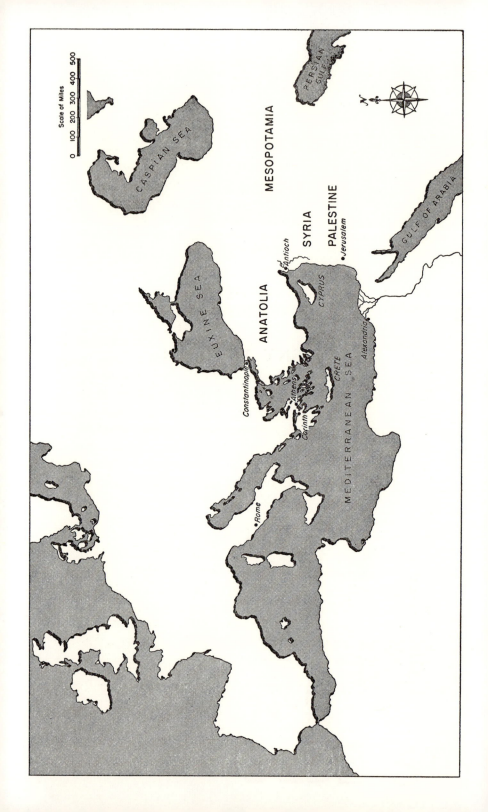

PROLOGUE

ANTIOCH IN HISTORY

IF a stranger ignorant of the history of the Moslem town of Antakiya in Syria had chanced to visit it a generation ago, he would have found little to suggest that beneath this sleepy, rather dingy town, part Turkish, part Arab, lay the ruins of one of the most famous and most beautiful cities of the Graeco-Roman world. He would have found remains of ancient city walls, of a Frankish citadel, of ancient aqueducts, the foundations of a hippodrome, a great rock carving of a human head and bust, a stone bridge of ancient lineage.

Still earlier, a century and a half ago, there was much more for a visitor to see. Some buildings had not been completely demolished by the steady plundering of ruins for building stone, and the Europeans who penetrated this far in the eighteenth and nineteenth centuries—and they had to be hardy travelers indeed to venture into the Syria of those days—found a whole series of ruins. They are preserved for us in the beautiful engravings of the well-traveled French artist Louis-François Cassas, who visited Antioch about 1785 (Figs. 6-11). They cast a spell upon generations of travelers and scholars—such names as Pietro della Valle, the learned Bishop Pococke, Carsten Niebuhr, Lady Hester Stanhope, Ernest Renan—a spell tinged with melancholy. For the traveler, whether learned or otherwise, the site of ancient Antioch was something quite different from the other great cities of the Graeco-Roman world, Athens, Rome, Alexandria, Constantinople. These cities indeed had never ceased to be known as the physical embodiment of the civilization they had molded and transmitted.

It was not so with Antioch. When in the seventh century Syria fell before the Moslem conquerors, most of the people of Antioch fled to other parts of the Empire, or to the West.

3

What became Antakiya survived as an isolated settlement, briefly prominent during the wars of Byzantium and the Moslems, and again during the Crusades, then for a long while little more than a village existing among the ancient ruins. But the life of ancient Antioch has been preserved for us in literature—Greek, Latin, Syriac—and it was here, while the city still lay buried, that its history was sought. From the histories, biographies, public orations, chronicles, personal correspondence, codes of laws, decrees of church councils—all the varied literature of the ancient world—one could recover something of the brilliance of ancient Antioch. The pioneer was the great German philologist Carl Otfried Müller (1797-1840), who in his study in Göttingen—it was still highly unsafe to travel in Syria in his day—worked through the ancient sources and the travelers' accounts and produced the first modern book on Antioch (*Antiquitates Antiochenae*, 1839), a work so well done that over a century later, though new information could be added to it, there was still little in it that needed correction. General Lew Wallace, when he sat down to write *Ben Hur* in the Governor's Palace at Santa Fe, used Müller's book as the source for his account of the topography of ancient Antioch.

The picture recorded in Müller's academic Latin showed Antioch as one of the cities in which ancient civilization reached its flowering. It was in its cities that the ancient world grew and prospered, and it was by means of its cities that the civilization was transmitted. Antioch had a special mission, first in transplanting Greek culture into Semitic Syria in the wake of the conquests of Alexander the Great, then as a vigorous Christian center in which Christianity and the Greek tradition were in time harmonized to form the new Christian Hellenic tradition which in turn was brought to a new fruition in Constantine the Great's new foundation, Constantinople, which as the center of Byzantine

culture preserved the Greek Christian heritage for transmission to the West at the Renaissance.

So it was that beneath the narrow winding streets of
Antakiya, lined with the blank walls of oriental houses, lay
the remains of a ruling city that was dominated in turn by
Zeus, Apollo and Aphrodite and by Christ and the saints.
The history of Antioch was made by the most varied per-
sonages and episodes. Apollo indeed was reputed to have
fathered the city's founder, Seleucus the First, the Conqueror.
The choice of the site was ascribed to Alexander the Great
himself. The patron goddess of Antioch, Tyche, became the
symbol of Good Fortune throughout the cities of the East.
King Antiochus Epiphanes, thought by some to be a mad-
man, by others a genius, organized one of the most magnificent festivals of the ancient world, with a procession including eight hundred young men wearing gold crowns, six
hundred royal pages bearing gold vessels, and two hundred
beautiful women sprinkling the crowd with scented oils from
gold vessels. Hannibal the Carthaginian visited Antioch to
seek help in his war against the Romans. The Roman governor Cassius here withstood a siege of the Parthians. Julius
Caesar, passing through Antioch during the civil war, endowed the city with magnificent buildings. Antony and Cleopatra sojourned in this beautiful spot.

It was in Antioch that St. Paul and St. Barnabas preached
in the streets, that the disciples were first called Christians,
that St. Paul planned his missionary journeys, and that St.
Peter was counted as the first bishop. Bishop Ignatius of
Antioch was considered so important as a martyr that he was
sent all the way to Rome to be executed by being eaten alive
by wild animals in the arena. Both Hadrian and Trajan
escaped death in one of Antioch's worst earthquakes—Trajan
conducted to safety, according to legend, by a supernatural
being who led him through a window of his bedroom.

When Roman control of Syria was challenged by the desert

dynasty of Palmyra, it was in a battle at Antioch that the power of Palmyra was finally broken, and the Palmyrene Queen Zenobia fled from the city at night, later to be captured and exhibited in the hippodrome at Antioch, mounted on a camel, and then displayed at Rome in a cage.

As first Christian emperor, Constantine the Great built the celebrated Great Church, the octagonal "Golden House," at Antioch, one of the most famous churches in the Christian world. The pagan emperor Julian, scholar, general, and energetic administrator, composed a witty satire on the people of Antioch, in repayment for their ridicule of his philosopher's beard. St. John Chrysostom, most gifted preacher of the ancient church, delivered his homilies in the cathedral and offered the terrified people comfort and encouragement after the great insurrection under Theodosius the Great. The learned empress Eudocia, daughter of a professor at Athens, passing through Antioch on a pilgrimage to Jerusalem, delivered an encomium of the city, seated on a golden throne in the senate chamber. Her graceful and courteous quotation from Homer was so applauded that the senate voted two statues of the empress in her honor.

Here was buried St. Symeon Stylites, greatest of the pillar saints, who had lived for thirty years on a column sixty feet high in the mountains east of Antioch. But paganism even in the sixth century was not dead, and it was possible for a Patriarch of Antioch to be accused of pagan sacrifices and dabbling in magic.

The history of the city was never characterized by moderation, and its last years came to a close with an unparalleled series of disasters. A devastating fire, two major earthquakes, a sack by the Persians, and a visitation of the plague, all within the seventeen years between A.D. 525 and 542, meant the end of the city's prosperity, and by the time the Arabs captured it in A.D. 637 it was not much more than a frontier fortress.

It is no wonder that the excavation of a city with such a history, and such a role in civilization, had long been a dream of archaeologists. Antioch remained the only major city of the Graeco-Roman world in which excavations had never been conducted, and it was a major event in the archaeological world when an American and French expedition organized under the auspices of Princeton University reached the town in the spring of 1932 and began soundings.

Although the outbreak of war in Europe brought the work to a stop in 1939 before it was possible to explore the whole of the site, the buried city did emerge once more as a living reality. As the results of the excavations became known to scholars, the fruitful interrelation of archaeology and literary tradition expanded our knowledge of ancient Antioch in every direction. The main lines of the topography were confirmed and clarified, the styles of domestic and public architecture emerged, and the successive stages of the expansion of the city plan became clear. But the major result of the excavations was the recovery of an extraordinarily handsome and extensive collection of ornamental mosaic floors from private houses and public buildings. Such evidence had been hoped for by the excavators, but the quantity of the floors discovered far surpassed expectations. Every aspect of life in Antioch was seen in a new light—art history, domestic life, intellectual and literary interests. A whole new chapter in the history of ancient painting presented itself. The life of ancient Antioch came before our eyes with a wealth of material, a richness of detail and a human charm not known for other cities of the Later Roman Empire. These floors, preserved in our museums, are some of the most precious relics of antiquity that have been preserved for us.

Just as, before the excavations, Antioch had been known chiefly through its authors, now the writings of the authors were themselves enriched as a result of the excavations. The Emperor Julian with his earnest philosophical and religious

7

writings and his acute satire on the pleasure-loving Antiochenes became an even more real figure when seen against the background of the figured mosaics of his era. The monumental history of Ammianus Marcellinus, the soldier-historian of Antioch, became more vivid through the new knowledge of the great public building program of the Emperor Valens (A.D. 364-378), of whose reign Ammianus was the chronicler. The orator Libanius, greatest pagan man of letters of Antioch in the fourth century and the first citizen of the metropolis in his day, left among his voluminous works an encomium of his native city which now, thanks to the confirmations of the excavations, becomes one of the most illuminating descriptions of ancient city civilizations that we possess.

So it is with everything found in the excavations. The mosaics with their pagan subjects furnish a new background for the sermons and didactic discourses of St. John Chrysostom. At the other end of the literary scale stands the local chronicler John Malalas, a not very well educated monk of the sixth century who compiled a history of the world in which Antioch played a leading part, now much easier to interpret and appreciate, for we can understand better Malalas' use of the local official sources. Antioch was fortunate in its native authors, and they have gained in stature—and in reality to us—as our knowledge of the city has revived and grown.

Antioch was founded where it was because of the strategic importance of the site, and it was in part as a consequence of its location that its history came to an end. But the physical disappearance has not been wholly irreparable. When a city is lost in this way it is through the labors of many scholars that it must be recovered—archaeologists, historians, philologists, art historians, architects. Inevitably some of the evidence—sometimes, indeed, most of it—has been destroyed by the passage of time and through the accidents of history.

The study and reconstruction of a city that has perished in this fashion is one of the most fascinating tasks a scholar can undertake. Literary sources, coins, inscriptions, mosaic floors, airplane photographs, chemical analyses, all are brought to bear; and if much has been lost, the ongoing city can nevertheless emerge. The past is part of the present—and through the present helps shape the future—and we come to realize that in its day Antioch played its part in the formation of our own world.

CHAPTER I

BEFORE ALEXANDER THE GREAT

In the Greek world, when a new city was to be founded, the greatest care was devoted to the choice of a site, for it was on the healthfulness, convenience, and safety of its location that the prosperity of the city would depend. Greek philosophers and city planners studied all these factors with close attention. Thus it was that when Syria became a part of the Greek world following the conquests of Alexander the Great (356-323 B.C.), the territory provided a site for a new Greek city that proved to be one of the finest situations in the ancient world. The whole history of Antioch and the development of its culture are a commentary on the natural advantages of its location and the happy choice that led Alexander's general, Seleucus Nicator, to build there in 300 B.C.

The neighborhood of the new foundation had long played an important part in the life of the peoples of that part of the world. In the geography of Syria, one of the principal factors influencing military and economic communications, in the northwestern part of the region, is the Amuk plain. Through it must pass all traffic between southern Anatolia and the coastal or western part of Syria and Palestine, and likewise all traffic between the northern part of Mesopotamia and the Mediterranean Sea. Fertile, well-watered, and enjoying a favorable climate, the plain attracted both nomadic and settled inhabitants, and in time it became densely populated and wealthy; today it is dotted with mounds formed of the ruins of ancient settlements. Commercial traffic through the plain flourished, and the successive powers that ruled this part of Syria established military controls there. The foundation of Antioch followed logically upon a long development of the region. Antioch was placed at the southwestern corner of the Amuk plain, at the point where the Orontes river, after flowing along the southern edge of the plain, enters a valley cut through the mountains, to continue its journey to the sea. Thus, thanks to its position, the city in antiquity controlled the network of roads, supplemented by the Orontes river, which passed through this region (Fig. 3).[1]

The site of Antioch is spectacular (Figs. 1-2).[2] The mountains which extend along the left bank of the river from the sea come to an end, at Antioch, in the magnificent Mount Silpius, which rises 1600 feet above sea level, the Orontes itself at this point being 300 feet above sea level (Fig. 3). At Antioch the Orontes, flowing from north to south, passes to the west of the city, which was almost entirely built on the left bank of the river and on an island in the river at the northern part of the city. The right bank, to the northwest and west of the city, was a flat plain which was not systemati-

---

[1] For accounts of the Amuk plain, see R. J. Braidwood, *Mounds in the Plain of Antioch, an Archaeological Survey* (The University of Chicago, Oriental Institute Publications, 18), Chicago, 1937, and L. Woolley, *A Forgotten Kingdom,* Penguin Books, 1953. On the road system of northern Syria in Roman times, see R. Mouterde and A. Poidebard, *Le limes de Chalcis,* Paris, 1945, with excellent maps. On the commercial routes, see M. P. Charlesworth, *Trade Routes and Commerce in the Roman Empire,* 2d ed., Cambridge, England, 1926, pp. 37-40; E. H. Warmington, *The Commerce between the Roman Empire and India,* Cambridge, England, 1928, pp. 18f, 35f, 86, 100; M. Rostovtzeff, *Caravan Cities,* Oxford, 1932, pp. 94f, with map on p. 2; C. G. Seligman, "The Roman Orient and the Far East," *Antiquity,* xi, 1937, pp. 5-30; M. Cary, *The Geographic Background of Greek and Roman History,* Oxford, 1949, pp. 169-172; H. H. von der Osten, "Anatolische Wege," *Eranos,* xlix, 1951, pp. 65-83, with map on p. 66.

[2] For a detailed description of the site, with numerous photographs and drawings, see J. Weulersse, "Antioche, essai de géographie urbaine," *Bulletin d'études orientales* (Institut Français de Damas), iv, 1934, pp. 27-79; also P. Jacquot, *Antioche, centre de tourisme,* Antioch, 1931, volume ii. Other modern views of the city are reproduced in the excavation reports, *Antioch-on-the-Orontes,* i-iii. Reproductions of old views, as well as modern photographs, may be found in Förster, "Antiochia," and in V. Schultze, *Antiocheia* (Altchristliche Städte und Landschaften, iii; Gütersloh, 1930).

cally settled; it was not brought within the walls in antiquity, and in the fourth century after Christ part of it served as a Campus Martius or military training ground. The road to Seleucia Pieria, the seaport of Antioch at the mouth of the Orontes, left the city by way of a bridge on the site of the present bridge (which incorporates some ancient masonry in its foundations), and followed the right bank of the river. Across the plain, to the west and north, ran the road to the Beilan Pass, Alexandretta, Cilicia, and the remainder of Anatolia.

The main part of the city, on the left bank of the Orontes, was built on relatively level ground between the river and the mountain. It formed an irregular oblong quadrilateral which varied in size and shape at different periods in the city's history (Fig. 5). Mount Silpius, stretching out roughly parallel to the river, confines the city on one of its long sides, as the river does on the other. From the short wall at the northern end of the city ran the road to Beroea (modern Aleppo) and to other parts of inland Syria and the south. From the southern end of the site the road to the suburb Daphne continued beyond it over the mountains to Laodicea-on-the-Sea, where it joined the road along the coast. Another entrance to the city, less used in antiquity, was at the Iron Gate (also known by its Arabic name, Bab el-Hadid), which stood at the ravine that divides Mount Silpius into two sections (Fig. 9). This was the terminus of a smaller and, for some purposes, shorter road that led to Apamea and to eastern and southern Syria; but this seems not to have been much used since it was narrow and, at the entrance to the city, precipitous.[3]

Towering above the city as if to shelter it, Mount Silpius offered a magnificent spectacle with its walls and citadel, and its massive and varied contours. On the side toward the city

[3] This road is shown in R. Dussaud, P. Deschamps, and H. Seyrig, *La Syrie antique et médiévale illustrée*, Paris, 1931, pl. 66.

the lower slopes of the mountain rose gradually from the plain, terraced in many places to provide sites for villas and public baths that commanded a sweeping view. After the first slopes, however, a steep rise gives the mountain the appearance of a huge wall. On the side of Mount Silpius away from the city the slope is everywhere more gentle, and it is possible to ascend to the top of the mountain from this side without great effort. As a result, a hostile force could reach the wall on the top of the mountain without difficulty; and if the fortifications were breached, the city lay at the mercy of the attacker. The Persians captured Antioch in just this way twice, in the third century and in the sixth century after Christ. Its vulnerability from the side of the mountain was the one drawback to the site; but evidently it was considered that the advantages of the location outweighed this hazard.

Through the break in the mountain marked by the Iron Gate flowed a winter torrent of great force, named Parmenios but also known colloquially as Onopnictes ("Donkey-drowner"). When swollen with winter rains, it ran down the slope of the mountain to empty into the Orontes. At other places the contours of the mountain led to the formation of similar but smaller torrents.

The position of the city below Mount Silpius created a special problem of drainage. During the rainy season which lasts from November to March, the enormous quantity of water which these rains sometimes precipitate in a few minutes cannot be carried off from the slope of the mountain by the various streams and ravines. As a result a heavy wash of loose stones, soil, and debris is carried down and deposited on the level part of the site between the mountain slope and the river. In antiquity such deposits were removed so far as possible, but in mediaeval and modern times the wash has accumulated and as a result the archaeological remains of the Hellenistic period are buried in some places to a depth of thirty feet or more.[4]

The Orontes today is a shallow and muddy stream, its bed altered and partly filled in by earthquake action. In ancient times it was navigable from its mouth as far as Antioch,[5] and the traffic on the river played a major part in the commercial life of the city. The original agora or market place lay on the bank of the river, and we hear of building materials for the original settlement being brought down the river on flat barges. The earthquake action that apparently raised the bed of the stream also filled in the arm of the river that ran between the island and the city proper, so that the island ceased to be such about the time of the Crusades.[6]

In ancient times, the suburb Daphne, five miles south of the city, was as famous as Antioch itself, and the city was sometimes (to distinguish it from the other Antiochs) called "Antioch near Daphne." The plateau of Daphne lies at a higher level than Antioch—the ancient texts speak of "going up to Daphne" from Antioch—and the road between them was lined with villas, gardens, inns, and all manner of pleasant places. Daphne was a picturesque garden spot, overlooking the Orontes (Fig. 3). It was made fertile and beautiful by numerous natural springs, which not only provided an ample supply of water for the local villas, baths and gardens, but furnished Antioch with a large part of its water, conducted to the city through aqueducts which skirted the lower slopes of the mountain. This abundant supply of water,

[4] See the observations of J. Lassus, *Antioch-on-the-Orontes*, I, p. 100, and W. A. Campbell's valuable description of the effects of a torrential rain witnessed during the excavations of 1938, with a photograph of the resulting flood (*Antioch-on-the-Orontes*, III, pp. 5f).

[5] Strabo, XVI, 2, 7, p. 751C; Pausanias, VIII, 29, 3; Libanius, *Antiochikos*, 262, cf. 265, translated by G. Downey, *Proceedings of the American Philosophical Society*, CIII, 1959, pp. 652-686.

[6] Förster, "Antiochia," p. 132.

still utilized today in modern Antakiya, was one of the principal reasons why Seleucus decided to build his city at Antioch (the area of Daphne itself is too small for a city). The famous local author Libanius, writing in the second half of the fourth century after Christ, embodied a classic description of Daphne in his panegyric of Antioch, which is matched by the scenes shown in the topographical border of the mosaic found in the excavations at Yakto, a modern part of the suburb (Figs. 45-59).[7]

In the same piece, Libanius describes flourishing suburbs all about the city, in addition to Daphne, and villas, baths, and churches have been excavated at various points without the walls, and sometimes at a distance from them.[8]

The terrain about Antioch and Daphne is varied, ranging from low hills and the slopes of the mountains to occasional plateaus and the flat plain of the Amuk region. In antiquity the hills and mountain sides were thickly wooded and the Amuk plain itself was forested at least in part.[9] Natural springs abounded, as a result of the presence underground of fissured calcareous rock that stored the winter rain. Where weak points in the rock occurred, springs were formed, as at Daphne, which flowed all year.[10] In the long, hot, and

[7] See Libanius, *Antiochikos*, 234-243; D. N. Wilber, "The Plateau of Daphne," *Antioch-on-the-Orontes*, II, pp. 49-56; and P. Bazantay, "Contribution à l'étude géographique de la Syrie: Un petit pays alaouite, le plateau de Daphné," *Haut-commissariat de la République Française en Syrie et au Liban, Bulletin de l'enseignement* (Publication du Service de l'instruction publique), XI, 1933-34, pp. 335-366.

[8] Libanius, *Antiochikos*, 231. A church was found at Machouka, along the road to Beroea (Levi, *Antioch Mosaic Pavements*, I, p. 368) and a bath at Narlidja, farther along the road (*ibid.*, p. 304). A tomb was excavated at Kara Bourk, near Narlidja (*ibid.*, p. 225). A Roman villa was excavated at Jekmejeh village, three miles west of the city on the rising ground at the edge of the Amuk plain (*ibid.*, pp. 28-34, 219). All these were chance finds, and more villas and settlements could doubtless be discovered if systematic search were made.

[9] Libanius, *Antiochikos*, 19, 25; Dio Cassius, XL, 29, 1-2.

[10] On the geology of the region around Antioch, see the studies of L. Dubertret, *La géologie et les mines de la France d'Outre-mer* (Publications

completely dry summer, the regularity of the water supply was one of the principal advantages of the site of Antioch and Daphne. Spring and autumn are brief.[11] The average annual temperature in the region of Antioch now varies between 59 and 68 degrees Fahrenheit, and the average annual precipitation in modern times is about 46 inches.[12]

A distinctive feature of the climate, in antiquity as well as today, was the wind which blew from the sea up the valley of the Orontes, from May to mid October. The wind began at noon and blew during the afternoon, evening, and night. By lowering the temperature and dissipating the humidity, this wind not only made life much more agreeable but favored the development of the summer crops by preventing them from being parched and scorched.[13]

The immediate neighborhood of Antioch, including the lower Orontes valley and the Amuk plain, was abundantly fertile,[14] and these regions, together with the suburban farms and truck-gardens around the city, supplied Antioch with a

---

du Bureau d'études géologiques et minières coloniales), Paris, 1932, pp. 362-377; "La carte géologique au millionième de la Syrie et du Liban," *Revue de géographie physique et de géologie dynamique*, VI, 1933, p. 303; "L'Hydrologie et aperçu sur l'hydrographie de la Syrie et du Liban dans leurs relations avec la géologie," *ibid.*, p. 357.

[11] See Libanius' description of the seasons at Antioch, *Antiochikos*, 29-33.

[12] C. Combier, "La climatologie de la Syrie et du Liban," *Revue de géographie physique et de géologie dynamique*, VI, 1933, pp. 319-346; idem, *Aperçu sur les climats de la Syrie et du Liban, avec carte au millionième des pluies et vents*, Beirut, 1945.

[13] Libanius devotes loving attention to his description of the breezes at Antioch, *Antiochikos*, 222-226. On the wind today, see Jacquot, *op.cit.* (above, n. 2), II, p. 349.

[14] E. Huntington's well-known theory of a change in the climate of Syria since antiquity, proposed in his *Palestine and its Transformation*, Boston, 1911, pp. 283-302, and summarized in his *Civilization and Climate*, 3d ed., New Haven, 1924, pp. 344f, is exaggerated. Huntington did not know the evidence to be found in Libanius. As a corrective to Huntington's statements, see the evidence for the climate in antiquity collected in a study of the now deserted parts of northern Syria by G. Tchalenko, *Villages antiques de la Syrie du Nord*, Paris, 1953-58, I, pp. 62-65.

variety of excellent products, though they were not able to fill all the city's needs.[15] The cereal crops were wheat and barley; the latter was regarded as an inferior grain, and in Antioch bread made from barley was eaten by poor people who could not afford wheaten bread.[16] Sowing of seed took place between the end of November and the end of December, as soon as the land, baked hard by the summer drought and heat, could be worked after the rains had begun. The harvest took place in May and June.[17] In the fourth century after Christ, at least, enough grain was normally grown to satisfy local needs; but a crop failure due to a drought could cause a famine.[18] Olives, olive oil, and wine were produced in abundance.[19] In such fertile ground, garden vegetables flourished. We are told that Antioch produced the best cucumber and we hear of the types of squash and pot-herbs which were common throughout the Near East.[20] Pulse (the edible seeds of beans, peas, etc.) is likewise mentioned.[21] The lilies of Antioch and its sister city Laodicea-on-the-Sea were famous, and the oil of lilies (also called "Syrian oil" in antiquity), which was in demand for medical use, was exported from Antioch.[22] Antioch produced a superior grade of oenanthe, picked from the wild vine, which was used for medical purposes.[23]

[15] Tchalenko, op.cit., I, p. 422, n. 3. On the products of Syria, see L. C. West, "Commercial Syria under the Roman Empire," *T.A.P.A.*, LV, 1924, pp. 159-189, and F. M. Heichelheim, "Roman Syria," in *An Economic Survey of Ancient Rome*, ed. by T. Frank, IV, Baltimore, 1938, pp. 121-257.

[16] Libanius, *Antiochikos*, 19, 23, and *Orat.* I, 8; Julian, *Misopogon*, 350B.

[17] Ammianus Marcellinus, XXII, 13, 4; Libanius, *Orat.* XVIII, 195; Julian, op.cit., 369A.

[18] We hear of several famines during the fourth century after Christ, the best known in the reign of the Emperor Julian (see the account of his reign below, Ch. VIII).

[19] Libanius, *Antiochikos*, 20, 23; Julian, op.cit., 369A.

[20] Athenaeus, II, 59B; *Antioch-on-the-Orontes*, III, p. 93 (fragments of graffiti on red stucco giving lists of foods).

[21] Julian, op.cit., 350C.

[22] Pliny, *Natural History*, XXI, 24; XXIII, 95.

[23] Pliny, op.cit., XII, 132f.

Various other sources of supplies came from the large domains of the upper Orontes valley and the plains of Beroea and Chalcis, as well as from the mountain region of the Belus, east of Antioch, which specialized in the production of olive oil, one of the principal products and exports of Syria.[24] Antioch partly consumed and partly assisted in the exportation of the products of these regions.

Wood for building and for fuel in houses, baths, and bakeries was taken from the thick forests around Antioch.[25] The cypresses of Daphne were highly prized, especially for building purposes.[26] The laurel was also grown in Daphne; the very tree into which the nymph Daphne was transformed, according to the legend, was shown there (Fig. 31).[27] The plane tree of present-day Antakiya appears to be represented in the topographical mosaic from Daphne (Fig. 54, No. 30).

Building stone, the basalt and limestone characteristic of this part of Syria, was quarried near Antioch,[28] but the finer marbles had to be imported. Though metal-working (especially in gold and silver) was an important craft at Antioch, there is no evidence that the metals were found near the city.[29]

Domestic animals were kept such as poultry, geese, pigs, sheep, and goats.[30] The catching of game birds is depicted on some of the mosaics found in the excavations.[31] A particular source of enjoyment and pride was the variety and abundance of the fish and shellfish available in the lake

---

[24] Tchalenko, op.cit. (above, n. 14), I, pp. 394f, 422-424.

[25] Libanius, op.cit., 19, 25.

[26] Libanius, op.cit., 236-238; Malalas, p. 204, 10ff; Procopius, Wars, II, 14, 5; Paulus Silentiarius, Description of St. Sophia, 524. The cypresses in the sacred grove at Daphne were protected by law (Cod. Iust. XI, 77).

[27] Eustathius' commentary on Dionysius Periegetes, 916 (Geogr. graeci minores, ed. C. Müller, IV, p. 378).

[28] Libanius, op.cit., 25.

[29] Athenaeus, V, 193D, quoting Polybius, XXVI, 1, 2.

[30] Julian, op.cit., 350B-C, 362B; Libanius, op.cit., 26.

[31] Levi, Antioch Mosaic Pavements, II, Pl. 23.

of Antioch (in the Amuk plain), in the river and in the sea; sea food apparently formed a major part of the diet of those who could afford it (Fig. 39).[32] The work animals of which we hear are the horse, the camel, and the donkey (Figs. 45-59).[33] Race horses were bred at Antioch, where racing was a popular pastime.[34] As late as the fourth century after Christ there were still wild animals in the mountains around Antioch, such as the lion, the tiger, and the fallow deer; and the ostrich and the hump ox are attested.[35] In antiquity, as today, there were scorpions and gnats. The famous wonder-worker Apollonius of Tyana set up a talisman, to drive them out of the city.[36]

Among the cities of the Graeco-Roman world Antioch was singularly blessed in its location and its natural advantages. Throughout its history it was known for its beauty and its comfort, and it was not without reason that Ammianus Marcellinus, the soldier and historian, who was born at Antioch, called his native city "the fair crown of the Orient."[37]

According to the local tradition of Antioch, before the time of Seleucus Nicator there were several Greek settlements on the site of the future city. These legends, preserved in the works of the Antiochene writers Libanius (fourth century after Christ) and Malalas (sixth century after Christ), have not yet been confirmed by archaeological evidence, and they

[32] Libanius, *op.cit.*, 258-260; Julian, *op.cit.*, 350B-C. A remarkably large number of the mosaics found in the excavations depict fish and shellfish of many kinds: Levi, *Antioch Mosaic Pavements*, II, Pls. 6, 31, 39, 41, 44, 50, 51, 62, 75, 152, 163, 182, 183 (see Levi's comment, I, p. 596).

[33] Libanius, *Orat.* L, 32; Julian, *op.cit.*, 355B, cf. 371A. Saddle horses appear in the topographical mosaic from Daphne (Figs. 46-47, 53, 58).

[34] Libanius, *Orat.* XLIX, 10.

[35] Libanius, *Epist.* 113 W.; see Dorothea M. A. Bate, "Note on an Animal Mosaic from Antioch-on-the-Orontes," *Honolulu Academy of Arts, Annual Bulletin*, I, 1939, pp. 26-31.

[36] Malalas, p. 264, 6ff.

[37] Ammianus Marcellinus, XXII, 9, 14.

have the sound of aetiological tales, though we do know that Greek traders were active in the neighborhood from early times.

The whole region has a very long history, much of which has been recovered only recently by archaeological explorations. One of the earliest records of the inhabitation of this area is the evidence of pottery, which shows a movement of peoples from Anatolia to Palestine via the Amuk route in the third millennium b.c.[38] This movement followed the north-south route linking Egypt and Anatolia, which has been called the "international highway," a route which Antioch in later times was destined both to profit from and control.

There is more evidence for the important traffic that passed between east and west across the Amuk plain. This has come in large part from the excavations at al-Mina and Sabouni, at the mouth of the Orontes, and at Tell Atchana (ancient Alalakh) and other sites in the Amuk plain.[39] Al-Mina was the harbor town of Sabouni; the two stood in much the same relationship as the Peiraeus and Athens. Alalakh was built on the road which ran inland from al-Mina and Sabouni. The archaeological discoveries show that these three places were all founded about 2000 b.c., if not earlier, and that Greek merchants lived at al-Mina and Sabouni from an early period. At this time northern Syria was occupied successively by Amorites, Assyrians, and Egyptians, then by Hurrians and Hittites. A very early Hittite building is a fourteenth century palace found at Alalakh. During all this period important trade was carried on with the west. Mycenaean and Cypriote

[38] Ruth B. K. Amiran, "Connections between Anatolia and Palestine in the Early Bronze Age," *Israel Exploration Journal*, II, 1952, pp. 89-103.

[39] L. Woolley, *A Forgotten Kingdom*, Penguin Books, 1953; idem, *Alalakh: An Account of the Excavations at Tell Atchana in the Hatay 1937-1949* (Society of Antiquaries, Reports of the Research Committee, 18), London, 1955; C. Clairmont, "Greek Pottery from the Near East," *Berytus*, XI, 1955, pp. 85-141.

Bronze Age pottery is common at al-Mina, Sabouni, and in the villages and towns of the Amuk plain, including Alalakh; and the products of Greece and the Greek islands continued to pass along this route down to the time of Alexander the Great. At first al-Mina and Sabouni were largely dependent upon trade with Cyprus, and the commerce with this island, which lay only sixty miles from the coast of Syria, must have been brisk; Mount Casius, at the mouth of the Orontes, is visible from Cyprus, so that navigation along this route was easy. In the seventh and sixth centuries trade was chiefly with Corinth and Rhodes; later Athens played the chief role.

A change came when the Aramaeans overran northern Syria in the fourteenth and thirteenth centuries, swamping the Amorites, Hurrians, and Hittites; and after the twelfth century Alalakh was deserted. However, al-Mina and Sabouni continued to flourish, and trade with Greece and the Greek islands was vigorous. It is at about this period that the local legends of Antioch put the arrival of certain Greeks, Cypriotes, and Cretans at the future site of Antioch.

Historically, the next great change in the region is its passing under the domination of the Assyrians, beginning in the ninth century. Here again a local Antiochene legend appears, in Libanius' story that the Assyrian Queen Semiramis built a temple at the place later called Meroë, five miles east of Antioch, in honor of Artemis, that is, the Assyrian deity, probably Anaitis, whom the Greeks would identify with Artemis.[40] The Semiramis of the Greeks was a legendary figure, famous as the builder of Babylon; she represents, almost certainly, the Assyrian Queen Sammuramat (844-782 B.C.), wife of Shamsi-Adad V, who after her husband's death acted as regent during the minority of her son Adad-Nirari III.[41] The story of her temple near Antioch appears only in

[40] Libanius, *Orat.* v, 42ff; *Antiochikos*, 59.
[41] M. Braun, *History and Romance in Graeco-Oriental Literature*, Oxford, 1938, pp. 6-13.

Libanius; it may be that the tale was a local Antiochene legend designed to provide a illustrious origin for the cult of Artemis.

Another relic of Assyrian rule near Antioch may be the place name Betagon or Bethdagon, which might have been named for the Assyrian god Dagan.

Jewish tradition, seeking to establish the antiquity of the Jewish community at Antioch, placed the meeting of Nebuchadnezzar and the Great Sanhedrin at Daphne, and attempted to identify Hamath and Riblah of the Old Testament with the site of Antioch. There seems to be no real basis for either tradition.[42]

Under Cyrus, Syria became a Persian satrapy and remained under Persian rule until the conquest of Alexander the Great. Libanius, after telling the story of Semiramis, goes on to describe the visit to the site of Antioch of the Persian king Cambyses (529-522 B.C.), who, accompanied by his wife Meroë, camped there in the course of his campaign against Egypt in 525 B.C.[43] The queen (who, Libanius says, gave her name to the place called Meroë) found that Semiramis' temple was ruinous, and she persuaded the king to restore it and increase its height, and she herself presented it with treasure. A festival in honor of Meroë was established, with resident priestesses, and in Libanius' day, in the fourth century after Christ, the temple was still standing.[44]

It was the Greek legends which were naturally much more significant for the people of Antioch, and these are recounted by Libanius and Malalas in detail. One was concerned with Io, the beautiful daughter of Inachus, king of Argos. Io was loved by Zeus and was driven from her home by Zeus' jealous consort Hera. In her wanderings, according to the local story, she came to Mount Silpius and died there.

---

[42] Kraeling, "Jewish Community," pp. 131f.

[43] Libanius, *Antiochikos*, 59-65.

[44] Libanius, *Orat.* v, 42.

Inachus sent his Argives, led by Triptolemus, to search for her, and though they did not find her, they were so struck by the attractions of the region of the future Antioch that they abandoned their task and settled on Mount Silpius, where they founded Iopolis.[45]

The next settlers came to the site when Kasos, son of Inachus, was moved by divine impulse to leave Crete and to bring the noblest of the Cretans with him to the region of the future city of Antioch, where they were gladly received by the Argives, and founded Kasiotis, at the acropolis on Mount Silpius. In time Kasos married Amyke the daughter of Salaminus, king of Cyprus, and the bride brought with her many of her people, who formed an important addition to the Argives and Cretans already settled on the spot. According to the legend as it appears in Malalas, Amyke when she died was buried 100 stadia (20 miles) from Kasiotis, for which reason, the chronicler says, the place of her burial was called Amyke. Of course the name of the Amuk region (a Semitic word meaning "hollow," "depth") is older than this legend; but it is interesting to see that tradition connected the Amuk plain with a Cypriote princess who ruled on Mount Silpius.

Another migration is supposed to have occurred when some of the children of Herakles were driven into exile by Eurystheus the king of Mycenae. The Herakleidae wandered in search of a home all through Europe and Asia, accompanied by many Eleans, and they finally chose the site of Antioch for their home and founded Herakleia, near the site which later became the suburb Daphne.[46] Finally, Malalas records

[45] The accounts of Libanius (*Antiochikos*, 44-52) and Malalas (pp. 28-30) differ somewhat; Libanius' is the more detailed, and is better designed for the glorification of Antioch. Strabo (XVI, 2, 5, p. 750C) also mentions Triptolemus' settlement at the site of Antioch. A mosaic showing Io guarded by Argos (an earlier episode in the story) was found in a house at Daphne: Levi, *Antioch Mosaic Pavements*, I, pp. 75-80, cf. p. 210.

[46] Libanius, *Antiochikos*, 56; Malalas, p. 201, 19ff.

that Perseus visited the Argives in Iopolis and built for them a Temple of Zeus Keraunios (Zeus the Thunderer).[47]

According to these legends, then, there were three Greek settlements in the region of the future Antioch. Iopolis (also called Ione) is spoken of as a *polis* or city, and seems to have stood on Mount Silpius. This settlement is said to have possessed a Temple of Io and a Temple of Kronos, both built by the inhabitants; a temple built by Triptolemus to Nemean Zeus, whose dedication was later changed to Zeus Epikarpios (Zeus the Fruit Bringer); and the Temple of Zeus Keraunios attributed to Perseus.[48] The other two settlements were Herakleia, near the site of Daphne, and Kasiotis at the acropolis on Mount Silpius. No temples in these two places are recorded.

These stories are typical of the legends of wandering heroes, which in ancient times grew up in connection with the foundation of cities;[49] obviously they were designed to help provide the people of Antioch with an illustrious origin. How much basis for the tales there may have been, we do not yet know; but it may be significant that the legends are in part associated with figures coming from Mycenae, Crete, and Cyprus, and that archaeological evidence shows that there were Greek traders who brought goods from these places to the Orontes valley and the Amuk plain. All this

---

[47] Malalas' confused account (pp. 37, 17ff) makes of Perseus the "king of the Persians" and (by confusion with Persian fire-worship) the temple he built is said to have been dedicated to "undying fire." The Medusa head of the coins of Seleucus I seems to be an allusion to the Temple of Zeus supposed to have been built by Perseus: E. T. Newell, *The Coinage of the Western Seleucid Mints from Seleucus I to Antiochus III*, New York, 1941, pp. 100f. A sarcophagus was found at Daphne decorated with the Medusa head and the head of Perseus: R. Mouterde, "Antiquités et inscriptions (Syrie, Liban)," *Mélanges de l'Université Saint Joseph*, xxvi, 1944-1946, pp. 40f.

[48] Libanius, *Antiochikos*, 51; Malalas, pp. 29, 15f; 30, 2f.

[49] For other examples, see A. H. M. Jones, *The Greek City from Alexander to Justinian*, Oxford, 1940, pp. 49f.

trade had to pass by the site of Antioch. While it might be expected that as a rule Greek traders in Syria before the time of Alexander the Great would remain in coastal towns, it seems by no means impossible that some Greek merchants might have pushed on beyond al-Mina and Sabouni and established themselves on the future site of Antioch. Antioch was the head of navigation of the Orontes, a day's journey by river from the sea,[50] and it was here that goods coming from the east could first be put into boats or on rafts to be carried down the river to al-Mina. Also the site of Antioch was an easy day's journey on foot for travelers going upstream; a messenger on foot, traveling rapidly, could make the round trip in one morning.[51] Likewise, the site of Antioch is approximately half way between al-Mina—Sabouni and the towns of the eastern part of the Amuk plain. Thus it is not difficult to believe that a Greek trading post and rest stop might have been established on the future site of Antioch. The tale of the Cypriote princess Amyke dwelling on Mount Silpius and then, after her death, being buried 100 stadia away, in "Amyke," especially suggests the connection between the site of Antioch and the plain.

After the various events, legendary and historical, which have been reviewed, we hear nothing further concerning the future site of Antioch until the conquest of Alexander the Great (333 B.C.). There were still Greeks at least in the neighborhood, for we know that al-Mina and Sabouni continued to prosper during the fifth and fourth centuries before Christ, and it was only when Seleucus the Conqueror founded Seleucia Pieria in 300 B.C. that the ancient port ceased to exist.

[50] Strabo, XVI, 2, 7, p. 751C; Pausanias, VIII, 29, 3.
[51] Libanius, op.cit., 41. In the reign of Diocletian, a body of rebellious troops took a day to march from Selucia to Antioch, stopping occasionally to plunder en route (ibid., 158-162).

CHAPTER II

THE CITY OF SELEUCUS
THE CONQUEROR

ACCORDING to the account of Libanius, the celebrated pane-
gyrist of Antioch, the plan for the foundation of the city
did not originate with Seleucus the Conqueror but with
Alexander the Great himself. After defeating Darius at the
battle of Issus, on the gulf of Alexandretta (October, 333
B.C.), Alexander moved on toward Phoenicia.[1] En route he
stopped at a spot east of the future site of Antioch where
there was a spring of remarkably sweet water beside the
mountain. Drinking this, Alexander exclaimed that it was
like his mother's milk, and gave her name, Olympias, to the
spring and built a fountain on the spot. Perceiving the beauty
of the site, Libanius goes on, Alexander desired to build a city
there, though of course he could not interrupt his campaign.
However, he made a beginning by founding a Temple of
Zeus Bottiaios, named for the Bottiaei who lived in the
region called Emathia, Alexander's homeland in Thrace. He
also established a citadel named Emathia.[2] Malalas mentions
a village named Bottia, which was on the level ground near
the Orontes where Seleucus later founded Antioch.[3]

The story of Alexander's visit and his declared intention
appears only in Libanius, and it may seem to have the sound
of a legend designed to secure for Antioch the claim to glory
enjoyed by the cities that had actually been founded by

[1] Arrian, *Anabasis*, II, 13, 7ff.

[2] Libanius, *Antiochikos*, 72-77, 87, 250. Malalas (p. 234, 11) records
the visit of Alexander but does not mention the plan to found a city.
Libanius mentions that in his own day the spring Olympias was converted
into a shrine. Malalas notes that the Emperor Tiberius built a public
bath near it. An anonymous epigram in the *Greek Anthology*, IX, 699,
purports to be an inscription set up at the spring to record Alexander's
naming of it.

[3] Malalas, p. 200, 14.

27

Alexander; every city in Syria would have been glad to boast of such a visit. Nevertheless there is nothing improbable in Libanius' account. The region of Antioch lay on a route which Alexander very likely followed in his march from Issus to Phoenicia, and the planting of a small colony and garrison of his Macedonian troops in such a strategic spot would be consistent with his actions elsewhere. It is not unlikely that Alexander, if he visited the region, perceived the possibilities of the site, and that the project for the foundation of a city there would have been formulated at that time in the minds of Alexander and his staff.[4]

About the foundation of Antioch we have fairly detailed information. After Alexander's death (323 B.C.) his generals divided up the territory he had conquered, and Seleucus, surnamed from his successes The Conqueror, eventually won Syria for his share. He proceeded to found, in the region which came to be known as the Seleukis in northwestern Syria, four "sister cities"—Antioch, Seleucia Pieria, Apamea and Laodicea-on-the-Sea—all named for Seleucus or for members of his family. The establishment of these four foundations—two seaports matched by two inland cities—represented a unified plan, and the archaeological evidence for the plan of the streets and for the size of the city-blocks suggests that at least two of the cities, Antioch and Laodicea, either were planned by the same architect or followed the same general specifications in their design. Seleucia Pieria, named for Seleucus himself, was originally the Seleucid royal headquarters and capital city in northwestern Syria, but before long Antioch eclipsed it and the other cities of the Seleukis. When these four cities were built, they formed a

[4] On Alexander's activities in colonization, see M. Rostovtzeff, *Social and Economic History of the Hellenistic World*, Oxford, 1941, I, pp. 130-134, 158, 472; A. H. M. Jones, *Cities of the Eastern Roman Provinces*, Oxford, 1937, pp. 238f; W. W. Tarn, *Alexander the Great*, Cambridge, England, 1948, II, pp. 232-259.

part of the practical Seleucid plan of colonization for military purposes, in which the establishment of cities inhabited by Macedonians and Greeks was to assure the domination of the new power in the conquered territory; and in this plan the four cities of northwestern Syria played a vital role.[5]

Seleucus won control of Syria by defeating his rival Antigonus at the battle of Ipsus in August, 301 B.C.[6] Antigonus had already, in 307/6 B.C., built a capital for himself, named Antigonia, five miles northeast of the site of Antioch, in a secure situation in a triangle of land bounded on the north by what was later known as the Lake of Antioch, on the south and east by the Orontes River, and on the west by the Arceutha river, which flowed out of the lake into the Orontes (Fig. 3).[7] The site was admirably suited for defense, and conveniently situated on the Orontes, but Seleucus would not use it as his capital. The foundation of a new capital would give him a prestige which the occupation of his defeated enemy's capital would not, and the destruction of Antigonia would be a gesture of power and magnificence which could hardly fail to impress Seleucus' subjects and rivals.

Seleucia Pieria, which was to be the capital, was the first of Seleucus' new cities to be founded.[8] The religious rites

[5] See the excellent discussion of the Seleucid policy in the foundation of cities by J. Sauvaget, *Alep*, Paris, 1941, pp. 34-36, with map (p. 36) of the new Seleucid cities in northern Syria.

[6] E. R. Bevan, *The House of Seleucus*, London, 1902, I, pp. 61ff.

[7] See the schematic map of Antigonia and its vicinity in P. Jacquot, *Antioche, centre de tourisme*, Antioch, 1931, II, p. 192. Traces of ancient buildings were found on the site in 1738 by the learned Bishop Richard Pococke during his tour of the East (*A Description of the East and Some Other Countries*, London, 1743-45, II, pt. 1, p. 188). Since Pococke's time the site has been cleared very thoroughly for agricultural purposes.

[8] The foundations of Seleucia Pieria and of Antioch are described by Libanius, *Antiochikos*, 85ff, 104; Malalas, p. 198, 23ff; cf. Diodorus Siculus, xx, 47, 5f. There is in addition an anonymous Arabic account of the foundation and construction of the new city, which, though it contains many of the conventional exaggerations and legendary tales characteristic

attending the foundation of a city were solemn and elaborate, for it was necessary to secure the favor of the gods, whose protection would ensure the prosperity of the city. Sacrifices had to be made both to the local divinities and to the deities under whose special protection the city was to be placed. In the case of a foundation by Seleucus, the special guardians of the city would be Zeus and Apollo, whom the king had taken as protectors and tutelary deities of himself and his house; indeed Apollo, in the official biography which had been developed for Seleucus, was reputed to be the king's father.[9]

So, according to the official account, preserved in the local chronicle of Malalas, Seleucus on the 23rd of the month Xanthikos (April), 300 B.C., ascended Mount Casius, which was sacred to Zeus, and made a sacrifice to the god, asking where he should found his city. In response an eagle, the bird of Zeus, appeared and seized the sacrificial meat and carried it to the site of Seleucia, thus indicating the spot where the city was to be built. Seleucus then performed the rites of founding and naming the city, and the archaeological evidence indicates that the residents of al-Mina and Sabouni were forcibly transferred to the new foundation.[10]

---

of such writings, may be based ultimately upon a factual record. The work is edited with an Italian translation by I. Guidi, *Descrizione araba,* pp. 137-161. A new edition, with English translation and commentary, has been prepared by William H. Stinespring (unpublished dissertation, Yale University).

[9] See A. D. Nock, "Notes on Ruler-Cult, 4: Zeus Seleukios," *J.H.S.,* XLVIII, 1928, pp. 38-41; M. Rostovtzeff, "Progonoi," *ibid.,* LV, 1935, pp. 56-66; idem, "Le Gad de Doura et Seleucus Nicator," *Mélanges syriens offerts à M. René Dussaud,* Paris, 1939, I, pp. 281-295; C. B. Welles, *Royal Correspondence,* pp. 108, 159, 183; J. Tondriau, "Souverains et souveraines Séleucides en divinités," *Le Muséon,* LXI, 1948, pp. 171-182; idem, "Comparisons and Identifications of Rulers with Deities in the Hellenistic World," *Review of Religion,* XIII, 1948-49, pp. 24-47; idem, "Bibliographie du culte des souverains hellénistiques et romains," *Bulletin de l'Association Guillaume Budé,* N.S., no. 5, 1948, pp. 106-125.

[10] L. Woolley, "Excavations at al-Mina, Suedia," *J.H.S.,* LVIII, 1938, pp. 1-30.

After completing the ceremonies at Seleucia, Seleucus, careful to sacrifice to the local gods, went to Iopolis to give thanks, and three days later, on the first of the month of Artemisios (May), he performed a sacrifice to Zeus Keraunios (The Thunderer) in the temple of that deity at Iopolis. Following this, Malalas continues, Seleucus went to Antigonia to sacrifice to Zeus on the altars built by Antigonus; and with the priest Amphion he asked the god to give a sign and tell him whether to occupy Antigonia, changing its name, or build another city in another place. Again an eagle appeared and seized the sacrificial meat, wrapped in flames, from the altar, and flew away. Seleucus put his son Antiochus on his horse and bade him follow the flight. The bird led Antiochus to the altar of Zeus Bottiaios. Here the eagle descended and placed the offerings on the altar, thus revealing that it was the divine will that a new city be built, and that this was its site.

Preparations were made for the new ceremony, and on the 22nd of Artemisios, in the twelfth year of Seleucus' reign, at the first hour of the day, as the sun was rising, Seleucus, with the priest Amphion, performed a sacrifice and laid the foundations of the walls at Bottia. He named the city for his father Antiochus[11] and at once began the construction of a temple to Zeus Bottiaios.[12]

The walls were built, and the streets outlined, by the archi-

[11] Fifteen other foundations of Seleucus were named Antioch. The ancient custom of using the same name in alternate generations of a family gave rise in antiquity to a lively scholarly dispute over the name of Antioch. Seleucus' father and son were both named Antiochus, and while many authorities maintained that the city was named for Seleucus' father (which would be in keeping with the custom in such cases), there were others who insisted that it was named for the son.

[12] As has been noted, Alexander the Great founded a temple to Zeus Bottiaios on the future site of Antioch. Probably the temple was really founded by Seleucus, and in later days a tradition grew up that it had been established by Alexander.

tect Xenarius.[13] The account of the laying out of the plan
of the city follows the conventional pattern of such events;
elephants of Seleucus' army were stationed to mark the sites
of the towers in the city wall, and the streets were traced
with wheat.[14] The size of the settlement did not fill the whole
site. Seleucus built on the level ground near the river in order
to avoid the wash from Mount Silpius. The settlement lay,
in an oblong shape, between the river and the road that in
Roman times became the colonnaded main street (Fig. 5).
The agora or market place, which is still the industrial and
commerical quarter of the modern city, lay along the bank
of the river.[15] The agora at Dura-Europos, a Seleucid military
colony founded at about the same time as Antioch, comprised
about eight city blocks,[16] and the agora at Antioch may have
been about the same size.

[13] In the Bonn edition, the name of the architect is printed as Xenaius
(p. 200, 21), but this is a misreading; the manuscript has Xenarius. According to Tzetzes, *Chiliades*, VII, 188, v. 176, Xenarius had three assistants, Attaeus, Perittas, and Anaxicrates, called "supervisors of the buildings," who later wrote accounts of the foundation of the city. In the
Museum at Beirut there is preserved a sculptured pilaster capital, made
during the fourth century after Christ, which shows a scene of the foundation of Antioch. On one side is a sacrificial altar beside which stands the
Tyche of Antioch, holding on her arm a small figure representing the
Apollo of Daphne. On the other side of the altar stands Seleucus Nicator,
preparing to sacrifice a bull. A Victory crowns Seleucus, and the eagle
of Zeus appears above the Victory's head. See H. Seyrig, "Scène historique
sur un chapiteau du Musée de Beyrouth," *Revue des études anciennes*,
XLII, 1940, pp. 340-344.

[14] Libanius, *Antiochikos*, 90. Some details of the account resemble the
tradition of the founding of Alexandria; see A. Ausfeld, "Zur Topographie
von Alexandria und Pseudo-Kallisthenes, I, 31-33," *Rheinisches Museum*,
LV, 1900, pp. 348-384, especially p. 381, and A. Ippel, "Ein Sarapisrelief in
Hildesheim," *Archäol. Anzeiger*, 1921, cols. 8f.

[15] Excavations could not be made in this area, but archaeological ex-
plorations show that the commercial quarters of modern Aleppo and
Damascus occupy the same area as the ancient market places; see Sauvaget,
Alep, pp. 47f.

[16] See F. E. Brown's study of the agora at Dura: *Excavations at Dura-
Europos, Preliminary Report of the Ninth Season of Work, 1935-1936*,
New Haven, 1944, p. 23.

Seleucus' city consisted of two separate quarters, one for the European settlers, the other for the native Syrians.[17] Each of these quarters had its own wall. The traces of walls preserved on the ground and found in the excavations, and the later development of the city plan, indicate that the quarter for the European settlers comprised about 370 acres, while that for the natives was smaller, being about 185 acres. Thus the two quarters together, ca. 555 acres, were less than one square mile (640 acres). Apamea, one of the sister cities of Antioch, occupied about 260 acres, while Laodicea covered about 543 acres.[18]

The analogy of other foundations of the period indicates that the city walls were built on a rectilinear plan.[19] Pottery found in the excavations shows that the area along the street which later became the main colonnaded street was a slum.[20]

Traces of the ancient streets are clearly preserved in the modern town with its surrounding fields and gardens (Fig. 4), and these show that the city was originally constructed on the gridiron plan, associated with the name of Hippodamus of Miletus, which was employed in many cities founded or refounded at this period. Recent investigations have shown that the arrangement of the streets at Antioch closely agrees with the city-plans of other Syrian cities, Beroea, Dura-Europos, Damascus, Apamea and Laodicea-on-the-Sea, all of which were either Seleucid foundations or Seleucid colonies refounded on the site of earlier cities.[21] The

[17] Strabo, xvi, 2, 4, p. 750C. See G. Downey, "Strabo on Antioch: Notes on his Method," *T.A.P.A.*, LXXII, 1941, pp. 85-95.

[18] See F. Mayence, "Les fouilles d'Apamée," *Académie royale de Belgique, Bulletin de la classe des lettres et des sciences morales et politiques*, ser. 5, vol. xxv, 1939, p. 333; J. Sauvaget, "Plan de Laodicée-sur-mer," *Bulletin d'études orientales*, IV, 1934, p. 111.

[19] Sauvaget, *Alep*, pp. 43f.

[20] See the report of J. Lassus, *A.J.A.*, XLIV, 1940, pp. 417f, and *Antioch-on-the-Orontes*, III, pp. 12-18.

[21] Sauvaget, *Alep*, p. 41; idem, "Plan de Laodicée-sur-mer," *Bulletin*

application of a standard plan is suggested by the fact that the city blocks at Antioch measure 367 x 190 feet, while those at Laodicea-on-the-Sea measure 367 x 186 feet (the difference in the short dimension presumably was caused by the circumstance that the site of Laodicea was a limited area with a special shape).[22] It would seem that Seleucus' four foundations in northwestern Syria were an example of what has been called "the mass production of new Hellenistic cities in Asia which took place under Alexander and his successors."[23]

The care given to the details of planning the city is reflected in the orientation of the streets. If the city had been mechanically laid out, the streets might have been planned in geometrical relationship with the river, with the long axis of the main thoroughfare running parallel with the river. Instead, the streets had no relation to the river, but were very carefully oriented with respect to the sun and the prevailing winds; they were laid out so as to take advantage of shade in the summer and sun in the winter, and the direction of the main avenues along the long axis was calculated so as to catch the regular breeze which blew from the sea up the valley of the Orontes in the summer.

Public buildings must have been constructed when the city was built and the Temple of Zeus Bottiaios, which Malalas says Seleucus built when he established the city, has been mentioned. There must have been other temples, public baths, and the necessary administrative and military installations, but we have no word about them. No record has survived of a theater, though it seems difficult to believe that one was not provided early in the city's history. How soon an

---

d'études orientales, VI, 1936, pp. 81-114; idem, "Le plan antique de Damas," Syria, XXVI, 1949, pp. 339-345, 356f.

[22] Measurements for the city blocks at Apamea are incomplete and there are none available as yet for Seleucia Pieria.

[23] R. E. Wycherley, How the Greeks Built Cities, London, 1949, p. 35.

aqueduct was built to bring water from Daphne to the city is not recorded.[24] A stadium existed at Daphne at least by 195 B.C. The analogy of other Hellenistic foundations would indicate that Seleucus built a citadel on the top of Mount Silpius.[25] It may be assumed that Seleucus, in addition to bearing the cost of the public buildings, granted the new settlers financial assistance for the construction of their houses, as well as providing them with building lots.[26]

Although the late writers who are our chief sources preserved only scanty information concerning public buildings, they were much more interested in the statues set up when the city was founded.

The best known was that of the goddess Tyche, the "Fortune" of the city. In the Hellenistic age, such a personification of Fortune reflected the current belief in a supernatural power which ordered the affairs of men.[27] When Antioch was founded, Seleucus commissioned the famous sculptor Eutychides of Sicyon, a pupil of Lysippus, to execute a statue of the Fortune of Antioch, and this may have been set up during the years 296-293 B.C.[28] Originally the statue was supposed to represent the good fortune that presided over the affairs of the people of Antioch, but from being a personification and a symbol, the Tyche, by an easy process, became a goddess, the protector of the city. The Tyche was also thought

[24] The anonymous Arabic account of the foundation of Antioch states that Seleucus I built an aqueduct to bring water to the city: Guidi, "Descrizione araba," p. 155. This source is so late and it exhibits so many dubious features that it is not clear how far it is to be trusted in such details.

[25] Sauvaget, *Alep*, p. 44.

[26] Such assistance on the part of Antigonus is attested in connection with the synoecism or joining together of the cities of Teos and Lebedos in 303 B.C.: Welles, *Royal Correspondence*, Nos. 3f.

[27] W. W. Tarn and G. T. Griffith, *Hellenistic Civilization*, 3d ed., London, 1952, pp. 316, 319, 340.

[28] Pliny, *Nat. Hist.*, xxxiv, 51; C. Robert, "Eutychides," *R.E.*, vi, cols. 1532f.

of as the guardian of the king, and in this capacity as well she would have been thought of as protector of the city.[29] The conception of Tyche, as it had been embodied in the statue of Eutychides, became immensely popular among the cities of the Hellenized East as a symbol of success, fertility, and prosperity.[30]

Eutychides' statue, which was to become the type of all other Tyche statues, was sculptured in bronze. It showed the goddess in her long robe seated on a rock representing Mount Silpius. With her left hand she supported herself on the rock, and in her right hand she held a symbolic sheaf of wheat. On her head a turreted crown represented the city wall. At her feet a nude swimmer symbolized the Orontes.

The marble statuette in the Vatican (Fig. 12) is probably the closest extant copy of the work of Eutychides.[31] The statue was set up under a stone roof supported by four columns. It was often represented on the coins of Antioch (Fig. 14, 16, 18),[32] and it appeared on souvenirs such as glass flasks

---

[29] Lily Ross Taylor, *The Divinity of the Roman Emperor*, Middletown, Conn., 1931, p. 32.

[30] M. Rostovtzeff, "Le Gad de Doura et Seleucus Nicator," *Mélanges syriens offerts à M. René Dussaud*, Paris, 1939, I, pp. 281-295. A list of the cities that placed the Tyche on their coins may be found in C. Bosch, *Die kleinasiatische Münzen der römischen Kaiserzeit*, Stuttgart, 1931, part II, vol. I, fasc. I, pp. 254-257.

[31] The statue is described by Malalas, pp. 201, 1f; 276, 6-9, and mentioned by Pausanias, VI, 2, 7. On the form of the work, and its later copies and imitations, see Jocelyn M. C. Toynbee, *The Hadrianic School, A Chapter in the History of Greek Art*, Cambridge, England, 1934, pp. 18, n. 1; 131-133; Gisela M. A. Richter, *The Sculpture and Sculptors of the Greeks*, 3d ed., New Haven, 1950, p. 295; Bosch, *op. cit.* (above, n. 30), pp. 253-258. The personification of Cilicia in a mosaic found at Seleucia Pieria is derived from the Tyche of Eutychides: Levi, *Antioch Mosaic Pavements*, I, p. 58; II, Pl. 9d. The Emperor Trajan later set up a copy of the statue in the theater at Antioch.

[32] L. Lacroix, "Copies de statues sur les monnaies des Séleucides," *B.C.H.*, LXXIII, 1949, p. 175; *B.M.C. Galatia etc.*, pp. 222, 225, 226, 229, 231f; Toynbee, *op.cit.* (above, n. 31), pp. 131-133.

and lamps which were manufactured for sale to visitors to the city.[33]

Other statues of special significance for the origin of Antioch were those of Zeus and Apollo, the founders and protectors of the Seleucid dynasty. Seleucus was officially identified with Zeus and his son Antiochus with Apollo. At Antioch, in addition to the cult statue in the Temple of Zeus Bottiaios, Seleucus set up a statue of Zeus Keraunios, "the Thunderer," in a temple that was attributed in later times to Perseus but was probably built by Seleucus.[34] This statue was sent from Antioch to Rome while M. Calpurnius Bibulus was Roman governor of Syria (51-50 B.C.).[35]

Two other statues commemorated events in the foundation. One was a stone eagle set up outside the city in honor of the bird of Zeus which had shown Seleucus the site on which the city was to be built.[36] In memory of this episode, an eagle was a favorite emblem on the coins of Antioch, not only in the Hellenistic period but in Roman times.[37] The other memorial of the foundation was an honorific statue of the priest Amphion who had assisted Seleucus in the sacrifices; this was placed outside the gate which was later called the Romanesian Gate, facing the open plain across the Orontes river from the city.[38]

To commemorate the destruction of his enemy's capital, and at the same time as a gesture of benevolence for the inhabitants of Antigonia whom he had brought to Antioch, Seleucus set up in the new city a bronze statue of the Tyche of Antigonia, who was shown holding before her the horn

[33] Gertrud Herzog-Hauser, "Tyche," *R.E.*, VII A 2, col. 1685.

[34] Malalas, p. 212, 2-4.

[35] The famous statue of Apollo at Daphne will be described below in the account of the foundation of Daphne.

[36] Malalas, p. 202, 6f.

[37] A. Dieudonné, "L'Aigle d'Antioche," *Revue numismatique*, ser. 4, vol. XIII, 1909, pp. 458-480.

[38] Malalas, p. 202, 19-21.

of Amalthia, the cornucopia. Like the figure of the Tyche of Antioch, this statue was sheltered under a roof supported by four columns, with an altar before it.[39]

The settlers who were transferred from Antigonia were Athenians by origin, and to provide for their accustomed worship Seleucus set up a great bronze statue of Athene, of the type called Athene Promachos, the goddess who had fought for her people.[40] The statue appears on coins of Seleucus I struck at Antioch (Fig. 15).[41] This statue, along with that of Zeus Keraunios, was sent to Rome during the governorship of M. Calpurnius Bibulus.

As a symbol of the union effected between the people of Antigonia, who worshipped Athene, and the subjects of Seleucus, who were under the tutelage of Zeus and Apollo, some of the coins issued at Antioch by Seleucus I show Athene and Apollo on the two sides of the same coin.[42]

For a sign of their gratitude to the king, the people who had come from Antigonia set up a bronze statue of Seleucus, with bull's horns added to the head.[43] This was an allusion to the king's celebrated feat of strength when he single-handed restrained a wild bull that had been brought for sacrifice to Alexander the Great and had broken loose from its ropes.[44]

Another episode in Seleucus' career was recalled by a statue set up by the king himself outside the city across the Orontes, showing a horse's head, with a gilded helmet near it. The event had become famous. After the death of Alexander the

---

[39] Malalas, p. 201, 5-11.   [40] Malalas, p. 201, 16-18.

[41] E. T. Newell, *The Coinage of the Western Seleucid Mints from Seleucus I to Antiochus III*, New York, 1941, pp. 96f; Lacroix, *op.cit.* (above, n. 32), p. 168.

[42] *Antioch-on-the-Orontes*, IV, pt. 2, Dorothy B. Waage, *Greek, Roman, Byzantine and Crusaders' Coins*, p. 3, nos. 1-7.

[43] Libanius, *Antiochikos*, 92.

[44] The story appears in several sources, e.g. Appian, *Syr.*, 57. For coins of Seleucus from the mint of Antioch which commemorate this exploit see Newell, *op.cit.* (above, n. 41), p. 101.

Great, when Seleucus became satrap of Babylon, Antigonus tried to do away with him, and Seleucus had to flee to Egypt to save his life. Later he was able to return and defeat Antigonus. The horse's head recalled the king's ride to safety and the helmet symbolized his final victory in battle. The group, Malalas writes, bore the inscription, "On this Seleucus fled Antigonus, and was saved; and returning and conquering him, he destroyed him."[45] A later source speaks of a place three miles from Antioch called Hippocephalus ("Horse's Head"), which is evidently the site of the statue.[46]

The inhabitants of Seleucus' city were gathered from a number of sources.[47] There were in the first place Macedonians, retired soldiers of Seleucus. There were also, if one is to believe the local accounts, some of the descendants of the Cretans, Cypriotes, Argives, and Herakleidae who had previously been settled on Mount Silpius. An important element must have been the Athenians from Antigonia who were re-settled in the new city.[48] There were also a number of Jews, some of whom were doubtless retired mercenaries of Seleucus' army.[49] There must have been a number of slaves, of diverse origins. Finally, there were the native Syrians who were assigned to their own quarter. Thus Antioch was a typical example of the Seleucid policy of settling Macedonians and Greeks at strategic points in the newly conquered territory in order to assure the security of the new regime.[50] In later times the people of Antioch seem

[45] Malalas, p. 202, 17-29. The horse's head appears as a counterstamp on coins of Seleucus; see Newell, *op.cit.* (above, n. 41), p. 97.

[46] Ammianus Marcellinus, xxi, 15, 2.

[47] Malalas, pp. 201f; Libanius, *Antiochikos,* 91f.

[48] Other inhabitants of Antigonia were re-settled in Seleucia Pieria: Diodorus Siculus, xx, 47, 6.

[49] Josephus, *Contra Apionem,* ii, 39; *Antiquitates,* xii, 119; *Bellum,* vii, 43ff. On the Jewish community, see the excellent account by C. H. Kraeling, "The Jewish Community at Antioch," *Journal of Biblical Literature,* li, 1932, pp. 130-160.

[50] The Seleucid policy is summarized by Sauvaget, *Alep,* pp. 34-36. There

to have taken more pride in their descent from their Athenian forebears than in their Macedonian origins.[51]

In the ancient world, population figures are notoriously scanty and unreliable, and Antioch is no exception. The local tradition, as preserved by Malalas, was that the number of Athenians whom Seleucus brought from Antigonia and the number of Macedonians who were settled in Antioch made a total of 5,300 "men."[52] On the analogy of similar figures elsewhere in the ancient sources, this would mean 5,300 free adult males, in addition to women, children and slaves, who would not be counted. The figure is interesting because it recalls the number 5,040 which Plato gives for the number of landholders and heads of households in the ideal city.[53] In the light of the standardization which has been observed in the city plans of the Seleucid foundations, the figure given for the size of the population of Antioch suggests that Plato's teaching concerning the ideal city was taken into account in determining the size of new colonies. The figure preserved by Malalas is comparable to the number 6,000 which the historian Polybius gives for the adult male citizens of Seleucia Pieria in 220 b.c.[54] We do not know what the average size of the family unit was at that time, but depending upon what would seem to be the minimum and the maximum in the ratio between adult male citizens and women and children, the total free population might have been something between 17,000 and 25,000—plus slaves and the native settlers, who would not be counted.[55] This might

is also a valuable treatment of the subject by M. Launey, *Recherches sur les armées hellénistiques*, Paris, 1946, pp. 331ff. On the composition and status of the native elements in such foundations, see V. Tscherikower, "Die hellenistische Städtegründungen," *Philologus*, Suppl. XIX, pt. I, pp. 190ff.

[51] Malalas, p. 211, 19; Evagrius, *Eccl. Hist.*, I, 20.

[52] Malalas, p. 201, 12-16.   [53] Plato, *Laws*, 737e, 740d-e.

[54] Polybius, v, 61, 1.

[55] See K. J. Beloch, *Die Bevölkerung der griechischen-römischen Welt*, Leipzig, 1886, p. 54.

seem to be a large population for a foundation such as Antioch.[56]

The suburb Daphne was always closely associated with Antioch, and its foundation was recorded in a traditional account as distinguished as that of Antioch itself. Indeed the natural beauty of Daphne, which made it one of the most celebrated spots in the ancient world, gave rise to a number of local legends, and the place had a rich mythological history of its own.

The original settlement of the site had been made by Herakles himself, according to one story, or, according to another, by the children of Herakles when they had been driven into exile by Eurystheus. Then, according to the local tradition, Daphne was the spot on which the maiden Daphne was transformed into a laurel tree to save her from the pursuit of Apollo (Fig. 31).[57] Other legends were connected with special aspects of the beauty of the suburb. A stream at Daphne was named for Ladon, the father of the maiden Daphne, who was supposed to have been the deity inhabiting the stream.[58] The cypress trees at Daphne, famous throughout antiquity, were connected with the youth Cyparissus, who was so saddened when he accidentally killed a pet stag that the gods in pity transformed him into a mourning tree.[59] One of the most celebrated local legends related that

[56] Tscherikower, *op.cit.* (above, n. 50), pp. 199f, concluded from his study of Hellenistic foundations that it is likely that cities such as Antioch did not usually possess more than 10,000 free citizens at the time of their foundation.

[57] Libanius, *Antiochikos*, 94. This must have been a favorite theme of local artists; it appears on a mosaic found in a house in Daphne (Levi, *Antioch Mosaic Pavements*, I, pp. 211-214), and there must have been other representations which have not been preserved. The story of Apollo and Daphne as told at Antioch differed from the versions current elsewhere; cf. Pausanias, VIII, 20, 2.

[58] Philostratus, *Life of Apollonius*, I, 16. A personification of Ladon appears on a mosaic of the Roman period in a house excavated at Daphne: Levi, *Antioch Mosaic Pavements*, I, pp. 205, 212f.

[59] Philostratus, *loc.cit.*

Daphne, rather than Mount Ida (the traditional spot) had been chosen, on account of its beauty, as the scene of the Judgment of Paris (Fig. 28).[60]

Fittingly, it was by divine direction that Seleucus was led to consecrate Daphne to Apollo. Libanius tells[61] how, after the foundation of Antioch, Seleucus once rode out to hunt at the place which was to become Daphne. Accompanied by his dogs, he approached the laurel into which the maiden had been transformed. "When he came to the tree, the horse stopped and smote the ground with his hoof, and the earth sent up a golden arrowhead." This proved to be inscribed with the name Phoebus, showing that it had belonged to Apollo. Libanius goes on, "I suppose that in his grief over the transformation of the maiden into a tree, Apollo had shot all of his arrows, and the tip of one, broken off, was hidden by the earth and preserved as a message for Seleucus, warning him to adorn the spot and to consider it a shrine of Apollo." As he held the arrowhead, a further sign was given to Seleucus. He "saw a serpent coming straight upon him, its head lifted in the air, hissing. But as the serpent came on, it simply looked at Seleucus mildly, and then vanished." As Libanius writes, this was a plain sign to Seleucus that the god walked abroad in this place. The king likewise recalled an oracle he had received from Miletus, in a time of adversity, which commanded him to make Daphne sacred to Apollo.

Seleucus proceeded to lay out a sacred enclosure in which he built the Temple of Apollo and planted the grove of cypress trees which were sacred to the god. The temple stood in the most beautiful part of Daphne, near the famous ever-

---

[60] Libanius, *Antiochikos*, 241. The Judgment of Paris is depicted on a painted glass bowl which, it has been suggested, may have been manufactured at Antioch some time between A.D. 250 and 350: see G. M. A. Hanfmann, "A Masterpiece of Late Roman Glass Painting," *Archaeology*, IX, 1956, pp. 3-7.

[61] Libanius, *Antiochikos*, 95-100.

flowing springs that provided pure water which was led in streams along the two sides of the shrine.[62] Libanius wrote that in Daphne, a spot free of troubles and noise, the Temple of Apollo was wholly set apart from care. No one could visit it without being freed from illness, from fear, or from sorrow. In the temple stood the famous statue of Apollo by the Athenian sculptor Bryaxis. The statue was acrolithic, that is, the extremities and exposed portions of the body were of stone, while the body itself was of wood covered with drapery or metal. Libanius writes that Apollo was shown playing and singing, holding his lyre in one hand, and in the other a golden vial with which, as he sang, he poured a libation on the earth. "My imagination (Libanius continues) places before my eyes the form, the delicacy of the shape, the softness of the neck in the marble, the girdle drawing together around the chest the gilded tunic. . . . Whose anger would not the statue lay to rest?" The god's hair and laurel crown were gilded, recalling his traditional association with the sun, and his eyes were two enormous violet stones. It was said that the statue was the equal in size of the statue of Zeus by Phidias at Olympia. We know its appearance from representations of it which appear on coins of Antioch (Fig. 17).[63] Bryaxis also executed a bronze portrait statue of Seleucus.[64]

[62] *Ibid.*, 98, 242.

[63] The temple and the statue are described by Libanius in his *Monody on the Temple of Apollo at Daphne* (*Or.* LX, 6, 9-11), which was written soon after the destruction of the temple in A.D. 362. See also Philostorgius, *Eccl. Hist.*, VII, 8. Further details are supplied by Ammianus Marcellinus, XXII, 13, 1. The sculptor's name is given by Cedrenus, I, p. 536, 11 Bonn ed. The work is mentioned also in pseudo-Chrysostom, *Hom. de S. Babyla contra Iulianum et gentiles*, 20. On the statue as a work of Bryaxis, see C. Robert, "Bryaxis," *R.E.*, III, cols. 916-920, and Gisela M. A. Richter, *The Sculpture and Sculptors of the Greeks*, 3d ed., New Haven, 1950, pp. 281-283. On representations of the statues on coins, see Richter, *op.cit.*, p. 281, with figs. 731f, and Lacroix, *op.cit.* (above, n. 32), p. 174.

[64] Pliny, *Nat. Hist.*, XXXIV, 73.

At a later date the temple is mentioned as being dedicated jointly to Apollo and Artemis.[65] When Artemis was added to the cult is not known; certainly there is no trace of her presence in the time of Seleucus.

The early history of the town of Daphne itself is not preserved. It was planned in the characteristic Hellenistic style with streets running in a quadrated pattern.[66] Its amenities must have attracted residents at once, and it soon became a famous and flourishing suburb. Beautiful in its own right, it was regarded as one of the special ornaments of Antioch. An easy walk from the city, it was a favorite resort of the citizens, and the wealthy built villas, private baths, and pleasure-houses there. Ordinary people could take their pleasure in the precinct of the Temple of Apollo, in the public baths, and in the restaurants and colonnades where refreshments and entertainment were offered. There was a large and fine theater, built to take advantage of the contours of the land. Hellenistic kings and Roman emperors spent their summers at Daphne, enjoying the water, the scenery, and the cool air. When the Olympic stadium was built, Daphne became the center of the local Olympic Games of Antioch, which rivaled those of Greece itself.

[65] This information is given by an inscription of Antiochus III dated in 189 B.C.: Welles, *Royal Correspondence*, No. 44.

[66] *Antioch-on-the-Orontes*, III, p. 28.

CHAPTER III

THE SELEUCID KINGS

FOR the years following the death of Seleucus, in 291/0 B.C., the sources for the history of Antioch are meager.[1] At the time of Seleucus' death Seleucia Pieria was still regarded as the Seleucid capital in northwestern Syria, for the king was buried there. When Antioch became the capital is not known. However, the city began to play an increasing role in Seleucid history with the accession of Seleucus' son, Antiochus I, and if it did not become the permanent capital at this time, it was frequently the royal residence.

While some details are not known, we are familiar with the main features of life at the Seleucid court at this time. The Seleucid government, as it eventually came to be centered in Antioch, was a personal regime of the king, modeled on the polity of the Macedonians who were the leaders in the formation of the new Seleucid state.[2] Power centered in the monarch, who conducted his affairs himself, with the help of a prime minister, who corresponded to the Persian vizier. The duties and powers of the prime minister might vary considerably, depending on the character of the king and on the influence which the prime minister was able to develop. It was possible for a prime minister to become immensely powerful and wealthy.

About him the king had his "Friends," *philoi*, a personal following, organized as a corps, wearing distinctive dress

[1] For the history of the Seleucid dynasty, reference may be made to E. R. Bevan, *The House of Seleucus*, London, 1902; A. Bouché-Leclercq, *Histoire des Séleucides*, Paris, 1913-1914; and the relevant chapters in the *Cambridge Ancient History*.

[2] On the Seleucid administration, see E. Bikerman, *Institutions des Séleucides*, Paris, 1938; Tarn-Griffith, *Hellenistic Civilization*, 3d ed., chapters III-V; C. Edson, "Imperium Macedonicum: The Seleucid Empire and the Literary Evidence," *Classical Philology*, LIII, 1958, pp. 153-170.

and insignia which were presented by the king himself. The special distinction of the "Friends" was that they had free access to the king and that they formed a council; they also accompanied him in war and went with him into battle.

Following the custom introduced by Alexander the Great, his cities, as a political gesture, paid the king worship, as to a god. Antiochus I deified Seleucus the Conqueror after his death. The Seleucids developed an official dynastic cult, which was brought into being at an early date and then was reorganized by Antiochus II or Antiochus III. The worship paid the king was primarily an expression of political loyalty, rather than of true religious feeling.

The Seleucids had adopted some features of the Persian administrative machinery found in operation at the time of Alexander's conquest, and the realm continued to be divided into satrapies, each governed by a satrap or by a satrap and a general. Probably Antioch, like other Seleucid cities, had a royal governor, *epistates*. Resident in the city, as capital, would be the high officers of the administration and the army, as well as the royal secretariat. The chief of the chancery, the royal *epistolographos*, was a very powerful individual.

In keeping with the character of the empire, there must have been a special group of officials charged with the maintenance and administration of the royal property and of the temples of the dynastic cult. One document illustrates the way in which such affairs were regulated.[3] This is the letter of Antiochus III, dated 12 October 189 B.C., on the appointment of a chief priest at Daphne. The document shows that all the sanctuaries at Daphne—not merely the principal shrine, the Temple of Apollo, but the others as well—were under the supervision of a single chief priest,

[3] This is an inscription found at Daphne by an American missionary in 1858, and sent by him to Yale University: Welles, *Royal Correspondence*, No. 44.

who was appointed by the king. Presumably the individual sanctuaries would also have their own special priests. The priest appointed by Antiochus III was a veteran of the royal army. His duties would not be onerous; but the king was evidently anxious to have the shrines of Daphne under the supervison of a man who could be trusted to administer this center which was of such unusual importance both financially and for religious purposes.

Probably later in the Seleucid period, Antioch had the political institutions of the Greek city or *polis*, with a council and a council-chamber (*bouleuterion*). The citizens were divided into tribes, of which there were eighteen in the fourth century after Christ. The non-Hellenic population was probably organized in corporate bodies (*politeumata*). These were quasi-political organizations, based on nationality, which were employed to provide political and administrative status for non-citizens of alien race. The members of the Jewish community at Antioch were organized in such a *politeuma*; those who wished to do so could doubtless become eligible for full citizenship by renouncing their faith and worshiping the city gods.

The Greek educational system was kept up with great care, as it was in all the new territory into which Greek civilization expanded during the Hellenistic period, and in a document of 246 B.C. (discussed below) we hear of the young men of the city undergoing the traditional training for citizenship in the gymnasium.

The founder's son and successor, Antiochus I Soter (281/0-261 B.C.), was so occupied by wars during his reign that he would not have had much time or money to devote to his cities. We do, however, hear for the first time of the intellectual activities that the Seleucids, like the other Hellenistic monarchs, encouraged at their courts. The Ptolemies in Egypt, the Seleucids, the Attalids in Asia Minor with their court at Pergamum, and the Antigonids in Macedonia, all maintained literary and artistic circles at their courts and thereby gave the intellectual world the most important support it received in those times.[4] The Seleucids, who never achieved the great wealth of the Ptolemies, did not found and maintain a splendid library and center for research such as the Egyptian rulers established in Alexandria, but they kept up their position by their patronage of scholars, poets, and scientists. The first such figure at the Seleucid court of whom we hear is the famous poet Aratus of Soli (ca. 315-240/39 B.C.), best known as the author of the astronomical poem *Phaenomena*, a technical treatise in poetic form, a type popular in those times. Aratus, who was the author of many other poems, had previously been at the court of the Macedonian king Antigonus Gonatas, but had left when Antigonus became involved in war with King Pyrrhus of Epirus. While he was at the Seleucid court, in the years 274-272 B.C., Aratus, at the request of King Antiochus, prepared a critical edition of the Odyssey, and he planned a similar edition of the Iliad, but this seems never to have been completed. Eventually Aratus returned to the Macedonian court.

In the reign of Antiochus II Theos (261-247/6 B.C.), both Antioch and Ephesus served as royal residences at different times. The reign was notable as the beginning of a period during which Egyptian influence was strong at Antioch. Antiochus for political purposes put aside his first wife Laodice and married Berenice, the daughter of Ptolemy Philadelphus, king of Egypt. Evidently it was understood that Berenice's issue should inherit the Seleucid throne. This marriage, which took place in 252 B.C., must have marked the beginning of close cultural and political ties between Antioch and Egypt. The relationship is exemplified by an episode described by Libanius, who tells the story not by way of illustrating the connection with Egypt but as proof that

[4] Tarn-Griffith, *Hellenistic Civilization*, 3d ed., pp. 269ff.

Antioch was so lovely that the gods themselves were eager to dwell in it.[5] Libanius relates that after the wedding of Antiochus and Berenice had taken place, Ptolemy of Egypt paid a visit to Antioch and was smitten with the beauty of the city's statue of Artemis—presumably the cult image which according to tradition had been set up by the Persian queen Meroë. Ptolemy was allowed to take the statue back to Egypt with him. The goddess was well cared for in Egypt, but she longed for her home in Antioch. She visited the king's wife with disease and revealed to the queen in dreams her desire to return to Antioch. So the goddess was restored to her temple and was given the name Eleusinia (according to popular etymology, "she who travels") in commemoration of the episode.[6]

Libanius tells of another incident that occurred at the same period, as a further illustration of the desire of the gods to dwell in Antioch. Some unidentified gods of Cyprus, who had always been honored in the island, were seized with a desire to migrate to Antioch. Taking the occasion of certain difficulties in Antioch, which Libanius does not describe, the gods impelled the people of the city to consult the Pythian oracle and then persuaded Apollo to declare that the only solution to the city's problems was the migration of the gods of Cyprus to Antioch. Libanius goes on to tell the picturesque conclusion of the story. "The king [at Antioch] sent to the island the men through whom he hoped to accomplish this migration. Then, since it was not possible either to carry the gods off openly or to tunnel into the temples secretly, they contrived the following plan. They said that they wished to fashion exact reproductions of the gods who were there.

---

[5] Libanius, *Antiochikos*, 109.

[6] One may detect in this story a certain parallelism with the accounts of Ptolemy III's taking back to Egypt from his campaign in the Seleucid kingdom (245 B.C.) images of Egyptian gods which had been carried off by Cambyses and the Persians; see Grace H. Macurdy, *Hellenistic Queens*, Baltimore, 1932, pp. 89f.

And when this was permitted, they worked at their carving lovingly night and day, while the priests remained at ease. The craftsmen carried the imitation to such a point of exactness that they removed the originals, and set the reproductions in their place, and embarked in the sight of the people of Cyprus, bearing off the originals, as though they were the new statues, and leaving, in the guise of the originals, those which had just been created by their skill. This success was not the result of the sculptors' skill, but of the gods' desire for the departure, for the sake of which they gave the craftsmen's hands more than their usual power." While we may not be prepared to accept this story literally, it must have had some basis in the introduction at Antioch of Cypriote cults or practices, possibly connected with the tradition of the migration to Antioch of a group of Cypriotes in the pre-Macedonian period. Some such connection is suggested by the fact that the type of Apollo seated on the *omphalos*, the hemispherical cult-stone in the temple at Delphi, which appears on the coins of the Seleucid kings, resembles the type shown on coins of Nicocles, king of Cyprus, struck between 320 and 310 B.C. It seems fairly clear that the representation of this type of Apollo at Antioch is a borrowing from Cyprus, evidently in connection with the oracle of Apollo which had been established at Daphne.[7]

[7] S. Reinach, *Cultes, mythes et religions*, 2d ed., Paris, 1908-1923, II, p. 354, n. 1; E. Babelon, *Rois de Syrie (Catalogue des monnaies grecques de la Bibliothèque Nationale)*, Paris, 1890, p. xlvii; L. Lacroix, "Copies de statues sur les monnaies des Séleucides," *B.C.H.*, LXXIII, 1949, pp. 169-175. Libanius, *Antiochikos*, 114, relates that the Egyptian goddess Isis migrated to Antioch in the reign of Seleucus II Callinicus (246-226 B.C.), but this story has been regarded as suspect and there is no other evidence for the introduction of Egyptian cults at Antioch at such an early period as this. Isis appears on coins of Antioch for the first time in the reign of Antiochus IV, ca. 168 B.C.: E. T. Newell, *Seleucid Mint of Antioch*, New York, 1918, pp. 25-27. In the Roman period Isis was popular at Antioch and important mosaics depicting her cult were found there: see D. Levi, "The Allegories

The death of Antiochus II in 247/6 B.C. was followed by a contest for the succession to the throne. Antiochus' first wife Laodice, who had been put aside in favor of the Egyptian princess, hoped to make her son (the future Seleucus II) king, while the Egyptian Berenice expected to secure the succession for her small son. Laodice, who had gone to Ephesus when put away by her husband, had powerful supporters in Asia Minor, while Berenice, who lived in Antioch, had her own circle of followers there.

When Antiochus died, an Egyptian naval force was dispatched to uphold the claims of Berenice for her son. The squadron occupied Seleucia Pieria without difficulty, perhaps by prior agreement. It sailed up the Orontes, and confronted Antioch with a foreign military force for the first time since its foundation.

The Egyptians were given an elaborate reception, described in an official report that may have been written by Ptolemy III himself.[8] The report states that the Egyptian ships set out from Seleucia with all the Egyptian officers plus the satraps and the generals whom they had found at Seleucia, except for those who were left behind on garrison duty. The writer took the time to note the beauty of the Orontes valley as seen from the ship, and recorded that the Egyptians were "struck with amazement" by the reception with which they were greeted at Antioch. They were met outside the gate of the city on the river bank by the satraps and the other high administrative officials and the chief military officers, as well as by the priests and the colleges of magistrates, all the young

---

of the Months in Classical Art," *Art Bulletin*, XXIII, 1941, pp. 258f, 270f; idem, *Antioch Mosaic Pavements*, I, pp. 49f, 163-166.

[8] This is the celebrated Gourob papyrus. A convenient edition, with bibliography of other publications, is that of M. Holleaux, *Etudes d'épigraphie et d'histoire grecques,* III: *Lagides et Séleucides,* Paris, 1942, pp. 281-310. A translation is supplied by E. R. Bevan, *A History of Egypt under the Ptolemaic Dynasty,* London, 1927, pp. 198-200.

men who were undergoing training in the gymnasium, and a great multitude of people. Crowned with garlands as a sign of rejoicing, and bearing the images of the gods into the road before the gate, they greeted the Egyptians with shouts and applause. The report continues,[9] "Though there were so many things [calculated to gratify us], nothing gave us so much pleasure as the intense loyalty of these people. When, then, we had sacrificed the victims presented to us by officers (?) and by private persons, the sun now verging to its decline, we immediately visited the Sister [Berenice], and after that attended to various matters which required our diligence, giving audience to the officers and the soldiers and to other people belonging to the place, and holding council on the general conduct of our affairs."

The succession thus seemed assured for Berenice's son. However, Laodice continued her efforts and eventually contrived to have Berenice and her son murdered in Daphne, where they had shut themselves up for safety. Berenice's devoted women buried her body secretly, keeping one of themselves in the queen's bed, and maintaining a pretense that Berenice had only been wounded. This fiction they managed to sustain until Ptolemy III, to whom word had been sent, came to Antioch for a second time with an army, not as a foreign invader, but to support the rightful heir to the throne.[10]

Ptolemy proceeded to take possession of all of Syria, and the Egyptians occupied Antioch for two years, 246-244 B.C. Many of the Greek cities, however, joined forces to drive the Egyptians out, and the youthful Seleucus II succeeded in occupying Antioch in 244 B.C., making the city his headquarters for his operations against the Egyptians. Seleucia

---

[9] Bevan's translation.

[10] Polyaenus, VIII, 50; Justinus, XXVII, 1; Jerome, *Commentary on Daniel*, XL (*P.L.*, XXV, 560); Valerius Maximus, IX, 10 ext. 1; IX, 14 ext. 1.

Pieria, by nature practically impregnable, remained in Egyptian possession until 219 B.C.[11]

Having already lost the original Seleucid domains, Seleucus II now found himself forced to abandon Asia Minor, which, after he had made it over to his younger brother Antiochus Hierax (236 B.C.), finally became a part of the Attalid kingdom. As a result of these developments, Antioch now became the principal seat of the Seleucid power, and to take care of the consequent increase in the population Seleucus II added a new quarter to the city. This was the island which lay in the Orontes, abreast of the original settlement of Seleucus I. A wall was built about the island, bridges were constructed, and the streets were laid out on the gridiron plan, the area being divided into four parts by two main streets which crossed each other at right angles in the center of the island (Fig. 2, No. 10; Fig. 5).[12]

Toward the end of Seleucus' reign Antioch was briefly the scene of a rebellion. This resulted from a plot made by Stratonice, the daughter of Antiochus I and sister of Antiochus II. Divorced by Demetrius II of Macedonia, she was living in Antioch. Stratonice schemed with her nephew Antiochus Hierax, the younger brother of Seleucus II, to overthrow Seleucus II and seize the whole kingdom. When the king was absent in Parthia, Stratonice raised a revolt in Antioch and Antiochus Hierax invaded Mesopotamia in order to harass Seleucus in Parthia. Seleucus, however, withdrew from Parthia and forced Antiochus out of Mesopotamia. He then recovered Antioch and executed Stratonice, who had fled to Seleucia Pieria.[13]

The brief career of Seleucus II's son, Seleucus III Soter (226-223 B.C.), was followed by the long and important

[11] Justinus, xxvii, 2; Polybius, v, 58.
[12] Strabo, xvi, 2, 5, p. 750C.
[13] Agatharcides in Josephus, *Contra Apionem*, i, 206 (*F.H.G.*, iii, p. 196, frag. 19).

reign of his younger brother, Antiochus III, the Great (223-187 B.C.). It was in these years that the fortunes of the Seleucid empire and of Antioch began to be increasingly affected by the growing power of Rome, which was inevitably becoming involved in the affairs of the Greek states in the eastern Mediterranean. As friction developed, Antiochus declared his position by giving protection to the arch-enemy of Rome, Hannibal, who visited Antioch in the summer of 195 B.C. to try to stir up war against the Romans.[14] In the inevitable conflict (192-189 B.C.) the new power in the West was victorious. The defeat of Antiochus at the battle of Magnesia (190 B.C.), followed by the treaty of Apamea (188 B.C.), marked the beginning of a new epoch in Seleucid history. The empire lost its military power, and the Romans exacted payment of a heavy annual tribute.

One immediate result of the war with Rome was a considerable expansion of the population of Antioch. At the end of the fighting King Antiochus found himself responsible for a number of veterans who were not otherwise provided for, and some of his supporters in Greece migrated to Antioch rather than remain in their homeland to suffer retaliations from the Romans. This influx of settlers, comprising, as Libanius writes,[15] "Hellenic stock, Aetolians and Cretans and Euboeans," was accommodated in the new quarter of the city on the island, the construction of which had been begun by Antiochus' predecessor. These settlers are the last Greek migrants to Antioch of whom we hear.

Before the defeat by Rome, Antiochus' reign was a period of increased royal revenues and general prosperity in Antioch. This prosperity was reflected in the heightened activity of the mint, and the coins of Antiochus III found in the excavations were far more numerous than those of any other Seleucid king.[16]

---

[14] Livy, XXXIII, 49.   [15] *Antiochikos*, 119.

[16] *Antioch-on-the-Orontes*, IV, pt. 2, Dorothy B. Waage, *Greek, Roman,*

In the reign of Antiochus III we hear for the first time of the public library at Antioch, though such a library must have been built very early in the city's history. Antiochus appointed to the librarianship Euphorion of Chalcis in Euboea, a well-known and learned poet who had a considerable influence in the intellectual world of that time.[17] Hegesianax, who wrote on grammar and history, and composed an astronomical poem, was one of the king's "Friends" and was frequently employed on diplomatic missions.[18]

Under Seleucus IV Philopator (187-175 B.C.), the son of Antiochus the Great, the Seleucid Empire had to adjust itself to the territorial losses it had suffered as a result of the war with the Romans. The economy was also seriously affected by the burden of the tribute paid to the Romans. Seleucus' monetary policy, as it has been reconstructed on the basis of his coinage, reflects the measures which were found necessary to reestablish public credit.[19]

If Antioch during the reign of Seleucus IV was preoccupied with economic readjustment, the accession of his brother Antiochus IV Epiphanes (175-163 B.C.) opens one of the most brilliant periods in the history of the city. One of the most remarkable members of the Seleucid dynasty, Antiochus IV possessed an energy, a vivacity, and a fertility of imagination which led him into activities that on occasion seemed to some people childish, to others insane. More active as a builder than any of his predecessors save the founder himself, Antiochus brought his capital to a point of luxury and magnificence that placed it among the foremost cities of antiquity.

Antiochus' buildings at Antioch and his displays of luxury

Byzantine and Crusaders' Coins, chart on p. 173. See Tarn-Griffith, *Hellenistic Civilization*, 3d ed., p. 143.

[17] Suidas, *s.v.* Euphorion.   [18] Athenaeus, IV, 155b.

[19] A. R. Bellinger, "The Bronze Standards of Antiochus III, Seleucus IV and Antiochus IV," *Numismatic Review*, II, no. 2, Oct. 1944, pp. 5f.

there were a part of the king's efforts to revive and strengthen the empire. To offset the diminution of the Seleucid territory, the loss of military power and the economic dependence on Rome, the king embarked on a vigorous campaign to unify his people by political, religious, and cultural bonds. He sought to strengthen the Hellenic religion and the ruler cult and to eliminate the separatist tendencies promoted by the religion of his Jewish subjects. As a part of this program he confiscated the property of the temples which (as in the case of the temple at Jerusalem) could be used to finance opposition or revolt. Antiochus regarded the ruler cult more seriously than any of his predecessors on account of its importance for his political program, and he spent much energy and treasure on the advancement throughout his realm of the cult of Olympian Zeus, the chief of the gods, with whom he identified himself.[20] The improvement of urban life everywhere in his empire was another means by which Seleucus sought to consolidate the diverse elements in his realm.[21] As a part of such a program, the enlargement and adornment of Antioch would enhance the prestige of the dynasty and win additional support among the people by whom Antiochus was immediately surrounded. One device by which the king sought to increase the loyalty of the people of his capital is shown in the coins minted at Antioch during his reign, which now for the first time bear both the name of the city and that of the king.[22]

Antiochus made himself famous by the regal magnificence

[20] See E. R. Bevan, "A Note on Antiochus Epiphanes," *J.H.S.*, xx, 1900, pp. 26-30, and Tarn-Griffith, *Hellenistic Civilization*, 3d ed., pp. 49f. On Zeus on the coins of Antiochus, see *BMC, Seleucid Kings of Syria*, p. 42, nos. 86f; E. T. Newell, *Seleucid Mint of Antioch*, New York, 1918, p. 28. One consequence of the added importance given to the cult of Zeus was the diminution of the cult of Apollo (Newell, p. 37).

[21] M. Rostovtzeff, *Social and Economic History of the Hellenistic World*, Oxford, 1941, p. 64.

[22] Newell, *op.cit.* (above, n. 20), p. 24; Babelon, *op.cit.* (above, n. 7), pp. 79-81.

of his benefactions to cities and the honors he paid to the gods—and not only in his own realm but in other cities of the Greek world, notably Athens.[23] In Antioch, his great beneficence was the addition to the city of a new quarter, named Epiphania for its founder. Evidently the new quarter was needed to provide for an increase in the population. Possibly the growth of Roman power in the East had impelled some Greeks to leave the lands which were now under Roman influence and seek out a city which was still free from alien domination. This extension brought the city to what was to be, substantially, its final form. It lay on the slope of Mount Silpius, adjacent to the original settlement of Seleucus which stood on the level ground near the river.[24] Thus the Hellenistic roadway that had run alongside Seleucus' settlement now bisected the city; this was the roadway which under the Romans became the colonnaded main street (Figs. 4, 5).

Epiphania was provided with an additional market-place or agora, so that like Miletus, Pergamum, and the Peiraeus, Antioch now boasted two agoras.[25] This was in keeping with Aristotle's recommendation that a city should have two agoras, located in different places, one a "free agora," kept clear of all merchandise and devoted to political and educational activities, the other an "agora for merchandise," devoted to commercial needs and located in the most convenient position for the purpose.[26] In Antioch, the "agora for merchandise" would continue to be the original one built by Seleucus near the river.

On the new agora Antiochus built a *bouleuterion* or council chamber.[27] This may have resembled the *bouleuterion* built

[23] Livy, XLI, 20.

[24] Malalas, pp. 205, 14-22; 233, 22ff.

[25] R. E. Wycherley, *How the Greeks Built Cities*, London, 1949, pp. 69-73; 78-80; Pausanias, I, 2, 3.

[26] Aristotle, *Politics*, VII, 11, 1-3 (1331a-b); cf. Wycherley, *op.cit.* (above, n. 25), p. 67.

[27] Malalas, pp. 205, 14-19; 234, 2f; cf. Libanius, *Antiochikos*, 125.

at Miletus in honor of King Antiochus by Timarchus and Heracleides, two wealthy Milesians who were influential ministers of the king. It has been suggested that the *bouleuterion* at Miletus was a copy of that at Antioch, or vice versa.[28] Antiochus also constructed a Temple of Jupiter Capitolinus, a token of the interest in things Roman he had gained in early life when he had been a hostage in Rome. This temple, the Roman historian Livy writes,[29] "had not merely its ceiling panelled with gold, but also its walls wholly covered with gilded plates." The chronicle of Malalas mentions "various other temples" which stood in the new quarter but does not record their names.

The expansion of Epiphania made necessary an increase in the water supply of the city, and Antiochus ordered the construction of a new aqueduct designed to tap the lively winter-torrent Parmenius (Fig. 5). The water diverted by the aqueduct during the rainy season was carried to cisterns placed along the terraced slope of the mountain. Two inscriptions in the cement wall of the channel of the aqueduct show that the work was done by the well-known Roman architect Cossutius, who was in charge of the work of Antiochus on the Temple of Olympian Zeus at Athens.[30] Possibly Cossutius also designed Antiochus' Temple of Jupiter Capitolinus at Antioch.

The magnificence of King Antiochus, and the wealth of Hellenistic Antioch, are famous from the description of the games which the king celebrated at Daphne about the year 167 B.C. The Roman general Aemilius Paullus, following

[28] This suggestion is made by H. Knackfuss in *Milet*, I, pt. 2, Berlin, 1908, p. 99; cf. W. B. Dinsmoor, *Architecture of Ancient Greece*, London, 1950, p. 297.

[29] Livy, XLI, 20, 9, transl. of E. T. Sage in the Loeb Classical Library.

[30] *Antioch-on-the-Orontes, II: Greek and Latin Inscriptions*, no. 90, p. 160 (*I.G.L.S.*, no. 825); cf. W. A. Campbell in *A.J.A.*, XLII, 1938, pp. 205f. On Cossutius' career, see Vitruvius, VII, praef. 15, and J. M. C. Toynbee, "Some Notes on Artists in the Roman World," *Latomus*, VIII, 1949, p. 310.

his victory over the Macedonians at the battle of Pydna (168 B.C.), had presented magnificent games to celebrate his victory, and Antiochus determined to outdo the Romans. Heralds and embassies were sent throughout Greece to invite the people to be present. Financial means were provided by the spoils of Antiochus' Egyptian campaign, by contributions from his friends, and by the property of the temples he had plundered.[31] The impression which these games must have produced may be gauged from the description of them by the contemporary historian Polybius:[32]

"The festival opened with a procession composed as follows. It was headed by five thousand men in the prime of life armed after the Roman fashion and wearing breastplates of chain armor. Next came five thousand Mysians, and immediately behind them three thousand Cilicians armed in the manner of light infantry, wearing gold crowns. Next came three thousand Thracians and five thousand Gauls. They were followed by twenty thousand Macedonians, of whom ten thousand bore golden shields, five thousand brazen shields and the rest silver shields. Next marched two hundred and fifty pairs of gladiators, and behind them a thousand horsemen from Nisa and three thousand from Antioch itself, most of whom had crowns and trappings of gold and the rest trappings of silver. Next to these came the so-called 'companion cavalry,' numbering about a thousand, all with gold trappings, and next the regiment of 'royal friends' of equal number and similarly accoutered; next a thousand picked horse followed by the so-called 'agema,' supposed to be the crack cavalry corps, numbering about a thousand. Last of all marched the 'cataphract' or mailed horse, the horses and men being armed in complete mail. . . . All the

[31] Polybius, xxx, 26, 9.

[32] Polybius, xxx, 25f, transl. of W. R. Paton in the Loeb Classical Library. The account is quoted by Athenaeus, v, 194; x, 439.

above wore purple surcoats in many cases embroidered with gold and heraldic designs. Next came a hundred chariots drawn by six horses and forty drawn by four horses, and then a chariot drawn by four elephants and another drawn by a pair, and finally thirty-six elephants in single file with their housings.

"It is a difficult task to describe the rest of the procession but I must attempt to give its main features. About eight hundred young men wearing gold crowns made part of it as well as about a thousand fat cattle and nearly three hundred cows presented by the various sacred missions and eight hundred ivory tusks. The vast quantity of images it is impossible to enumerate. For representations of the gods and spirits mentioned or worshipped by men, and of all the heroes were carried along, some gilded and others draped in garments embroidered with gold, and they were all accompanied by representations executed in precious metals of the myths relating to them as traditionally narrated. Behind them came images of Night and Day, of Earth and Heaven, and of Dawn and Midday. The quantity of gold and silver plate may be estimated from what follows. The slaves of one of the royal 'friends,' Dionysius, the private secretary, marched along carrying articles of silver plate none of them weighing less than a thousand drachmae,[33] and six hundred of the king's own slaves bearing articles of gold plate. Next there were about two hundred women sprinkling the crowd with perfumes from golden urns, and these were followed by eighty women seated in litters with golden feet and five hundred in litters with silver feet, all richly dressed. . . . When the games, gladiatorial shows and beast-fights, which lasted for thirty days . . . were over, for the first five succeeding days every one who chose anointed himself in the gymnasium with saffron ointment out of gold jars; of these there were fifteen, and there were the same number of jars with

[33] About eleven and a half pounds.

ointment of cinnamon and spikenard. On the succeeding days ointments of fenugreek, marjoram and orris were brought in, all of exquisite perfume. For banqueting there were sometimes a thousand tables laid and sometimes fifteen hundred, all furnished with the most costly viands."

In prosperous times Antioch was a center for the production of luxury goods and of gold and silver work, and the enumeration of the objects carried in the procession shows what the activity of the workshops must have been at this period. King Antiochus himself took a lively interest in the work of the artists at Antioch and he must have given them splendid commissions.[34]

One monument of Antiochus' time, the rock-hewn bust traditionally known as the Charonion, is still to be seen on the mountainside above the city (Fig. 13).[35] The head of the figure is veiled, and on its right shoulder stands a smaller draped figure (now much weathered) which appears to wear a *calathus*, a lily-shaped basket of a type carried in processions in honor of Demeter. Examination of the bust has shown that it was never finished. The story preserved by Malalas is that during Antiochus' reign the city was visited by a plague in which many people perished.[36] A seer named Leios, Malalas writes, commanded that a great "mask" be carved out of the mountain overlooking the city; "and inscribing something on it he put an end to the pestilential death. This mask the people of Antioch call the Charonion." No writing is visible on the preserved sculpture, but an inscription might have been destroyed, for the face of the bust has been badly battered and a portion of the chest is missing. Professor Elderkin believes that the name Charonion indicates that the bust was thought to represent a deity of the

---

[34] Polybius, xxvi, 1, 2, quoted by Athenaeus, v, 193d.

[35] See R. Perdrizet and C. Fossey, "Voyage dans la Syrie du Nord," *B.C.H.*, xxi, 1897, pp. 79-82, and G. W. Elderkin, "The Charonion," *Antioch-on-the-Orontes*, i, pp. 83f.

[36] Malalas, p. 205, 8-13.

underworld who had been appeased and had brought to an end the affliction which sent many souls to Charon.

Our account of the reign of Antiochus IV may close with a notice of the Jewish community at Antioch, which comes into prominence in connection with the king's conflicts with his Jewish subjects in Judaea. Judaea, previously under Egyptian rule, had come into Seleucid possession in 200 B.C. The Jews there were already divided into two parties, those who maintained strict observance of Jewish law and customs, and the "liberal" Hellenizers, who were willing to conform, at least in some outward matters, to the practices of the alien culture which now dominated them. When Antiochus IV came to the throne, he found himself involved in a series of factional troubles among the Jews which had originated before his time. The situation in Palestine put special difficulties in the way of Antiochus' program to unify his subjects. Factional fighting among the Jews was followed by rebellion, and Antiochus finally found himself forced into an outright attack on the Jewish religion. He plundered the temple in Jerusalem, carrying off the sacred vessels and materials to Antioch, and rededicated the shrine to Olympian Zeus.[37] Warfare between the government forces and Jewish nationalist bands led by Judas Maccabaeus continued until after the death of Antiochus, whose forces were too weak to defeat the rebels, and the king's attempt to integrate the Jews into a unified Hellenic state came to nothing.

All this time the Jews who lived in Antioch must have found themselves in a difficult situation, and the non-Jewish majority in the city can hardly have remained on friendly terms with them. The Antiochene Jews of this period lived in a quarter of their own near the southern end of the city, where there was a synagogue. There was also a Jewish settlement near Daphne. The former Jewish High Priest Onias III lived there after he had been supplanted by his brother

---

[37] I Maccabees, I, 20-24; cf. Kraeling, "Jewish Community," p. 146.

and rival Jason. In the course of a quarrel with Menelaus, a member of the faction that opposed his own, Onias took refuge in the Temple of Apollo. He was treacherously induced to leave the sanctuary and killed.[38]

Among the Jews themselves, Antioch later was sometimes reputed to be the scene of the martyrdom of the priest Eleazer and of the seven Maccabaean brothers and their mother, who were executed by Antiochus IV for refusing to abandon their religion; their tombs were shown in the synagogue Kenesheth Hashmunith, which was named for the mother of the Maccabees. The best evidence indicates that the martyrdoms took place in Jerusalem, but the story illustrates the prominence which the Jewish community at Antioch was able to claim for itself.[39]

After the death of Antiochus IV (163 B.C.) the Seleucid realm was never again to play a part as a world power. Rome was now the dominant nation, and from this time the history of the Seleucid house, and of Antioch, is one of steady decline. The meager sources for the most part yield only the bare outline of continual struggles for the throne among rival claimants whose resources were limited and uncertain. Antioch was repeatedly the scene of intrigue, revolution, and street fighting. For a short period (149-147 B.C.) Antioch and Seleucia Pieria joined together in a league in an effort to introduce popular rule, but the people evidently did not have sufficient strength to maintain this. About this time, in 148 B.C. and 130 B.C., we hear of the first of the earthquakes that afflicted Antioch throughout the rest of its history; this part of Syria lay in an earthquake belt and Antioch repeatedly suffered damage.

One violent scene, typical of many at this period, has sur-

---

[38] II Maccabees, IV, 33-38.

[39] See Kraeling, "Jewish Community"; J. Obermann, "The Sepulchre of the Maccabean Martyrs," *Journal of Biblical Literature*, LI, 1932, pp. 250-265; E. Bikerman, "Les Maccabées de Malalas," *Byzantion*, XXI, 1951, pp. 63-83.

vived from the reign of Demetrius II, who in 147 B.C. made his way to the throne by overcoming his rival Alexander Balas. When he was safely established, Demetrius made the mistake of discharging his native troops and retaining in his service only some Cretan mercenaries whom he had been employing. The people of Antioch sympathized with the discharged troops, and feeling against the king grew. Alarmed, Demetrius ordered the discharged soldiers to be disarmed. When those who had weapons in their possession refused to give them up, the Cretans tried to take them by force, and did not scruple to kill even women and children in the process.

Demetrius had appealed for help to the Jewish leader Jonathan, and three thousand picked Jewish mercenaries were sent to Antioch to support the king.[40] When they learned of the arrival of the alien reinforcements, the people of Antioch seized what arms they could and blockaded the palace, attempting to get the king in their hands. Demetrius sent out his mercenaries and the Jewish troops, and they were forced back. The Jewish soldiers, retreating to the roofs of the palace, hurled missiles down on the people, and fired the houses adjoining the palace. The citizens began to retreat before the rapidly spreading fires, hoping to save their own homes and possessions, and the Jews pursued them from above, leaping from roof to roof. When he saw that the mob was disorganized, the king sent his troops out to attack the citizens from the narrow streets. So many of the citizens were killed that the survivors speedily surrendered. The Jewish soldiers, evidently with the king's approval, plundered the city.

The ending of the revolt was followed by the punishment of the rebels and the confiscation of their property by the royal treasury. Syria was filled with citizens of Antioch who had fled their city in fear and hatred of the king and sought

---

[40] Josephus, *Antiquities*, XIII, 133-142; I Maccabees, XI, 44-53.

an opportunity to strike back.[41] The use of Jewish mercenaries also contributed greatly to the growing unpopularity of the Jewish community at Antioch.[42]

Such episodes were all too symptomatic of the history of the city at this period. Occasionally, however, there were times when a capable ruler was able to bring back a measure of order and prosperity for a brief period. Such was Antiochus VII Euergetes Sidetes (138-129 B.C.). An able man, Antiochus VII set out to restore the Seleucid power, and made substantial progress. The accounts of his luxurious mode of living, though doubtless exaggerated, indicate that some degree of prosperity had been recovered.[43] By the year 130 B.C. the king considered that he was in a position to undertake the reconquest of the lost Seleucid possessions in the East, but he was defeated by the Parthian army and killed. His soldiers were slain or made captive, and as the news was brought back every house in Antioch was filled with mourning.[44]

The death of Antiochus VII, the last able king of the line, marked the end of the Seleucid dynasty as an effective force. From this time until the occupation of Syria by the Romans in 64 B.C., the history of Syria, and of Antioch, is a depressing record of growing weakness and dissolution.[45] There were continual struggles for the throne between legitimate members of the Seleucid dynasty and usurpers. Characteristic of these contests was a sordid episode (123/22 B.C.) which occurred when one of the pretenders, Alexander Zabinas, found himself in need of funds with which to maintain himself in power. He removed from the Temple of

---

[41] Josephus, *Antiquities*, XIII, 142; Diodorus Siculus, XXXIII, 4, 3f.

[42] Kraeling, "Jewish Community," pp. 146f.

[43] Athenaeus, v, 210d; Justinus, XXXVIII, 10.

[44] Diodorus Siculus, XXXIV, 17.

[45] The best account of this period is that of A. R. Bellinger, "The End of the Seleucids," *Transactions of the Connecticut Academy of Arts and Sciences*, XXXVIII, 1949, pp. 51-102.

Zeus the solid gold image of Victory which the statue of
Zeus was holding, excusing the sacrilege by saying jokingly
that "Victory had been offered to him by Zeus." This was
the statue of Zeus set up by Antiochus IV. A few days later
it was discovered that Alexander was secretly attempting
to have the huge golden statue of Zeus himself removed
from the temple, and the people gathered quickly to prevent
this desecration. Alexander collected the royal treasure and
fled at night toward Seleucia Pieria. The news of his sacrilege
preceded him and the gates were shut against him. Setting
out along the coast toward Posidium, he was overtaken by
a great storm. His attendants deserted him, and he fell into
the hands of brigands, who took him to the camp of the
legitimate king, Antiochus VIII. Here he was executed—or,
according to one account, allowed to commit suicide.[46]

In the barren history of the city in these days we get some
glimpses of its intellectual life. The celebrated Greek poet
Archias, later to be a client of Cicero, was born in Antioch
in the latter part of the second century B.C. Cicero wrote
that Antioch, at the time when Archias grew up there and
gained a distinguished place for himself by his intellectual
gifts, was "a renowned and populous city, the seat of brilliant
scholarship and artistic refinement."[47] At some time between
114 B.C and 92 B.C. a Museum with a library was built with
money left in his will by a merchant of Antioch named
Maron, who had settled in Athens and, like other Syrian
businessmen who had gone abroad, left to his native city
some of the money he had made in commerce.[48] The Museum
and library were built on the new agora in Epiphania. They

---

[46] Justinus, xxxix, 2, 5f; Diodorus Siculus, xxxiv, 28; Josephus, *Antiquities*, xiii, 269; Eusebius, *Chronicle*, i, pp. 257f ed. Schoene. A somewhat similar story of the purloining of a gold statue is told of Antiochus IX Cyzicenus (114-95 B.C.); cf. Clement of Alexandria, *Protrepticus*, iv, 52, 3.

[47] Cicero, *Pro Archia*, 4, transl. of N. H. Watts in the Loeb Classical Library.

[48] Malalas, p. 235, 18ff.

were destroyed by the fire that ruined this agora in A.D. 23/4.

From this period there also survives one token of the commercial relations between Antioch and the western lands, in the form of a Greek dedication in honor of the city of Antioch set up at Delos, soon after 88 B.C., by one Lucius Granius.[49] The dedication consisted of a small inscribed altar which bore a statuette; the altar has been preserved but the figure is lost. From his name, Lucius Granius could have been either a Roman merchant or a freedman of Syrian origin, and the dedication was made either because he was a native of Antioch or was bound by intimate ties to the city. The offering illustrates the close connections that must have existed between Antioch and the free port of Delos, which for some years had been serving as the principal commercial link between the eastern Mediterranean and Italy. While the dedication of Lucius Granius is the only surviving one concerning Antioch, we know that many Roman and Syrian merchants lived at Delos, and the commercial relations between this center and Antioch must have been extensive.[50]

In the twelve years between 96 B.C. and 84 B.C. there were six kings of Syria, and on two occasions there were two kings reigning—or claiming to reign—at the same time. The resources of the contestants must have been exhausted, and it is not surprising to read[51] that the people of Syria began to think of turning to outside help in the hope that some foreign king might be able to restore order and security, and keep the land from being invaded and pillaged. Among the various possibilities the final choice was Tigranes of Armenia.

The accounts of Tigranes' occupation of Syria differ. Ac-

---

[49] J. Hatzfeld, "Les italiens résidants à Délos," *B.C.H.*, XXXVI, 1912, p. 40, no. 6, and pp. 212-214, no. 34 (*Inscriptions de Délos*, no. 2355, cf. no. 2612).

[50] On the Roman and Syrian traders at Delos, see Rostovtzeff, *op.cit.* (above, n. 21), pp. 702, 741f, 778, 787ff, 791.

[51] Justinus, XL, I, 1-4.

cording to one tradition[52] Tigranes came peacefully, by invitation, and his reign was tranquil and prosperous. Other sources, however, speak of a conquest by force.[53] Probably the oriental elements in the population, plus those of Greek descent who were weary of Seleucid rule, summoned and supported the Armenian prince, while he inevitably met opposition in some quarters as a foreign usurper. Certainly Tigranes could not have taken over the rule of Syria as he did without the approval of an important part of the population. Economically, the country was in a very poor state; Tigranes when he arrived found currency so scarce that some of the bronze coins had been in circulation in Antioch for forty years.[54] Any change in leadership might have seemed welcome.

Tigranes' viceroy for the fourteen years during which he ruled the country (83-69 B.C.) was his general Magadates, who presumably made his headquarters at Antioch.[55] The mint of the city began to issue coins in the name of Tigranes as *basileus*, "king," suggesting that Tigranes at first was careful to present himself as a Hellenic ruler, or as a successor to Hellenic rulers. At the same time, the Tyche of Antioch, as portrayed by Eutychides, appeared on the coins, for the first time in the history of the city (Fig. 14). Later, however, the coins began to bear the oriental title "king of kings," and Tigranes became "pompous and haughty in the midst of his great prosperity" and began to observe the ceremonial of an oriental court.[56] The autonomous cur-

---

[52] Justinius, XL, 1, 2—2, 1.

[53] Appian, *Syr.*, 48; Strabo, XI, 14, 15, p. 532C; XVI, 2, 8, p. 751C; Eutropius, VI, 14, 2; Josephus, *Antiquities*, XIII, 419.

[54] *Excavations at Dura-Europos, Final Report*, VI: A. R. Bellinger, *The Coins*, New Haven, 1949, p. 114, nos. 112, 112a.

[55] Appian, *Syr.*, 48f.

[56] Plutarch, *Lucullus*, XXI, 3, transl. of B. Perrin in the Loeb Classical Library; G. Macdonald, "The Coinage of Tigranes I," *Numismatic Chronicle*, ser. 4, vol. II, 1902, pp. 193-201.

rency issued by the mint of Antioch disappears in 72 B.C., an indication that by this time Tigranes had abandoned whatever pretence he may once have made of observing the forms of Hellenic government, and had finally converted his rule to an oriental despotism. The regime of the deliverer at last became "intolerably grievous" to the Greeks.[57] An earthquake occurring at about this time was interpreted as a portent of coming disaster.[58]

An opportunity for a change presented itself. Rome had been at war with Mithradates of Pontus, and in 72 B.C. the Roman commander Lucullus had forced Mithradates to take refuge in Armenia under the protection of Tigranes. In an effort to put an end to the war, Lucullus sent his brother-in-law Appius Clodius Pulcher to Antioch to demand that Tigranes hand Mithradates over to the Romans. Tigranes happened to be absent in Phoenicia engaged in operations against Cleopatra Selene, who was attempting to place her son Antiochus (the son of Antiochus X) on the throne. Clodius waited in Antioch for the return of Tigranes and took the opportunity to intrigue with the dissatisfied element in the population both in Antioch and in other cities, which sent representatives to him secretly. Clodius promised the assistance of Lucullus against Tigranes. Tigranes when he returned refused to surrender Mithradates and this amounted to a declaration of war.[59] Tigranes set out to defend Armenia and the Armenian government and its forces withdrew from Syria. Lucullus invaded Armenia and defeated Tigranes (69 B.C.).

When Tigranes left Syria, Antiochus the son of Antiochus X set himself up as Antiochus XIII Asiaticus, with the support of Lucullus and the consent of the people of Antioch.[60]

---

[57] Plutarch, *Lucullus*, XXI, 3. [58] Justinus, XL, 2, I.

[59] Plutarch, *Lucullus*, XXI, 7; Josephus, *Antiquities*, XIII, 419-421.

[60] Appian, *Syr.*, 49; Justinus, XL, 2, 2 (who says that Antiochus XIII was called to the throne by Lucullus).

Antiochus reigned at Antioch in 69/8 B.C. He was defeated in a battle the details of which are not known, though it was probably with one of the Arab chieftains who from time to time in this unsettled period attempted to establish principalities for themselves in this region. This defeat provided the occasion for a revolution in Antioch. The king managed to remain in power, but the leaders of the rebellion escaped and joined forces with another claimant to the throne, Philip II, son of Philip I; and the Arab chief Aziz undertook to place Philip II on the throne. Antiochus XIII for his part obtained the support of another Arab chieftain, Sampsigeramus. The two Arabs, however, made a private agreement to dispose of the two weak Seleucid rivals and divide the kingdom between themselves. Sampsigeramus captured Antiochus, but Philip heard of the plan of Aziz in time to escape to Antioch, where he would be safe.[61]

By this time it was clear to the Roman government that the Seleucid princes could not hope to maintain order in the northwestern corner of Syria, around Antioch, which was serving as a refuge for the Cilician pirates, and it was plain that if the pirates were to be suppressed, the Romans must have some control of this region.[62] The Roman government hesitated to annex Syria at this time, and instead tried the experiment of supporting the Seleucid ruler as a client king, and it was in this status that Philip II reigned in Antioch 67-65 B.C. In 67 B.C. Q. Marcius Rex, the governor of the province of Cilicia, paid a visit to Philip in the course of which (by order of his government) he made arrangements

---

[61] Diodorus Siculus, XL, 1a-1b.

[62] For further details, see G. Downey, "The Occupation of Syria by the Romans," *T.A.P.A.*, LXXXII, 1951, pp. 149-163, and A. R. Bellinger, "The Early Coinage of Roman Syria," *Studies in Roman Economic and Social History in Honor of A. C. Johnson*, Princeton, 1951, pp. 58-67. For the background of conditions in Cilicia, see also R. Syme, "Observations on the Province of Cilicia," *Anatolian Studies Presented to W. H. Buckler*, Manchester, 1939, pp. 299-332.

for building a palace and a circus at Antioch, as a token of Roman support and interest in the city and in an effort to bolster Philip's prestige with his subjects, some of whom at least must have favored Roman intervention at this point.[63] There may already have been a colony of Italians living in Antioch, and Roman commercial circles had well-developed interests in Syria.[64] On the same occasion the Roman official asked Philip for a contribution toward the cost of the operations which were being carried on against the Cilician pirates. The contribution cannot have been a large one, but it would be politically important as a token of "cooperation" on the part of the Seleucid government. The circus which Marcius ordered built is evidently the one on the island in the Orontes, still visible in ruins (Fig. 5).[65] Before this time, apparently, the only other circus at Antioch had been at Daphne. The location of the palace is not specified; it may have stood, like the circus, on the island.

Soon after Marcius' visit to Antioch, Clodius, who had been captured by the Cilician pirates and then released, went to the city, where he proceeded to stir up trouble, declaring that he would assist the people of Antioch against the Arabs, with whom they were having difficulties. The details of what followed are not clear, though we are told that Clodius nearly lost his life. It has been conjectured that the disorders for which Clodius was responsible cost Philip II his throne, for we hear nothing further of him. Sampsigeramus, after Clodius' failure and return to Rome, set free his prisoner Antiochus XIII, who once again occupied the throne at

---

[63] Malalas, p. 225, 7-11.

[64] See Rostovtzeff, *op.cit.* (above, n. 21), p. 991.

[65] The circus is dated by archaeological evidence in the first century B.C. (*Antioch-on-the-Orontes*, I, p. 40), and since the financial resources of the last Seleucid kings were hardly such that they could have built such a structure, the circus on the island must be that constructed by Q. Marcius Rex.

Antioch during the year 65/4 B.C.[66] While Antiochus XIII was in power, Pompey defeated Mithradates, and in 64 B.C. the Roman commander came to Antioch to make a settlement of the status of the city. With his arrival a new chapter in the history of Antioch begins.

[66] Cassius Dio, xxxvi, 17, 3; Appian, *Syr.*, 70. As a conjecture, it may be suggested that when Clodius went to Antioch, he found that Sampsigeramus was plotting to expel Philip and place Antiochus on the throne, and that Clodius then offered his assistance against Sampsigeramus; he might even have offered to obtain Roman military support for Philip. The disorders might then have arisen when a local party which distrusted Rome tried to drive Clodius out of the city. It is interesting to speculate whether there may have been some connection between the visits to Antioch of Marcius Rex and Clodius, for Marcius Rex was married to a sister of Clodius. See Walter Allen Jr., "Claudius or Clodius?" *Classical Weekly*, xxxiii, 1937, pp. 107-110.

CHAPTER IV

THE COMING OF THE ROMANS

WHEN it became evident that both for military security and for the protection of Roman commercial interests it was necessary to take over Syria as a Roman province, Antioch, as the largest city in northwestern Syria and as the Seleucid capital, already an important military, administrative and commercial center, was obviously the city that should be the capital of the new province.

Pompey granted *libertas*, a technical status of administrative "freedom," to Antioch, as he did to other cities in Syria, including Seleucia Pieria.[1] This "freedom" in reality meant only that the city was allowed to manage some of its internal affairs, though in all important matters it was under Roman control. To augment this appearance of "freedom," Pompey repaired the *bouleuterion* or council-house, which had fallen into disrepair.[2] He also granted additional land to the sacred grove at Daphne, which he particularly admired. Pompey's freedman Demetrius had great influence in Antioch at this time.[3]

With Roman assistance, Antioch must have recovered without difficulty from the effects of the last years of the Seleucids. Roman commercial interests, which had exercised strong influence to procure the annexation of Syria, rapidly took advantage of the occupation of the new province.[4] Roman

[1] Porphyrius of Tyre, *F.H.G.*, III, p. 716, frag. 26. On this conception of "freedom," see A. H. M. Jones, "Civitates liberae et immunes," *Anatolian Studies Presented to W. H. Buckler*, Manchester, 1939, pp. 103-117.

[2] Malalas, p. 211, 18.

[3] Eutropius, VI, 14, 2; Festus, XVI, 4; Plutarch, *Cato the Younger*, 13; *Pompey*, 40; Julian, *Misopogon*, 358b-c.

[4] J. Dobiáš, "Les premiers rapports des Romains avec les Parthes et l'occupation de la Syrie," *Archiv orientální*, III, 1931, pp. 215-256; J. Hatzfeld, *Les trafiquants italiens dans l'Orient hellénique*, Paris, 1919, pp. 142, 374f.

73

merchants quickly established themselves at Antioch, and by 48 B.C. the colony of Roman citizens engaged in business in the city was a flourishing and influential one.[5] A portrait head of a young Roman, found at Antioch and now in the museum there, may date from about this period.[6]

Syria was made a proconsular province, governed by consuls who went to this post on the expiration of their terms of office. Characteristically, we hear that the first proconsul, Aulus Gabinius, had to take measures to control the activities of the *publicani* or "publicans" who according to the Roman system obtained by contract the right of collecting taxes.[7] The governor's regulation of the exactions of the publicans may reflect an effort to hasten the economic recovery of the land.

A war with the Parthians, launched by the governor M. Licinius Crassus in 54 B.C., had unfavorable results, and in 51 B.C. the Parthians invaded Syria and penetrated as far as Antioch. C. Cassius, who had succeeded Crassus as governor, shut himself up in Antioch, and the Parthians, who did not know how to conduct a siege of a fortified place, found they were unable to take the city.[8]

The next governor, M. Calpurnius Bibulus, seems to have administered the province efficiently and beneficially. He obtained from the people of Antioch, as a gift to the Roman people, the statues of Athene and of Zeus the Thunderer which had been set up by the founder Seleucus. These were sent to Rome and placed in the Capitolium, with inscriptions

---

[5] Caesar, *Civil War*, III, 102.

[6] F. Poulsen, "Portrait hellénistique du Musée d'Antioche," *Syria*, XIX, 1938, pp. 355-361.

[7] Cicero, *De provinciis consularibus*. See Eva M. Sanford, "The Career of Aulus Gabinius," *T.A.P.A.*, LXX, 1939, pp. 64-92.

[8] Dio Cassius, XL, 29, 1; Cicero, *Ad familiares*, II, 10, 2; *Ad Atticum*, V, 21. The Parthians must have taken the opportunity to plunder the unprotected suburbs of Antioch.

recording the gift. Eventually the statue of Zeus, at least, seems to have been returned to Antioch.[9]

The city became directly involved in the civil war between Julius Caesar and the Senate which began in 49 B.C. When Caesar defeated Pompey at Pharsalus (48 B.C.), the people of Antioch declared against Pompey, who had taken flight in the direction of Syria.[10] Caesar, after spending the winter of 48-47 B.C. in Alexandria, set out in the spring of 47 B.C. on his way to Pontus to put down Pharnaces, a client king who had taken the opportunity to seize power in Asia Minor. On his way through Syria, Caesar paused at various cities to bestow rewards for the support he had received from them. On 16 April he entered Antioch.[11] Whether by accident or design, this was the 23rd of the month Artemisios in the local calendar, the day following the anniversary of the foundation of the city by Seleucus. Caesar remained in Antioch about nine days and then continued his journey. He issued a decree bestowing "freedom" on Antioch—presumably in terms which would make the gift seem to be an improvement over the "freedom" received from Pompey.

Caesar also continued the notable series of public buildings constructed in Antioch by the Roman government through the agency of Q. Marcius Rex and Pompey.[12] The most famous of Caesar's buildings was the basilica which he called after his own name, the Kaisarion, the oldest basilica in the East for which evidence has been preserved.[13] It stood opposite the Temple of Ares, near the stream Parmenius (Fig.

---

[9] Malalas, p. 212, 1-8; Libanius, *Antiochikos*, 116.

[10] Caesar, *Civil War*, III, 102.   [11] Malalas, p. 216, 7ff.

[12] Malalas, p. 216, 19ff.

[13] See G. Downey, "The Architectural Significance of the Use of the Words *Stoa* and *Basilike* in Classical Literature," *A.J.A.*, XLI, 1937, pp. 197-199; A. M. Schneider, "Basilica Discoperta," *Antiquity*, XXIV, 1950, pp. 131-139; E. Sjöqvist, "Kaisareion: A Study in Architectural Iconography," *Opuscula Romana*, I, *edidit Institutum Romanum Regni Sueciae* (*Acta Instituti Romani Regni Sueciae*, series in 4°, XVIII, 1954), pp. 86-108.

5). The location was a central one, for in the reign of Valens (A.D. 364-378) part of the Kaisarion was demolished so that its site could be used as a part of Valens' new forum. The basilica contained an open court and a vaulted apse, and was probably similar in plan to the Kaisarion, later used as a Christian church, which Caesar built in Alexandria.[14] Outside the apse stood statues of Caesar and of the Tyche or Fortune of Rome.[15] These statues show that Caesar, with his statesmanlike plans to Romanize the empire, was bent on transmuting into a new form and preserving the elements of the Hellenistic ruler cult and of the cult of the personification of Rome. These cults were later developed more systematically by Augustus in the official worship of Roma and Augustus.[16] The statue of Caesar himself outside the Kaisarion doubtless came in time to serve in the cult of the Deified Julius, which was recognized under Augustus.[17]

Other measures carried out at Antioch under Caesar's orders included the rebuilding of the Pantheon, which was dilapidated; the building of a new theater on the slope of the mountain (or the rebuilding of an old one; the source is not precise); the construction of an amphitheater, likewise on the slope of the mountain; the building of an aqueduct designed to supply the needs of the people who lived on the upper part of the mountain; and the construction of a public bath on the upper part of the mountain, served by this aqueduct.[18] The Roman policy of introducing the Roman way of life into the Greek East is well illustrated by the construction of the amphitheater designed to accommodate the gladiatorial fights and other brutal sports which the Romans enjoyed. The earliest Roman amphitheater now known is the

[14] Strabo, xvii, 1, 9, p. 794C; Malalas, p. 217, 10-12.

[15] Malalas, pp. 216, 19-21; 286, 16ff; 290, 18-20; 338, 19ff.

[16] See David Magie, *Roman Rule in Asia Minor*, Princeton, 1950, pp. 447-449; 1295-1298; 1613f.

[17] Cassius Dio, li, 20, 6ff; Magie, *op.cit.*, p. 447.

[18] Malalas, p. 216, 21ff.

temporary structure built at Pompeii ca. 80 B.C., and the first permanent building of this character in Italy was set up in 29 B.C.; thus Caesar's structure at Antioch was erected at a time when such buildings were just becoming popular.[19] The work done in connection with the theater also shows how important Caesar considered the entertainment of the people to be.

When Caesar concluded his visit to Antioch he left behind him in charge of Syria a young relative, Sextus Julius Caesar. Early in 46 B.C. Q. Caecilius Bassus, an adherent of Pompey's, engineered a mutiny among the troops in the course of which Sextus Caesar lost his life. Struggles continued between the supporters of the two parties. After the assassination of Caesar in 44 B.C., C. Cassius arrived at Antioch from Italy and as an interloper succeeded in winning the support of the people of Syria and of the troops stationed there. In raising money, he seized property of the Jews in Antioch.[20] Finally, he was able to compass the defeat of the legitimate governor, Cornelius Dolabella, who had reached Syria after him. We have Cicero's account of Dolabella's effort, on one occasion in 43 B.C., to dislodge Cassius from Antioch.[21]

Antioch continued to share with the rest of the Roman world the unsettlement and uncertainties that followed Caesar's death. The power passed to the triumvirate of Antony, Lepidus, and Octavian, and in time Antony set out for the East (41 B.C.) in order to raise money to pay the troops; in any such tour Antioch was one of the places which would have to be visited.[22] Antony restored to the Jews of Antioch and other cities property seized by Cassius;[23] and

---

[19] See D. S. Robertson, *A Handbook of Greek and Roman Architecture*, 2d ed., Cambridge, Eng., 1945, pp. 283-289, 351.

[20] Josephus, *Antiquities*, XIV, 319-323. The Jews in Tyre, Sidon, and Aradus also suffered.

[21] Cicero, *Ad familiares*, XII, 15, 7, cf. XII, 14, 4; Cassius Dio, XLVII, 30, 2.

[22] Plutarch, *Antony*, 24.

[23] Josephus, *Antiquities*, XIV, 319-323.

he received, in Daphne, a deputation of influential Jews, who wished to secure his support against Herod's pretensions in Palestine.[24] Antony reorganized the province of Syria, and we hear that his acts there caused many disturbances; possibly a curtailment of the titular "freedom" of Antioch was a part of his policy.[25]

From Syria, Antony went to Alexandria, where he became involved with Cleopatra; and the Parthians, taking advantage of this distraction of his interests and of the dissatisfaction with Antony in Syria, determined to invade the province (spring, 40 B.C.). The Parthian army was commanded by Pacorus, son of the Parthian king Orodes. Pacorus defeated Decidius Saxa, Antony's governor of Syria, who fled first to Antioch and then to Cilicia, where he was captured and executed. Antioch surrendered to the Parthians, who occupied all of Syria and Phoenicia with the exception of Tyre.[26]

The new regime proved popular. The Syrians, the historian Cassius Dio writes, "felt unusual affection for Pacorus on account of his justness and mildness, an affection as great as they had felt for the best kings that had ever ruled them."[27]

The foreign regime lasted until the Parthians were driven out of Syria by Antony's forces in the summer of 39 B.C.[28] A year later, Antony reached Syria and took over the task of punishing King Antiochus of Commagene, who had aided the Parthians. While he was besieging Antiochus in Samosata, Herod, whom Antony had chosen to be client-king of Judaea, came to Antony's assistance, marching by way of Antioch.[29] After the surrender of Samosata, Antony put Gaius Sosius

---

[24] Josephus, War, I, 243-245; Antiquities, XIV, 324-326.

[25] Cassius Dio, XLVIII, 24, 1-3; E. T. Newell, "The Pre-Imperial Coinage of Roman Antioch," Numismatic Chronicle, ser. 4, vol. XIX, 1919, p. 94.

[26] Cassius Dio, XLVIII, 24, 3, and 25, 3ff. See N. C. Debevoise, A Political History of Parthia, Chicago, 1938, pp. 109-111.

[27] Cassius Dio, XLIX, 20, 4, trans. of E. Cary, Loeb Classical Library.

[28] Debevoise, op.cit. (above, n. 26), pp. 111-116.

[29] Josephus, Antiquities, XIV, 439f.

in charge of Syria and himself left the province. Herod seems to have gone to Antioch at this time, presumably in order to act in concert with Sosius. Sosius and Herod now set out against the Hasmonean Antigonus (Mattathias), who had usurped Herod's place in Jerusalem.[30] Antigonus surrendered Jerusalem in the summer of 37 B.C. Sosius eventually sent the usurper to Antony at Antioch, and there he was put to death.[31]

Antony, after an absence in the West, returned to Syria in the late autumn of 37 B.C. to prepare for the campaign he was planning against the Parthians. He sent Fonteius Capito to bring Cleopatra to Syria, and when she arrived he married her. The wedding, though none of the extant sources happen to say so specifically, presumably took place in Antioch.[32] As a wedding gift, Antony presented Cleopatra with territories in Syria and Palestine, and recognized as his children the twins she had borne him in 40 B.C. He named them Alexander Helios and Cleopatra Selene. While he was in Antioch, Antony, who was now the master of the whole East, bestowed many gifts of titles and crowns of tetrarchies and kingdoms.

In the spring of 36 B.C. Antony set out on his conquest of Parthia. His elaborate expedition failed, and he was forced to return to Antioch in the autumn with only a handful of his troops.[33] During the next few years Antony was still busy with his plans for the reconquest of the eastern possessions of Alexander the Great and the Seleucids, and here again Antioch served as his military headquarters.

All this time Octavian's power and popularity, especially in Italy, had been growing, and Antony's conduct increased

---

[30] *Ibid.*, 447f.

[31] Strabo, frag. 15, *F.H.G.*, III, p. 494; Josephus, *Antiquities*, XIV, 488-490; *War*, I, 357; Cassius Dio, XLIX, 22, 6.

[32] Plutarch, *Antony*, 36.

[33] Florus, II, 20, 10; Orosius, VI, 19, 1.

the rivalry between the two former colleagues. Octavian at length determined to go to war against Antony, and Antioch was the scene of one final, and quite minor, episode in the struggle. A band of gladiators enrolled in Antony's service had been training in Cyzicus; and when they heard of Antony's need for assistance, they tried to make their way to Egypt to join him. When they passed by way of Antioch they were overpowered by Q. Didius, the governor of Syria, with the aid of forces provided by Herod of Judaea, and were made to settle in Daphne.[34]

With Antony's defeat at the battle of Actium in September of 31 B.C., followed by his suicide in Alexandria, a year later, another phase in the history of Antioch came to an end. The victory of Octavian was to introduce a new era in the Roman world.

Antony had carried on Caesar's policy for the Romanization of Syria by presenting himself both as a Roman magistrate and as a divine heir to the divine Seleucid rulers.[35] It remained for Octavian as Augustus to follow the same course among the more stable conditions of the peace which he brought to the Roman world.

Antioch was now free of the vicissitudes of political fortune that had beset it almost constantly since the power of the Seleucids began to decline. The dawn of the golden age founded by Augustus brought to the city, with the blessings of peace, the material prosperity which it was to enjoy for many years. The Augustan Peace was to unify the Empire as a whole and to reconcile the Greek East to Roman rule. Pompey and Caesar had begun the process of fitting Antioch into the Roman scheme by the construction of public buildings; but their work was only a beginning. It remained for Augustus as emperor (31 B.C.—A.D. 14) and for Agrippa and

[34] Cassius Dio, LI, 7, 2-6 and 9, 1; Josephus, *War*, I, 392.
[35] *BMC Galatia etc.*, p. 157, no. 52; M. Grant, *From Imperium to Auctoritas*, Cambridge, Eng., 1946, pp. 368-375.

the Emperor Tiberius (A.D. 14-37) to effect the physical trans-formation of Antioch as the metropolis of Roman Syria. Augustus visited the city twice, in 31-30 B.C. and again in 20 B.C., and so had firsthand knowledge of the beauty and importance of Antioch.

In Augustus' new plan for the government of the prov-inces, Syria, because of its strategic importance, was given the highest rank, that of an imperial province, governed by a legate (*legatus Augusti propraetore*) of consular or prae-torian rank, who was appointed by the emperor for an in-definite number of years. The legate was assisted by a *pro-curator* of equestrian rank, in charge of financial matters, who was appointed by the emperor and was responsible, not to the legate, but directly to the emperor. The legate had under his command legions (originally three, sometimes four, later sometimes two) which were permanently sta-tioned in the province. The legate and the *procurator* had their headquarters at Antioch. Although the city was called "autonomous," meaning that it managed some of its internal affairs, the presence of the legate and the *procurator* must have overshadowed all the activities of the municipality.

One of the major events in the history of Antioch under Augustus was the foundation of the local Olympic Games, which in time became one of the most famous festivals of the Roman world. A senator of Antioch named Sosibius, who accompanied Augustus to Rome after one of his visits to Antioch, and died in Rome, bequeathed his property to his native city, with the provision that the income be used to present games every four years for thirty days during the month of Hyperberetaios or October.[36] At first the games (not yet specifically called Olympic Games) were presented regularly. Soon, however, the officials charged with their

---

[36] Malalas, p. 224, 22ff. See the chapter "Die antiochenischen Olympien" in A. Schenk von Stauffenberg, *Die römische Kaisergeschichte bei Malalas*, Stuttgart, 1931, pp. 412-443.

administration began to abuse their trust, diverting the money from Sosibius' estate to their own pockets, and by the time of Claudius (A.D. 41-54) the festival had ceased to be presented. The citizens of Antioch petitioned Claudius for a reorganization of the festival, and this was granted, the games now being called Olympic.

But the reign of Augustus was chiefly notable in Antioch for the new buildings with which the Roman authorities began the transformation of Antioch into a Roman capital. The building program symbolized as well the prosperity of the Augustan age, which Antioch with the rest of the Empire enjoyed. These buildings, begun under Augustus, were continued under Tiberius, and King Herod and Agrippa had an important share in the work. Herod of Judaea was famous as a munificent builder and a long and impressive list of his enterprises can be drawn up;[37] he was also an enthusiastic supporter of the Roman regime, and eager to do honor to Augustus.

Associated with Agrippa's name was a new quarter of the city, named for its founder; this included a public bath.[38] Outside the city, on the slope of the mountain, at a spot where there was a spring to furnish water, Agrippa built another bath, which later came to be called, from its setting, "The Bath in the Vineyards." The addition of a new zone of seats to the theater, carried out in Agrippa's name, indicates that there had been an increase in the population. Later Agrippa cleared the hippodrome of the rubbish with which it had been encumbered as the result of an earthquake, and attended an entertainment held to mark the restoration of the building.[39]

One of the principal undertakings of this period was the

[37] F.-M. Abel, *Histoire de la Palestine*, Paris, 1952, I, pp. 363-380.
[38] Malalas, p. 222, 15ff.
[39] Malalas, p. 225, 3ff. This is the only record of the earthquake that made the hippodrome useless.

construction of a great colonnaded street, two Roman miles in length, which ran through the city along the line of the earlier Hellenistic street, and now formed the main street of the city. This thoroughfare, one of Antioch's chief claims to fame in antiquity, was among the earliest monumental avenues of which we have knowledge; it was roughly contemporary with the colonnaded streets of Olba and Pompeiopolis in Cilicia,[40] though the street in Antioch must have been larger than those of the Cilician cities. Herod first supplied the paving of the street, then Tiberius built the roofed colonnades that lined the thoroughfare, and erected *tetrapyla* at each main cross street. These highly ornamental structures, covering the crossing of the streets with vaulted stone roofs supported on four columns, one at each corner of the crossing, were adorned with mosaic work and marbles. At intervals all along the length of the street stood bronzes and statues.[41] The roadway was about 31 feet wide and each of the flanking porticos was about 32 feet wide (Fig. 5).[42] The street served to unify the plan of the city, which had now reached almost its maximum extent.

The name of Tiberius is also connected with the completion and improvement of Epiphania, the quarter established by Antiochus IV Epiphanes. Three temples, as well as other edifices, were constructed or reconstructed.[43] Foremost among these was the Temple of Jupiter Capitolinus, evidently the temple built by Antiochus IV, which Tiberius restored. Another temple built at this time was that of Dionysus,

[40] Robertson, *op.cit.* (above, n. 19), pp. 291f, 359; R. E. Wycherley, *How the Greeks Built Cities*, London, 1949, p. 32.

[41] Malalas, pp. 223, 17-19; 232, 17ff; Josephus, *War*, I, 425; *Antiquities*, XVI, 148.

[42] These are the measurements at the beginning of the second century of the Christian era, as determined in the excavations (J. Lassus in *A.J.A.*, XLIV, 1940, p. 417); presumably they represent the original size of the street.

[43] Malalas, p. 233, 10ff.

before which stood two statues of the Dioscuri, Amphion and Zethos, the sons of Antiope and Zeus. The placing of the statues indicates that this temple was built on a podium or raised foundation approached by a flight of steps, with the statues standing on the flanking walls of the steps. The third temple mentioned is that of Pan, which stood "behind the theater." This may have been associated with a cavern or grotto sacred to the god which was located on the slope of Mount Silpius.

The theater was again enlarged by the addition of another zone of seats. This further addition, coming so soon after that of Agrippa, indicates that the population of Antioch had continued to grow. Another enlargement of the theater was to be made by the Emperor Trajan, and this was to be final.

One important part of the program carried out at this time was the provision of further protection against the washing of soil and debris brought down from Mount Silpius by the winter rains. What the arrangements for drainage and protection were, we do not know, since the only evidence that has been preserved is a story of a talisman set up at this time to protect the city against the winter torrents. The story of the talisman procured by Tiberius from a seer named Ablakkon evidently represents a product of local folklore designed to explain the results achieved by the emperor's engineers.

Still other building undertakings were executed by Tiberius' orders. One was the "Eastern Gate," on top of which stood a stone statue of the she-wolf nursing Romulus and Remus, a symbol of Roman sovereignty.[44] The gate presumably stood at the eastern end of the colonnaded main street, where it would be the first monument to be seen by travelers arriving at Antioch from the hinterland of Syria.

In the same region Tiberius built a public bath near the

[44] Malalas, p. 235, 3ff.

84

spring to which Alexander the Great was supposed to have given his mother's name, Olympias; this was in the eastern part of the city, on the slope of the mountain.[45]

Tiberius had given Antioch much, and in gratitude for his benefactions, the senate and people of Antioch erected a bronze statue of the emperor on a column of Theban stone in an open plaza in the colonnaded street; Malalas calls the spot "the omphalos of the city," which suggests that it was circular in plan.[46] This plaza seems to have been placed at the point at which the course of the main street, crossing the stream Parmenius, changes direction slightly (Fig. 5). This very slight change in the axis of the thoroughfare was a subtle and effective architectural device, offering a monumental composition at the end of the view, as one proceeded along the street toward the center of the city. If the street had been a perfectly straight line throughout its length, one would have seen only an endless vista of the colonnades on either side disappearing into the distance.

During Tiberius' reign, in the year A.D. 23/4, there was a major fire at Antioch.[47] Its effects were the more severe because it broke out at night and burned for some time before it was discovered. It destroyed the greater part of the agora in Epiphania, including the council house and the shrine of the Muses with the library which had been built with the bequest of Maron, the Antiochene merchant who had emigrated to Athens.

Only one other untoward event disturbed the history of the city under Tiberius; but this episode, the mysterious death of Germanicus, was sensational indeed. Germanicus, son of Tiberius' brother Drusus, had been Augustus' favorite grandson, and Tiberius had been forced to adopt him and make him senior, in the family, to his own son Drusus. Germanicus was handsome, affable and popular, but not

---

[45] Malalas, p. 234, 11-17; Libanius, *Antiochikos*, 72-74, 250.
[46] Malalas, p. 233, 4-6.   [47] Malalas, p. 235, 15ff.

conspicuously able, and there was good reason for Tiberius to view his public career with some misgivings. In A.D. 17, a complicated political situation had been created in the East by internal disorders in Parthia and Armenia, accompanied by discontent in Syria and Palestine over the size of the tribute imposed on these provinces. Germanicus was sent to the East on a special mission, with extraordinary powers; but in order to provide a check on the young man, whom he did not wholly trust, Tiberius also sent Cn. Piso to Syria as governor of the province. Piso was a harsh, unyielding man of the old Republican type, and he might be expected to curb Germanicus' actions if necessary. Germanicus made himself popular wherever he went, and treated the people of the provinces with signal generosity. However, he was also indiscreet in his official conduct, and on his return to Antioch from a vacation in Egypt (A.D. 19), differences of policy between Piso and Germanicus came to a head, and Germanicus dismissed the governor.[48] Soon after Piso's departure from Antioch, Germanicus became seriously ill. The contemporary description of his symptoms indicates a severe fever; but he was convinced that Piso had poisoned him, and there were those who said that Piso had acted at Tiberius' orders. When Germanicus died, aged thirty-three (10 October A.D. 19), his unclothed body was displayed "in the forum" at Antioch, but there was doubt whether signs of poisoning appeared on it. A cenotaph was erected at Antioch, presumably in the forum where the body had been exhibited, and a further memorial, in the form of a catafalque, was set up in Daphne, where Germanicus had died.[49]

Among the children of Germanicus who witnessed his death was the future Emperor Caligula (A.D. 37-41), then seven years old. Pious respect for the scene of his father's death may have been one cause of Caligula's noteworthy generosity toward the city after he became emperor.

[48] Tacitus, *Annals*, II, 69ff.   [49] *Ibid.*, II, 83.

Antioch was always in close touch with the eastern part of Syria and the states beyond, and all during the reigns of Augustus and Tiberius the city must have been a center in the constant planning and diplomatic activity that attended the difficult and delicate task of maintaining equilibrium among the vassal states in the East. This contact with the eastern lands, which always played an important part in the life of Antioch, is illustrated by the way in which King Vonones of Armenia found refuge in the city when he was forced out of his country by the Parthian king Artabanes. For political reasons the governor of Syria, Creticus Silanus, allowed Vonones to live in Antioch with his accustomed luxury and to keep his royal title.[50]

Another illustration of the ties with the East and of the cosmopolitan character of the city is afforded by the story of the Babylonian Jewish emir Zamaris, who during the governorship in Syria of C. Sentius Saturninus (9-6 B.C.) migrated from Babylon to Antioch accompanied by a retinue of one hundred relatives and five hundred mounted bowmen.[51] Evidently Zamaris was a wealthy landowner who found it necessary for some political reason to flee from his home, and it is significant to find that it was Antioch that attracted him. The city's advantages, for such a man, would have been that it lay in a rich agricultural district, where he might be able to resume his farming activities; that it possessed an important Jewish community; and that as the capital of Syria it offered at once the protection of the Roman government and the possibility that some advantageous political connection might be made with this government, which might perhaps find some use for the services of the emir's private army. Zamaris came first to Daphne, but the governor, Saturninus, who evidently did not wish to have so large a group of organized and armed foreigners so near

[50] *Ibid.*, II, 4 and 68; Josephus, *Antiquities*, XVIII, 52.
[51] Josephus, *Antiquities*, XVII, 23-27.

the capital, assigned to him a place called Oualatha near Antioch, in which there was a Jewish community. Eventually Zamaris left Antioch at the invitation of King Herod, who offered him special inducements to settle in Batanea, in Transjordania.

CHAPTER V

CAPITAL OF SYRIA

BY THE END of Tiberius' reign, Antioch had been transformed, in its physical aspect, from a Hellenistic to a Graeco-Roman city, and prosperity had been recovered. From this point the history of the city is that of the capital of Roman Syria. The sources, though not abundant for this period, give us insights into different aspects of the life of the metropolis.

The principal event in the history of Antioch in the reign of Caligula (Gaius), A.D. 37-41, was a severe earthquake which occurred on 9 April A.D. 37.[1] The emperor immediately responded with assistance. In this early part of his reign Caligula had at his disposal the considerable sums left in the treasury by Tiberius,[2] and the assistance which he provided for the rebuilding of the city must have been substantial.

Three officials were sent from Rome to carry out the work of restoration: Salvianus, who had the title of legate, and two senators named Lurius Varius and Pontius. All three made gifts to the city from their own funds, building public baths and a Trinymphon adorned with statues, to be used for weddings.

A legend related that after the earthquake a seer named Debborius set up a talisman in the city to protect it against future earthquakes.[3] This consisted of a porphyry column, placed "in the middle of the city," which bore a bust on which was inscribed the words "unshaken, unthrown." At some time before the reign of Domitian (A.D. 81-96) the column was struck by lightning which consumed the bust but left the shaft standing, though scarred. The basis for this legend is not clear; the story could easily have grown up

[1] Malalas, p. 243, 10ff.
[2] Suetonius, *Caligula*, 37; Cassius Dio, LIX, 2.
[3] Malalas, p. 265, 12-18.

concerning an empty column which had once borne an imperial statue.

At Antioch, the reign of Claudius (A.D. 41-54) is known chiefly for a famine, an earthquake, and the reorganization of the pentaeteric festival of the city into its Olympic Games.

The famine, caused by failures of crops in Syria, Palestine and Egypt, affected Antioch for several years. A flood of the Nile caused a shortage of grain in Egypt from about A.D. 44 to 46 or 47, and this would have affected the price of grain in Antioch. More direct results would have been felt from the shortage of grain which occurred in Judaea and all Syria in A.D. 46 or 47. At this time the Christian community at Antioch sent assistance to the Christians in Jerusalem to relieve the distress there.[4]

The earthquake (the date of which is not recorded) damaged Ephesus, Smyrna, and many other cities of Asia Minor, as well as Antioch. At Antioch it destroyed the temples of Artemis, Ares, and Herakles, as well as "a number of houses."[5] The roofed colonnades along the main street also seem to have been damaged. The emperor granted relief to all the cities affected.

The Olympic Games of the city were established in A.D. 43/4, replacing the festival founded under Augustus which had fallen into disuse.[6] The new games were to consist of scenic and athletic contests, including theatrical, dramatic, and musical events and races in the hippodrome. The games were to be held in every fifth year, for thirty days beginning with the new moon in the month of Hyperberetaios (October). The games were not, however, celebrated regularly. Pretexts for interruptions were found in wars, earthquakes, fires, and various other public calamities, and the games

---

[4] Acts 11:27-30; Orosius, *Hist.*, VII, 6, 12; K. S. Gapp, "The Universal Famine under Claudius," *Harvard Theological Review*, XXVIII, 1935, pp. 258-265.

[5] Malalas, p. 246, 13-19.   [6] Malalas, pp. 224, 22ff; 248, 5ff.

came to be held only at intervals of fifteen or twenty years, and on a total of six occasions, until a reorganization took place in the reign of Commodus (A.D. 180-192).

The principal events of which we hear in the history of Antioch under Nero (A.D. 54-68) are those connected with the Jewish rebellion. For a number of years the Greeks of Syria, Palestine, and Egypt had been hostile toward the Jews because of their privileged position as exempt from military service, and because they were not obliged to worship the emperor in the official state cult. The Jews at the same time had a serious grievance in the effect of Roman taxation, which made agriculture unprofitable for them and forced many men to seek a living through brigandage. Combined with these conditions were other factors. Their faith made the Jews a religious rather than a political community. Moreover, within this community there was the serious division between the Sadducees, who favored cooperation with Rome, and the Pharisees, whose religious intolerance generated hostility to Rome. All this made for a situation that was bound to produce a major outbreak.

The crisis developed gradually. Under Caligula there was an outbreak at Antioch, during the governorship of P. Petronius (A.D. 39-41/2), which resulted in a pogrom, and although the privileges of the Jews at Antioch and elsewhere were confirmed by Claudius in A.D. 41, the basic sources of friction remained.[7] In A.D. 66 massacres at Caesarea in Palestine and in Jerusalem touched off a full-scale national revolt of the Jews, and there were risings against them in other cities of Syria and Palestine. In the winter of A.D. 66-67, Nero appointed his general Vespasian to the governorship of Judaea, with command of a large army with which he was to suppress the rebellion. Traveling overland via the Hellespont, Vespasian proceeded to Antioch, where he planned

---

[7] Malalas, p. 244, 18ff; Josephus, *Antiquities*, xix, 279-285. On the history of the Jewish community at this period, see Kraeling, "Jewish Community," pp. 148ff.

to assemble his forces. The rebellion in Palestine inevitably inflamed anti-Jewish feeling in Syria, and only the occasion for an outbreak was wanted. Just after Vespasian's arrival in Syria, a renegade Jew of Antioch named Antiochus, son of the chief magistrate of the Jews at Antioch, seized the opportunity to stir up an attack on his own people.[8] He entered the theater when a public assembly was being held and accused the Jews of a plot to burn the whole city in one night; he likewise delivered up, as accomplices in the undertaking, some foreign Jews whom the state of public opinion had made it possible for him to have arrested. Feeling was sufficiently strong to make the people of Antioch burn to death on the spot the men who had been handed over to them. Then they set out to attack the Jewish community. Antiochus suggested that the Jews be compelled to offer pagan sacrifices; a few complied but most refused and were massacred. Antiochus then seems to have been given some sort of authority, and he proceeded to compel the Jews to give up their observance of rest on the seventh day. This outbreak was to be followed by another, led by the same Antiochus, after the fall of Jerusalem.

Nero's death (9 June A.D. 68), which brought to an end the Julio-Claudian dynasty, was followed by a year in which the various legions, as Tacitus says, discovered the fatal secret of the empire, namely that the emperor could be nominated elsewhere than in Rome. Thus the troops in various parts of the empire nominated in succession four emperors, Galba, Otho, Vitellius, and Vespasian. The first three were overthrown in turn, and Vespasian emerged as the founder of a new dynasty, that of the Flavians. In Vespasian's rise to power, Antioch and the province of Syria played a major part, exemplifying for the first time the importance of the province in the contests for the succession to the imperial office. By reason of the presence in Syria of three or at some

[8] Josephus, *War*, VII, 46-53.

periods four legions, plus a detachment of the fleet stationed at Seleucia Pieria,[9] the legate of the province was the most powerful of the provincial governors, and repeatedly the governor of Syria influenced the choice of a new emperor, until Septimius Severus, to put an end to this potential source of danger to the emperor and his succession, divided Syria into two new provinces, Syria Coele (in the north) and Syria Phoenice (in the south).[10]

On the news of Nero's suicide, Vespasian, who had almost ended the Jewish war and was now preparing for the final attack on Jerusalem, decided to suspend operations until his command could be confirmed by Nero's successor.[11] The eastern troops took the oath of allegiance to Galba, Otho, and Vitellius in succession.

Vespasian at first allowed events to take their course; but with C. Licinius Mucianus, the legate of Syria, he watched the situation, and the two men, who between them controlled a large army, came into close consultation. Vitellius' rule provoked dissatisfaction, and by the summer of A.D. 69 it became apparent that the eastern troops, having watched three emperors created by the western legions, would be willing to put forward a candidate of their own; and it was plain that Mucianus or Vespasian might be this candidate. Mucianus had no ambition for the office, and preferred to support Vespasian.[12]

On 1 July A.D. 69, Vespasian was proclaimed emperor at Alexandria. Mucianus returned to Antioch, administered

[9] Concerning the legions that were stationed in Syria at different times, see H. M. D. Parker, *The Roman Legions*, Oxford, 1928, pp. 91f, 119, 126-128, 137-140, 145, 149, 158f, 162f. On the detachment of the fleet based at Seleucia Pieria, see H. Seyrig, "Le cimitière des marins à Séleucie Piérie," *Mélanges syriens offerts à M. R. Dussaud*, Paris, 1938, I, pp. 451-459.

[10] Britain was almost as powerful as Syria in matters affecting the imperial succession.

[11] Tacitus, *Histories*, II, 4; V, 10; Josephus, *War*, IV, 497f.

[12] Tacitus, *op.cit.*, I, 10; II, 4-7, 73f, 76f.

the oath of allegiance to his own troops there, and addressed the people of the city, who had hurriedly gathered in the theater to show their loyalty to the new regime. Here Mucianus cleverly put into circulation a rumor that Vitellius intended to transfer the legions of Germany to Syria, where service was easy and life pleasant, and in exchange to send to Germany, with its harsh climate and laborious duties, the legions which were stationed in Syria. This infuriated not only the troops, who had grown fond of Syria, but the civilians who had formed many ties of friendship and marriage with the soldiers.[13] Before 15 July, all Syria had pledged allegiance to Vespasian.

In the preparation for war, Antioch, as would be expected, played a large part. Gold and silver coins were struck at the mint and the city was one of those in which arms factories were established. Fresh troops were enrolled and veterans recalled to service, and Vespasian held a series of conferences in the city.[14] Titus was entrusted with the completion of the war against the Jews. Mucianus defeated Vitellius and occupied Rome by the end of A.D. 69.

Titus began his operations against Jerusalem in the spring of A.D. 70, and completed the conquest of the city in late August. After the city and the temple had been razed, Titus made a triumphal tour in Palestine, pausing to hold games and spectacles. During this tour, in November A.D. 70, a great fire broke out in Antioch, destroying the "tetragonal agora" with the government administrative offices, the record office, and the law courts. The flames were prevented only with difficulty from spreading to the whole city. Antiochus, the renegade Jew who had instigated a persecution of his former co-religionists in the winter of A.D. 66-67 by accusing them of a plot to fire the city, now repeated his charges. The people of the city rushed against the Jews, but were restrained by

[13] *Ibid.*, II, 78, 80f.
[14] *Ibid.*, II, 82; Josephus, *War*, IV, 630f.

the acting governor of Syria, Cn. Pompeius Collega. Collega, telling the people that the matter would have to be laid before Titus, made an investigation and determined (the Jewish historian Josephus says) that no Jews had any part in the affair, but that the fire had been started by certain men in financial straits who imagined that they could save themselves by burning the public records and so destroying the evidence for their debts.[15]

Titus in his triumphal tour came in due course to Antioch. He was given an enthusiastic reception, and men, women, and children streamed out from the city for a distance of over three miles to meet him. With their greetings and acclamations they mingled a running petition to him to expel the Jews from Antioch. To this request Titus made no reply; he remained in Antioch for a time and then proceeded to Zeugma on the Euphrates to receive a congratulatory deputation from Vologeses, the king of Parthia. He then returned to Antioch. The senate and people invited him to visit the theater, where the whole population assembled to greet him. Again a request for the expulsion of the Jews was made, and when this was denied, the people asked that the privileges of the Jews and their special rights of citizenship be abolished, and that the bronze tablets on which their privileges were inscribed be taken down. This request Titus likewise refused. However, in order to provide some compensation for these refusals, he did present to the people of Antioch (whose good will it was desirable to keep) a part of the Jewish spoils, which would serve as perpetual memorials in Antioch of the humiliation of the Jews. Outside the city gate on the road

[15] Josephus, *War*, VII, 39, 54-62, 96. A similar case of the burning of archives in a time of trouble is illustrated by striking archaeological evidence from Palmyra, where excavations have shown that documents were thrown into the market place and burned when the Romans occupied the city in A.D. 272 after the defeat of Zenobia, queen of Palmyra; see H. Seyrig, "Cachets d'archives publiques de quelques villes de la Syrie romaine," *Mélanges de l'Université Saint Joseph*, XXIII, 1940, pp. 103-105.

to Daphne he set up bronze figures which were supposed to be the Cherubim from the Temple (actually the Cherubim no longer existed, and the figures which Titus set up were either imitations, or winged figures which were called cherubim). On the gate itself Titus place a bronze figure of the Moon with four bulls, facing Jerusalem. This group was supposed to commemorate the fact that Jerusalem had been captured by moonlight, but in reality it must have been a symbol of the eternity of the Empire.[16] The location of all these figures was in itself an affront to the Jews, since there was a Jewish quarter in this part of the city. The region came to be known as "The Cherubim" and a famous statue of Christ later stood there.[17]

In Daphne, a theater was built (on the site, it was said, of a synagogue which was destroyed to make room for it). This bore the Latin inscription EX PRAEDA IVDAEA, "From the Jewish Spoils," and a statue of Vespasian was placed in it.[18] The theater found in the excavations seems to be identical with this one.[19]

During Domitian's reign (A.D. 81-96) Antioch received a visit from Apollonius of Tyana, the famous Pythagorean philosopher and wonder-worker.[20] Apollonius presented the city with some of the talismans for which he was celebrated. One, a protection against the north wind, was placed on the Eastern Gate; another, against scorpions, consisted of a bronze scorpion, on top of which was placed a small column, was set in the middle of the city. The wonder-worker also

[16] On the Moon and the Sun as symbols of Eternity in the imperial symbolism of this period, see H. Mattingly and E. A. Sydenham, *Roman Imperial Coinage*, London 1923ff, II, p. 7.

[17] Josephus, *War*, VII, 96-111; *Antiquities*, XII, 121-124; Malalas, pp. 260, 21ff; 281, 4f; G. Downey, "The Gate of the Cherubim at Antioch," *Jewish Quarterly Review*, XXIX, 1938, pp. 167-177.

[18] Malalas, p. 261, 8-12.

[19] D. N. Wilber, "The Theatre at Daphne," *Antioch-on-the-Orontes*, II, pp. 57-94.

[20] Malalas, p. 264, 6ff.

prescribed an annual ceremony that would act as a charm against gnats.

As capital of Syria, Antioch provided the first step in the careers of many Roman young men of good family who were going through the traditional course of military and civil offices. Typical of such careers was the sojourn of Pliny the Younger, who was in Antioch in A.D. 81 or 82 as a junior officer of the third legion.[21] The young man—he was about twenty—doubtless spent no more time on his duties than was necessary, and one may be sure that he was in Antioch as much of the time as was possible. Pliny writes that while he was in Syria he became closely acquainted with the philosophers Artemidorus and Euphrates of Tyre, the latter a popular Stoic preacher.

Another military tribune in Syria at about this time was Trajan, the future emperor, whose father, M. Ulpius Traianus, was governor of Syria from A.D. 76/7 to 79. At this time Trajan acquired the knowledge of Syria and of Antioch which led him to show them special marks of favor when he became emperor.

Antioch played a prominent part in Trajan's reign (A.D. 98-117) as headquarters for the preparations for the Parthian war, one of the chief glories of the epoch, by means of which the boundaries of the Roman Empire were carried to the greatest limits they ever reached.[22] When he landed at Seleucia Pieria on his way to begin the campaign, Trajan dedicated to the Zeus of Mount Casius, with a prayer for the success of the coming expedition, two engraved silver cups and a gilded aurochs' horn, spoils of his campaign in Dacia. The dedication was commemorated in Greek verses by Trajan's ward and nephew by marriage, the future Emperor Hadrian, who had been chosen to act as governor of Syria during the operations against the Parthians.[23]

---

[21] Pliny, *Letters*, I, 10; III, 11; VII, 16, 31; VIII, 14.

[22] See F. A. Lepper, *Trajan's Parthian War*, Oxford, 1948.

[23] *Anth. Pal.*, VI, 332.

Trajan made his ceremonial entry into Antioch on 7 January, A.D. 114, and spent the remainder of the winter there, making preparations for the campaign.[24] At about this time Trajan ordered the construction of an additional aqueduct to bring water from Daphne to Antioch and enlarged the theater. Both projects evidence an increase in population. A new public bath was built, named for Trajan, in connection with the aqueduct. Hadrian seems either to have completed Trajan's work, or to have repaired it after the earthquake of A.D. 115.[25]

In the spring of A.D. 114 Trajan set out for Armenia, which he conquered easily, and then proceeded to annex Mesopotamia, spending the winter of A.D. 114/5 in the field. Late in A.D. 115 he returned to Antioch for the winter, in order to rest and plan further operations.

During his stay, the city suffered one of the most severe of its many earthquakes. The disaster began at dawn on 13 December A.D. 115.[26] Because of the emperor's presence, the city was filled with soldiers and with civilians who had come for business or for pleasure. The shocks continued for several days and nights, and the destruction, both in Antioch and in Daphne, was considerable. Many people were killed, including M. Pedo Vergilianus, one of the consuls for the year. Trajan himself escaped with a few slight injuries. It was reported that a being of supernatural size had appeared and had led him to safety through a window of the room in which he was sleeping. During the remainder of the earthquake he lived in the open in the circus. The future Emperor Hadrian, then governor of Syria, was likewise in the

[24] Malalas, p. 272, 18ff.

[25] Malalas, p. 276, 1ff. Archaeological evidence shows that Trajan's aqueduct was built before the earthquake: Levi, *Antioch Mosaic Pavements*, I, p. 34.

[26] A vivid description of the catastrophe is preserved in the account of Cassius Dio, LXVIII, 24f. Malalas records the disaster more briefly, p. 275, 3-10. A passage in Juvenal, *Sat.*, VI, 411, seems to refer to this earthquake.

city when the earthquake occurred. After the disaster, the survivors, in gratitude for their preservation, built a Temple of Zeus Soter, "Zeus the Savior," in Daphne.

In antiquity, earthquakes were often taken as manifestations of divine wrath, and this time the Christians were held responsible because of their attempts to upset the worship of the traditional gods. Elsewhere is given an account of how Ignatius, the bishop of the city, was arrested, condemned, and sent to Rome, where he was executed by being eaten alive by wild beasts in the arena. Other executions took place in Antioch itself.[27]

How much of Trajan's varied building activity in Antioch was occasioned by the damage caused by the earthquake cannot now be determined. We hear of the restoration of the colonnades along the main street which sounds almost certainly like repair of earthquake damage,[28] the construction of the Middle Gate, a monumental arch near the torrent Parmenius, bearing a statue of the she-wolf suckling Romulus and Remus;[29] the restoration of the theater, in which was placed a statue of Calliope, who ranked as a tutelary deity of the city; and a Temple of Artemis at Daphne.[30]

After the end of the Parthian campaign, Trajan set out for Rome from Seleucia Pieria, in August A.D. 117; but he died suddenly in Cilicia a few days later. Hadrian, who had been left in Antioch as governor of Syria, soon departed for Rome, having given orders for the construction in Antioch of a temple in honor of the deified Trajan, which is described as "small and very graceful."[31]

Coming to the throne when the Roman Empire had reached its greatest development, Hadrian (A.D. 117-138)

---

[27] See below, Ch. VI.

[28] Malalas, p. 275, 21f.

[29] Malalas, p. 275, 13ff.

[30] Malalas, p. 277, 11.

[31] *Scriptores Historiae Augustae* (hereinafter called *S.H.A.*), *Hadrian*, v, 9f; Aurelius Victor, *Epitome*, XIV, 2; Suidas, *s.v.* Iobianos. The temple was turned into a library by the Emperor Julian, and was burned by the Emperor Jovian.

devoted his restless energy and remarkable creative ability
to the supervision of the government and the development
of the cities of the empire. He travelled, in every part of the
Roman world, for nearly twelve of the twenty-one years of
his reign, everywhere planning new buildings and public
works. Antioch, which he visited three times, was among
the many cities which received notable benefits at his hands.

At Antioch, Hadrian's name was remembered for his valuable improvements to the water supply of the city.[32] He built
an aqueduct (or completed one begun by Trajan—the source
is not clear), and at Daphne he constructed an elaborate
reservoir designed to conserve and control the water of the
famous springs. This was called a "theater," from its plan
and its façade, which resembled the background of a contemporary theater. Into this reservoir was directed the water
of one of the springs, named Saramanna, which had not
previously been controlled. The reservoir also received water
that formerly had flowed out through a wild ravine in a
torrent going down through Daphne to the Orontes; this was
now brought under control by means of a wall. The reservoir
itself was equipped with a set of five adjutages or efflux
pipes of different sizes by means of which the rate of flow
through the aqueduct leading to the city could be regulated.[33]
At the upper end of the reservoir, at the point where the
water from the springs entered it, was built a Temple of the
Nymphs which contained a great seated statue of Hadrian
depicted as Zeus, holding the celestial sphere. The reservoir
appears in the topographical border of the mosaic of Yakto,
which shows some of the notable monuments of Antioch
toward the end of the fifth century after Christ (Fig. 59,
No. 51). Hadrian also rebuilt the installation at another of the
springs, named Pallas, which had been damaged (presumably by the earthquake), and constructed a channel for the

[32] Malalas, p. 277, 20ff.
[33] See Frontinus' description of Roman adjutages, De aquis, 1, 23-34.

distribution of its water to Daphne. He closed the spring called Castalia, evidently because it had become inactive.[34] The dedication of the work at Daphne was celebrated at a special festival, on 23 June A.D. 129, while Hadrian was visiting Antioch.

In the Antonine Age which succeeded the reign of Hadrian, the tranquillity of the Roman world was unbroken, and Antioch, along with the remainder of the empire, enjoyed one of the greatest periods of prosperity and security the Roman state had ever known. Antoninus Pius (A.D. 138-161) paved with Theban granite the main colonnaded street and all the other streets of Antioch. The work was commemorated in a stone inscription (now lost) placed on the Gate of the Cherubim, where the operation was begun.[35] There was a fire at Antioch during Antoninus Pius' reign, but we have no details concerning it.[36]

Under Marcus Aurelius (A.D. 161-180) we hear of Antioch chiefly as the scene of the pleasures of the emperor's colleague Lucius Verus (A.D. 161-169), who had been sent to the East to take command in the war against the Parthians. When he arrived, Verus spent his time in luxurious living, moving between Daphne, where he spent the summers, Laodicea-on-the-Sea, where he passed the winters, and Antioch, where he stayed the remainder of the time.[37] In Antioch, Verus occupied himself with gladiatorial shows and hunting, and he was ridiculed by the citizens. He was on bad terms with Annius Libo, the governor of Syria, but fortunately he entrusted the conduct of the war to three generals who were able soldiers, Statius Priscus, Avidius Cassius, and Martius Verus. Avidius Cassius, a native Syrian who had already achieved eminence as a military commander and was famous

---

[34] Ammianus Marcellinus, xxii, 12, 8. This was later reopened by the Emperor Julian.

[35] Malalas, p. 280, 20ff. [36] S.H.A., Antoninus Pius, ix, 2.

[37] S.H.A., Verus, vii, 1-10.

as an iron disciplinarian, was put in charge of training the Syrian legions, which had become debauched and demoralized. To indicate the extent to which the troops had become corrupted, one writer thought it sufficient to comment that they were "given over to the behavior of Daphne."[38]

After the capture of Seleucia on the Tigris, in December A.D. 165, the Roman forces were stricken with an epidemic disease, probably (from the contemporary accounts) smallpox. The cause and treatment of the disease were unknown. Returning to Syria, the troops brought the disease with them; and for fifteen years it ran through the whole Roman world, causing many deaths.[39] Antioch was the first large center that the infected army reached and the loss of life must have been considerable.

In the middle of the following year, Verus returned to Rome, taking with him a number of actors, musicians, and other entertainers from Syria and Egypt.[40]

For almost ten years we hear nothing of the history of the city. Then, in mid-April of A.D. 175, it became one of the two chief centers of the revolt of Avidius Cassius. Cassius had been governor of Syria in A.D. 165 while he was in command of the Parthian war. Later he was given an extraordinary command over the whole of the East, while the emperor was busy with wars in the northern part of the empire. By the spring of A.D. 175 the empire appeared to be in such a state of difficulty that Cassius (perhaps instigated by the empress, who anticipated her husband's early death) judged it opportune to proclaim himself emperor. He had a reputation for harshness, but he had some claim to popularity in Syria, being a native of Cyrrhus, and he controlled Egypt, the granary of the empire. What success he might eventually

[38] *S.H.A., Avidius Cassius*, v, 5.
[39] *S.H.A., Verus*, viii, 2-3; Cassius Dio, lxxi, 2, 4; Ammianus Marcellinus, xxiii, 6, 24.
[40] *S.H.A., Verus*, viii, 7-11.

have had we cannot judge, for his revolt was brought to an end, after three months and six days, when he was murdered by two army officers.

The emperor had already set out for the East before Cassius' death. When he reached Syria he adopted a policy of clemency toward the rebels, and he pardoned communities which had sided with Cassius, with the exception of Cyrrhus and Antioch, which had been the centers of disaffection. At first he refused even to visit Antioch; and he abolished the local games of the city and forbade all public meetings. These measures were necessary precautions against further plotting and revolution. Later, however, the emperor relented and did pay a visit to Antioch.[41]

Commodus (A.D. 180-192), the unworthy son of Marcus Aurelius, became acquainted with Antioch when he visited it in company with his father during the imperial tour in the East in A.D. 175-176,[42] but he was never in the city again. Commodus' principal interest was his own pleasures, and the government was largely conducted by his favorites. It is characteristic of the emperor's devotion to athletics and spectacles of all kinds, in which he himself liked to appear as a performer, that most of what is known of the history of Antioch during his reign is concerned with the Olympic Games and other festivals of the city. In this respect the history of Antioch seems to be characteristic also of other eastern cities under Commodus.

As has been mentioned, the games and spectacles of Antioch, including the Olympic Games, had been abolished by Marcus Aurelius in A.D. 175-176 as a punishment for the city's support of Avidius Cassius. Apparently soon after Commodus became sole emperor, the people of Antioch, knowing his passion for games and entertainments, presented a petition asking for permission to resume the Olympic Games and

[41] S.H.A., *Marcus Antoninus*, xxv, 8-12; *Avidius Cassius*, IX, 1.
[42] S.H.A., *Commodus*, II, 3.

other festivals, and requesting as well that the financial arrangements for the games be reorganized.[43] The petition was granted and the games were resumed in A.D. 181. The original endowment of the games was transferred to the public treasury to protect it against misuse. The games were to be celebrated for forty-five days during July and August. The principal official, in charge of the actual performance of the games, had the traditional and honorable title of Alytarch (chief police officer). The Alytarch was always one of the most prominent citizens of Antioch, and he was supposed to contribute generously to the cost of the festival. During his tenure of office he received divine honors, as the representative of Zeus, in whose honor the games were held. He did not sleep under a roof or in a bed, but carried out an ascetic ritual of sleeping in the open air, in the courtyard of the Kaisarion. He wore a white robe ornamented with gold, a crown adorned with rubies and pearls and other precious stones, and white sandals, and carried an ebony rod.

The secretary of the games was appointed by the senate and people of the city; he received the honors paid to Apollo, and wore a white robe and a solid gold crown in the form of laurel leaves. A third official, a youth called the *amphithales* (the term meaning that both his parents were living), was also chosen by the senate and people. He wore a white silk robe and a crown woven of laurel leaves, containing a gold bust of Zeus; and he received the honors paid to Hermes. The Alytarch was supposed to distribute largess to the people during his occupancy of office, and we hear of a free distribution of bread on one occasion.

To signalize the restoration of the games, new buildings for use in the festival were erected. The most important of these was the Xystos, a covered running-track of the Greek

[43] Malalas, pp. 283, 1-290, 2, is the source of our knowledge of the reorganization of the Olympic Games and of the other festivals and entertainments.

type, with a colonnade and seats, which could be used during rainy weather or during excessive heat. The Xystos was a part of an important complex of public buildings; it stood near the Temple of Athene, which was restored on this occasion, and on the other side of it Commodus built a public bath named for himself. At the lower end of the Xystos was built a temple to Olympian Zeus, the patron of the games.

Other festivals and entertainments at Antioch were reorganized at the same time. In the decree by which the Olympic Games were reestablished, Commodus also made provision for payment out of public funds for the support of several entertainments. Among these the best known was the Maiouma, a survival of an old Syrian cult, which in the time of Commodus had come to be an orgiastic nocturnal festival honoring Dionysus and Aphrodite; celebrated every three years, in May, it acquired a reputation for licentiousness. Commodus' decree provided for the purchase with public money of lamps, candles and other supplies and equipment. Another entertainment which became a public charge was the series of horse races which, Malalas says, were held weekly on the day of the Sun. A third appropriation was made for the hunts of wild beasts which were held in connection with the festivals of Ares and Artemis. Provision was now made to assure the supply of animals, which, it seems, were being used up more rapidly than they could be collected; Commodus' decree ordained that in each period of four years, hunts were to be held only during forty-two months, while they were to be suspended for six months during which animals were to be assembled. Finally, the emperor's decree provided for the public support of mimes and dancers. In gratitude for all these benefactions, the people of Antioch set up a bronze statue of Commodus. We know from an inscription[44] that there was a festival at Antioch

---

[44] *Fouilles de Delphes*, III, pt. 1, no. 550, line 34 (Waddington, No. 1257).

named for the emperor (*Komodeion*). This was probably an existing festival renamed.

The peace and prosperity of the Antonine Age came to an end with the death of Commodus (A.D. 192), and when the emperor died without an heir, Syria once more was the scene of a struggle for power. The contests of A.D. 193-194 were the prelude to a century of growing weakness and uncertainty for the whole empire.

After Commodus' death two emperors, Pertinax and Didius Julianus, were proclaimed and then assassinated in quick succession (A.D. 193), and a third aspirant, Pescennius Niger, appeared in Syria. Pertinax, so far as we know, had no connection with Antioch during his brief reign (January-March, A.D. 193), though he had begun his military career in Syria and later had been governor of the province. However, during the even briefer reign of Didius Julianus (March-June, A.D. 193), Antioch, along with the remainder of Syria, had a prominent role. The proclamation of Didius Julianus was unpopular with the people of Rome and they at once began to call for help from the armies, and especially for assistance from Pescennius Niger, the governor of Syria, and his troops.[45] Pescennius was proclaimed emperor in Antioch by his soldiers, and he proceeded to make the city his headquarters, using the mint to issue his own coins, and receiving delegations from the rulers of the frontier states to the east.[46] At about the same time P. Septimius Severus, the governor of Upper Pannonia, was proclaimed emperor by his legions.

It was during the reign of Didius Julianus that the Plethrion was built to accommodate the wrestling contests in the Olympic Games.[47] If the archetype of such structures received its name from the land measure *plethron*, it would have been either 100 feet long, or 10,000 square feet in area. It had two

---

[45] Cassius Dio, LXXIV, 13, 5.   [46] Herodian, II, 7, 9ff.

[47] Malalas, p. 290, 14-20. Libanius' tenth oration is concerned with enlargements of the Plethrion in the fourth century.

rows of stone seats for spectators, and was located near the Kaisarion, the Xystos and the Bath of Commodus.

After Didius Julianus was killed (1 June A.D. 193), it was the first task of the new emperor, Septimius Severus (A.D. 193-211), to deal with Pescennius Niger, who was collecting strong support in Syria and was actually more popular in Rome than Severus himself. Many of Pescennius' troops were from Antioch, and almost all the young men of the city had joined his forces.[48] Early in July, Severus left Rome and, gaining control of Asia Minor, forced Pescennius to fall back on Antioch, where he collected fresh troops and resources.[49] Here Pescennius was distracted by the jealousy and rivalry between Antioch and Laodicea-on-the-Sea, which had declared for Severus.[50] The two armies met in the spring of A.D. 194 at Issus and Pescennius was defeated. He fled on horseback to Antioch and found the city full of lamentation for its men who had fallen in the battle. Pescennius realized he could expect no more backing from Antioch and he fled, with some of his soldiers. He hid in one of the suburbs, but was discovered by the cavalrymen who were searching for him, and they beheaded him on the spot. Antioch surrendered to the imperial troops.[51]

Septimius Severus, in order to guard against any future attempt by a governor of the powerful province of Syria to make himself emperor, divided the province into two, Syria Coele and Syria Phoenice. Special punishment was devised for Antioch, not only because of its favor to Pescennius Niger, but because its citizens, always independent in spirit, had seen fit to make fun of Septimius Severus when he was stationed in the city in A.D. 179 in command of the Fourth Legion.[52] For punishment, Septimius had at his disposal

---

[48] Herodian, III, 1, 4.   [49] Herodian, III, 2, 10.

[50] Herodian, III, 3, 3.

[51] Herodian, III, 4, 6; Cassius Dio, LXXV, 8, 3; Ammianus Marcellinus, XXVI, 8, 15.

[52] *S.H.A., Severus*, IX, 4.

a peculiarly effective device. Laodicea-on-the-Sea had from the beginning been jealous of Antioch, which, originally equal with Laodicea in rank, had soon surpassed it in importance.[53] The people of Antioch, never noted for tact or modesty, very likely took no trouble to ease any of the numerous and varied causes of neighborly friction which formed a regular feature of life in the Greek cities.[54] Laodicea did possess many advantages in which it could take pride.

The emperor took full advantage of this situation. Antioch was deprived of its title of metropolis and its position as capital of Syria, and was reduced to the administrative status of a "village" of Laodicea, which was made the capital.[55] Severus conferred many other benefits on Laodicea and presented it with public buildings. As a further humiliation to Antioch, the emperor removed the local Olympic festival from the city and combined it with the games he instituted at Issus in commemoration of his victory there. This measure was also necessary politically, since the opposing factions in the circus were active political parties and were potential sources of revolution.[56] A similar measure had been taken by Marcus Aurelius, who abolished the games and public assemblies of Antioch after the city had supported the rebel Avidius Cassius; and the same treatment was adopted by Theodosius I after the riot of A.D. 387, when Antioch was again made a "village" of Laodicea.

While Antioch was in disgrace, it served as the head-quarters for Severus' war against the Parthians (A.D. 197-198).[57] Eventually the city was restored to favor. Severus

---

[53] Theodoret, *Hist. eccl.*, v, 20, 2.

[54] For examples of feuds between cities, see A. H. M. Jones, *The Greek City from Alexander to Justinian*, Oxford, 1940, p. 249.

[55] Justinian, *Digest*, L, 15, 1, 3.

[56] The account of Malalas is confused; see G. Downey, "Malalas on the History of Antioch under Severus and Caracalla," *T.A.P.A.*, LXVIII, 1937, pp. 141-156.

[57] See G. J. Murphy, *The Reign of the Emperor L. Septimius Severus*

was anxious to conciliate public opinion, and his wife, Julia Domna, was a native of Syria. Late in A.D. 201 Septimius visited Antioch in order to show that the city was no longer in disfavor. While he was there, the emperor celebrated the coming of age ceremony of his son, the future Emperor Caracalla, and immediately thereafter the two entered upon a joint consulship—a rare event—on 1 January A.D. 202. Coins of Antioch issued in this year show the Tyche of Antioch, evidently as a token of the rehabilitation of the city.[58] The emperor also presented two public baths to the city.[59]

Caracalla, when he became emperor (A.D. 211-217), had good reason to be well disposed toward Antioch, which he had visited several times as a child; and the chief city of Syria would have a special claim on him in that his mother, the brilliant and masterful Julia Domna, was a member of a native royal dynasty of Emesa. The emperor not only restored to the city its Olympic Games, but did this with noteworthy promptness, so that the celebration could be held in the traditional Julian leap-year, in the summer of A.D. 212.[60] Caracalla also revived the civic pride of Antioch by removing it from the control of Laodicea and by giving it the title of colony, a coveted epithet though by now politically meaningless.[61]

The emperor stayed in Antioch twice when he went to the East in an effort to unite the Roman and the Parthian Empires. His first visit was made in May A.D. 215, and he was given an enthusiastic reception, in gratitude for his favors to the city. He proceeded to indulge in all the pleasures

---

from the Evidence of the Inscriptions, Diss., University of Pennsylvania, 1945.

[58] S.H.A., Severus, xvi, 8; A. R. Bellinger, The Syrian Tetradrachms of Caracalla and Macrinus (American Numismatic Society, Numismatic Studies, 3), New York, 1940.

[59] Malalas, p. 294, 17ff.   [60] See above, n. 56.

[61] Justinian, Digest, L, 15, 1, 3 and 8, 5.

Antioch could offer. At this time his health was so under-
mined by his excesses that he was unfit for business, and his
mother, Julia Domna, took charge of the affairs of state.[62]
Later in the year a sedition in Alexandria took Caracalla
away from Antioch, but he returned late in the same year
and spent the winter of A.D. 215-216 in the city, continuing
his efforts to gain control of Parthia.[63] We hear of his presiding, on 27 May A.D. 216, at the appeal of a lawsuit connected with the Temple of Zeus Hypsistos at Dmeir, in the
plain east of Damascus; one of the lawyers participating
was the distinguished Egnatius Lollianus.[64] Then, diplomatic
efforts having proved unsuccessful, Caracalla was forced to
undertake the invasion of Parthia, and he left Antioch in
the summer of A.D. 216. During his absence his mother remained in Antioch, charged with the task of sorting the
official communications which arrived for the emperor, and
sending on only those which needed immediate attention.[65]

Caracalla was assassinated in eastern Syria, in April A.D.
217, and the praetorian prefect Macrinus was proclaimed
emperor in the field. He at once sent for his son Diadu-
menianus, who had been staying in Antioch, and had him
proclaimed Caesar. Macrinus then returned to Antioch and
proceeded to consolidate his position, distributing a largess
to the people. He ordered Caracalla's mother Julia Domna
to leave Antioch, but she either killed herself or died of the
effects of a disease.[66] Macrinus, instead of going to Rome,
remained in Antioch to supervise the Parthian war, and An-

[62] Herodian, IV, 8, 6; Cassius Dio, LXXVIII, 18 and 20, I.

[63] Herodian, IV, 8, 6 and 9, 8.

[64] P. Roussel and P. de Visscher, "Les inscriptions du temple de Dmeir,"
Syria, XXIII, 1942-43, pp. 173-194. The suit was concerned with the tenure
of the priesthood of the temple.

[65] Cassius Dio, LXXVIII, 18.

[66] Cassius Dio, LXXIX, 23; Herodian, IV, 13, 8.

tioch became a kind of eastern capital, its mint acting as an imperial mint.[67]

Macrinus was unable to maintain himself in power and he was eventually defeated by the forces of Julia Maesa, the sister of Julia Domna. Julia Maesa was thus able to put on the throne her grandson Elagabalus (A.D. 218-222), a depraved youth of fourteen who had been serving as a priest of the native temple in Emesa.[68] Elagabalus after his accession remained in Antioch for several months, until his position was secure. In Rome, after three years of religious mania and fantastic excesses, he was murdered.

Severus Alexander (A.D. 222-235), who at the age of fourteen succeeded his cousin Elagabalus, was a person of far different character and upbringing. Honest and virtuous, he had been kept away from the influence of Elagabalus and trained for the responsibilities of power. During his reign he was under the tutelage of his mother Julia Mamaea.

By the year A.D. 230 the rise of the new Sassanid Empire, succeeding the Parthian state, presented a serious challenge to the Roman world. For the next two generations the Roman emperors had constantly to struggle against the Persian menace, and in these efforts Antioch was destined to play a major role.

The years after the death of Severus Alexander (A.D. 235) were filled with the contests for power of a whole series of emperors (A.D. 235-244), and little is known of the history of Antioch. At the same time the new threat was rising in the East. The Persian king Sapor I (A.D. 241-272) pressed on with imperialist plans for the conquest of Syria and Asia Minor. A peace was made in A.D. 249, but discontent and alarm were growing in Antioch, and even a certain amount of pro-Persian sentiment began to appear there as people lost confidence in the ability of the emperors to keep the

[67] Herodian, v, 2, 3ff; Bellinger, *op.cit.* (above, n. 58).
[68] Herodian, v, 4, 1ff; Cassius Dio, LXXIX, 31.

Persians out of Syria. There was in fact enough friendly feeling toward Persia in Antioch to make possible a pro-Persian coup.[69] An adventurer does indeed appear just at this time, in the person of Mariades, whose Semitic name was hellenized as Kyriades.

The accounts of Mariades' career differ in details.[70] He was wealthy and well-born. Because of peculation of some sort he had to leave Antioch, and he fled to Persia. Apparently he was able to organize a pro-Persian party in the city before he left. Then he accompanied Sapor when the king invaded Syria in A.D. 253. Antioch was captured and burned, and we hear that Mariades and his supporters played a part in the taking of the city.

When the Persians withdrew from Antioch, they took with them a number of captives, whose technical knowledge and skills Sapor was anxious to utilize. Among those deported was Demetrianus, the bishop of Antioch. The captives were settled in Persia, where they were later to be joined by others who were carried away after the second capture of Antioch in A.D. 260.

The year A.D. 253 saw the accession of a new emperor, Valerian (A.D. 253-260). He hastened to the East to organize an attack on the Persians and one of his first undertakings was the rebuilding of Antioch. In the course of this work he constructed a fortified camp on the island, the foundations of which Diocletian later used when he built a palace.[71]

The Persians continued their attacks on Syria, and captured Dura in A.D. 256. Valerian mounted a counter-offensive which came to grief in the summer of A.D. 260 when the Roman army was disabled by sickness, and finally the emperor him-

[69] See J. Gagé, "Les Perses à Antioche et les courses de l'hippodrome au milieu du IIIe siècle, à propos du 'transfuge' syrien Mariadès," *Bulletin de la Faculté des Lettres de Strasbourg*, XXXI, 1953, pp. 301-324.

[70] The sources are the *S.H.A., Trig. tyran.*, 11; Ammianus Marcellinus, XXIII, 5, 3; Malalas, p. 295, 20ff; Peter Patricius, frag. 1 (*F.H.G.*, IV, p. 192).

[71] Malalas, p. 306, 21f. By mistake the chronicler calls Valerian Gallienus.

self was taken prisoner by the Persians. Sapor then invaded Syria and once more captured Antioch. The details have been lost. Whether the traitor Mariades was again active in this campaign is not certain.[72]

The deportation of captives to Persia was repeated, and a second group of learned and skilled inhabitants of the city were taken to Persia where the king was anxious to make use of their services. The Christians were given land and dwellings and proceeded, under the tolerant regime of the Persians, to build churches and monasteries. Sapor rebuilt the city of Gondisapor, which had become ruinous, and settled some of the captives there, naming the place Beh-az-Andêw-i-Sâpûr, which may be translated "Sapor's Better-than-Antioch."

The rulers of the caravan city Palmyra had been hoping to take advantage of the struggle between Rome and Persia to establish their own independence, and Prince Odenath of Palmyra now offered to support the Romans, planning in this way to expand his own power. The new emperor Gallienus (A.D. 260-268) welcomed Odenath's help, and the Palmyrenes were able to drive the Persians back to the Euphrates. Gallienus in gratitude appointed Odenath to the supreme command of the Roman forces in the East. Odenath proceeded to win control of most of the cities of Syria, and when Ballista and Quietus set themselves up as usurpers in Antioch, he defeated them.[73] Syria was thus nominally brought under the control of Gallienus, though Odenath was the actual master of the East, and it was Odenath and the Palmyrene troops who saved the eastern lands of the Roman Empire from the Persians. After Odenath was assassinated in A.D. 266/7 he was succeeded by his wife Zenobia, who remained in actual control of Syria.

Antioch had come under Palmyrene domination along

---

[72] Ammianus Marcellinus, XXIII, 5, 3.

[73] *S.H.A.*, *Gallieni*, III, 1-5; *Trig. tyran.*, XIV, 1f; XV, 4f; Zonaras, XII, 24.

with the remainder of Syria, though it remained nominally under the rule of Gallienus. At this time the leading figure in the city was its bishop, Paul of Samosata.[74] Paul came from the Semitic part of Syria and represented the Semitic interests rather than those of the Graeco-Roman element in the population. He was entrusted with civil as well as ecclesiastical functions, and enjoyed the support of Palmyra and acted as representative in Antioch of the Palmyrene regime. Paul was accused by his enemies of being heretical and of receiving bribes. He clothed himself with worldly honors and wished to be called procurator rather than bishop, "strutting about in the market-places, reading and dictating letters as he walked in public, and attended by a bodyguard."[75] He was also accused of setting up as a magistrate with a private audience chamber. An effort was made to depose Paul at a church council called at Antioch in A.D. 264, but no result was achieved. Four years later a second council did depose Paul and elected as bishop Domnus, the son of Paul's predecessor Demetrianus; but Paul, relying on the support of Palmyra, refused to lay down his office.[76]

Antioch continued under the control of Palmyra until the accession to the imperial throne of the famous general Aurelian (A.D. 270-275). One of Aurelian's first problems was the spreading power of Palmyra, which now dominated Egypt and parts of Asia Minor as well as Syria. Queen Zenobia, thinking that Aurelian was fully occupied with other difficulties, took the opportunity to proclaim the complete independence of Palmyra (A.D. 271). Her son Waballath took the title of Augustus and had appropriate coins struck in his name at the mints of Antioch and Alexandria.

Aurelian now took action and marched to Asia Minor,

[74] See G. Bardy, *Paul de Samosate, étude historique,* 2d ed., Louvain, 1929.

[75] Eusebius, *Eccl. hist.,* VII, 30, 2-17, transl. of Oulton and Lawlor in the Loeb Classical Library.

[76] Eusebius, *Eccl. hist.,* VII, 30, 19.

which he reconquered in the early part of A.D. 272. A substantial force of the Palmyrene army under command of the general Zabdas, and accompanied by Zenobia herself, was waiting in Antioch, which Aurelian could be expected to make his first objective in Syria.[77]

Apparently planning to circle about Antioch and cut the escape route to the south, Aurelian did not approach the city by the direct Pagrae-Antioch road, but took the route which skirted the eastern side of the Lake of Antioch.[78] From this he would reach the Antioch-Beroea road, along which he could move on Antioch from the east. Somewhere along the Antioch-Beroea road east of the crossing of the Orontes at the town of Gephyra the Romans encountered a large force of Palmyrene cavalry. This seems to have represented a major part of the Palmyrene forces at Antioch.

On learning that he would have to face the Palmyrene cavalry, Aurelian detached his infantry and sent it across the Orontes, since he knew it could not stand against the Palmyrene horse. He ordered his cavalry not to do battle at once, but to simulate withdrawal, so that the Palmyrenes might be worn out by the heat and the weight of their heavy armor. The Romans fell back along the highway toward Immae, a village that lay in the direction of Beroea, and when it was seen that the Palmyrenes were showing signs of fatigue, the Romans turned on them and won a complete victory. Those of the Palmyrenes who could do so, escaped to Antioch. The Palmyrene general Zabdas probably realized that the people of the city, on learning of the disaster, would rise in favor of Aurelian, whose clemency during his recovery of Asia Minor had become known in Antioch; moreover, knowledge of the superiority of the Roman army would turn the local population against the Palmyrene regime.

[77] Zosimus, I, 50, 2.
[78] See G. Downey, "Aurelian's Victory over Zenobia at Immae, A.D. 272," *T.A.P.A.*, LXXXI, 1950, pp. 57-68, with map.

Immediately after the battle, therefore, he let it be known that he had defeated and captured Aurelian, and paraded through the streets a man who resembled the emperor. The trick succeeded, and Zabdas and Zenobia were able to flee from Antioch that same night with the remainder of their forces, leaving a rear guard behind them. They went by way of the road through Daphne which led to Apamea, Epiphania, and Emesa. The rear guard established itself on a height above Daphne.

On the next day, when he learned of Zenobia's flight, Aurelian gave up his plan for an infantry assault on Antioch, and the city opened the gates and welcomed him. The emperor proclaimed an amnesty, and people who had fled from the city returned. It is a tribute to the strength of Aurelian's military discipline that he was able to keep his troops from plundering the city. The Palmyrene rear guard was easily dislodged from its stronghold at Daphne and annihilated. Aurelian pursued the Palmyrenes and defeated them, and Zenobia was eventually captured at the Euphrates. She was taken to Antioch and exhibited in the hippodrome mounted on a camel, then was sent to Rome for further public display.[79]

Aurelian was assassinated in A.D. 275; but he had succeeded, even during his brief reign, in restoring the political unity and financial stability of the empire. Antioch, which for more than thirty years suffered repeatedly from Persian conquest, pillage, depopulation, destruction, and finally Palmyrene domination and the civil and ecclesiastical disturbances which rose about Paul of Samosata, had in the last few years of Aurelian's reign enjoyed a brief period of tranquillity.

Under Aurelian's successor Probus (A.D. 276-282) Antioch received special assistance toward its recovery, including a free distribution of wheat, at public expense.[80] There was also a building program for the restoration of the physical

[79] Malalas, p. 300, 11-17.
[80] Malalas, p. 302, 9-11.

damage to the city; a functionary named Julius Saturninus was placed in charge of the work.

At the death of Probus, a brief struggle for power ended with the choice of Diocletian (A.D. 284-305), which brought the empire to a new phase. Diocletian transformed the empire from a principate to an absolute monarchy, putting into effect changes which the whole course of recent history had demonstrated were necessary. Order had to be restored, the civil administration reorganized, taxation and currency reformed and stabilized; the imperial throne and dynastic succession had to be safeguarded and the defense of the frontiers assured. The rise of Christianity posed a political problem for which a solution must be found.

It was Diocletian's merit that he had not only the insight but the practical ability to organize his program of reform. Antioch shared with the other cities of the empire the new security and prosperity made possible by the new regime of Diocletian. The emperor himself visited Antioch on a number of occasions and his benefactions to the city prepared it for the important role it was to enjoy under the first Christian emperors.

The best known of Diocletian's buildings at Antioch was the imperial palace, which was constructed on the island at some time before A.D. 298 (Fig. 5).[81] Designed for the use of the emperor and his court when he visited Antioch, the palace was modeled on the standard plan of the fortified camp of the Roman army, and the building at Antioch served as the prototype of the famous palace which Diocletian later erected at Salona for a residence during his retirement. The choice of Antioch as a place where a palace should be

[81] See further G. Downey, "The Palace of Diocletian at Antioch," *Annales archéologiques de Syrie*, III, 1953, pp. 106-116. The palace is dated by the circumstance that it appears in the background of the scene on the triumphal arch of Galerius at Thessalonica in which Galerius is shown celebrating the triumph of A.D. 298, which was held at Antioch; see K.-F. Kinch, *L'arc de triomphe de Salonique*, Paris, 1890, p. 37.

built illustrates the importance of the city as a military and administrative headquarters.

From the description of the palace by Libanius we know that it occupied the space between the middle of the island and the outer branch of the river.[82] Along the river, the wall was surmounted, at the second story, by a covered portico in which the emperor could walk and enjoy the air and the view. There were towers at either end of this gallery, and between the palace and the river there was a road which led from the city across a bridge to the suburbs.

As at Constantinople and Thessalonica, the palace was adjacent to the hippodrome. The ceremonies and spectacles of the hippodrome played an important part in the political and ceremonial life of the emperor, so that it was essential that palace and hippodrome be closely integrated.

Other buildings at Antioch reflect the strengthening of the defenses of the eastern frontier. Arms factories were built at Antioch, Edessa, and Damascus. There were two at Antioch, one devoted to the production of shields and weapons, the other to the making of coats of mail.[83] Diocletian also built granaries at Antioch to assure regular supplies of grain for both civilian and military use.[84] The mint of Antioch was reorganized and took its place in the new monetary system in which all mints throughout the empire now came under direct imperial control and produced coins of a uniform type.[85] Likewise we hear of five baths built by Diocletian, of which one was named for the emperor and stood on the island near the hippodrome.[86] Another bath was reserved for the use of members of the senatorial order.[87]

The Olympic Games of Antioch were of special interest

[82] Libanius, *Antiochikos*, 205-207.
[83] Malalas, p. 307, 20-23; *Notitia Dignitatum*, Or., xi, 18ff.
[84] Malalas, p. 307, 2-5.
[85] See W. Ensslin, *Cambridge Ancient History*, xii, pp. 403f.
[86] Malalas, pp. 306, 22ff; 308, 3-5.
[87] Malalas, p. 308, 3-5.

to Diocletian because they were held in honor of Zeus, the patron deity of the emperor and his dynasty. To do honor to his protector, Diocletian rebuilt the Olympic stadium at Daphne, and in the stadium he constructed shrines of Olympian Zeus and of Nemesis.[88] Diocletian also on one occasion acted as Alytarch, or presiding official, at a celebration of the games, probably in A.D. 300, a year in which he spent much time in Antioch.[89]

[88] Malalas, p. 307, 5-16.
[89] Malalas, p. 310, 7ff.

CHAPTER VI

THE EARLY CHRISTIAN COMMUNITY

THE STORY of the early Christian fellowship at Antioch, where the disciples were first given the name of Christians (Acts 11:26), is one of the city's chief claims to distinction; and in the development of the Christian community Antioch served as a connecting link between antiquity and the modern world.

In the time of Christ, a special religious situation had grown up in Antioch which was to make the city peculiarly fertile ground when Christianity reached it. Antioch had shared, with other centers in which Hellenistic religion and philosophy had flourished, the changes characteristic of the late Hellenistic age, in which the old religious cults and philosophies were tending to become matters of individual belief, as people sought religious satisfaction for their own problems and aspirations.[1] In addition the city, as a meeting point of the Greek and the Oriental civilizations, filled with orientalized Greeks and hellenized orientals of all classes and all degrees of education, had come to contain, as part of its normal daily existence, not only the old established Hellenic cults, of Zeus, Apollo, and the rest of the pantheon, but the Syrian cults of Baal and the mother-goddess—partly assimilated to Zeus and Artemis—as well as the mystery religions with their doctrines of salvation, of death and re-generation, and their promises for the after life. As one of the largest cities of the Roman Empire and one of the great commercial centers of the ancient world, with business con-

---

[1] A. D. Nock, "Early Gentile Christianity and its Hellenistic Back-ground," in *Essays on the Trinity and the Incarnation*, ed. by A. E. J. Rawlinson, London, 1928, pp. 51-156; H. R. Willoughby, *Pagan Regeneration*, Chicago, 1929; A. D. Nock, *Conversion*, Oxford, 1933.

nections in all parts of the empire, Antioch saw the coming and going of people of all sorts, bringing news of events everywhere in the Roman world. Another factor of prime importance was the presence of a large and ancient Jewish community. This community had attracted to its ceremonies and its teachings numbers of Gentiles who found in Judaism an ethical doctrine that was more satisfactory to them that the pagan teaching.[2] Thus Antioch was peculiarly receptive to the new message.

When the persecution broke out in Jerusalem after the execution of Stephen, many of the followers of Jesus fled from the city and traveled as far as Phoenice, Cyprus, and Antioch, preaching to Jews.[3] In Antioch, however, some of the refugees, Hellenist (Greek-speaking) Jews who came from Cyprus and Cyrene, began to preach not only to Jews but to Greek-speaking pagans as well.[4] A man of Antioch of Gentile blood named Nicolaus had been an early proselyte and became one of the seven deacons in Jerusalem.[5] Whether, when the persecution occurred, he went to Antioch with the early missionaries, we are not told, but it is easy to believe that he would have wished to do so, rather than remain in hiding in Jerusalem.[6]

The efforts of the Hellenist Jews in Antioch met with great success, and thus the mission to the Gentiles was born. Most of the early converts were doubtless Gentiles who had already been attracted to Judaism, and the conversion of other Gentiles would follow readily in a large cosmopolitan city such as Antioch where traditional barriers of race,

[2] Josephus, *War*, vii, 43-45; Kraeling, "Jewish Community," p. 147.

[3] Acts 11:19.

[4] Acts 11:20f. A good account of the early mission at Antioch is provided by W. L. Knox, *St. Paul and the Church at Jerusalem*, Cambridge, Eng., 1951, pp. 156-198.

[5] Acts 6:5.

[6] See K. Bauer, *Antiochia in der ältesten Kirchengeschichte*, Tübingen, 1919, pp. 19f.

nationality, and formal religion would easily be submerged.[7] For both religious and philosophical needs, the new teaching was unique and superior to anything that could be found elsewhere.[8] A practical reason for the success of the early mission to Antioch was that the city, as the capital of Syria, was governed by a legate, and enjoyed a reasonable degree of public order. There was less opportunity for mob violence such as had occurred in Jerusalem, which was subject to the procurators of Judaea, officials who were inferior not only in rank, but apparently in ability to the legates of Syria.[9]

When the elders in Jerusalem heard of the surprising work that was going on in the Syrian capital, they sent Barnabas, a native of Cyprus like some of the early missionaries in Antioch,[10] to inspect the undertaking and report on its success and prospects. Barnabas as a Cypriote would have felt quite at home in Antioch, and the people of the city would have recognized him as a member of a neighboring community with which they were familiar. He made further conversions, and seeing that the mission was prospering, he went to Tarsus, where Paul was now living, and asked him to come to Antioch to help in the work. Barnabas and Paul remained in Antioch for a year teaching, and many people were converted.[11] The local tradition was that they preached in a street called Singon or Siagon ("jawbone") near the Pantheon.[12] The death of Stephen seems to have taken place about A.D.

[7] On the role of Antioch and other non-Jewish centers in the spread of Christianity, see especially Bauer, *op.cit.*, pp. 23-25; D. W. Riddle, "Environment as a Factor in the Achievement of Self-Consciousness in Early Christianity," *Journal of Religion*, VII, 1927, pp. 146-163; M. C. Tenney, "The Influence of Antioch on Apostolic Christianity," *Bibliotheca Sacra*, CVII, 1950, pp. 298-310.

[8] For an excellent statement of the reasons for the early success of Christianity, see Nock, "Early Gentile Christianity" (cited above, n. 1), pp. 154-156.

[9] On this important point, see Knox, *op.cit.* (above, n. 4), p. 156.

[10] Acts 11:22-26. [11] Acts 11:26.

[12] Malalas, p. 242, 11f. The location of the Pantheon is not known.

34 or possibly 36,[13] and the mission to Antioch would have begun soon after that. Barnabas was apparently sent there about A.D. 38. The chronology of Paul's conversion (though this is disputed) and of his sojourn in Cilicia following it would put the beginning of the labors of Paul and Barnabas in Antioch at about A.D. 40.[14]

The result of this work was the emergence of a community different from the original group of the followers of Christ in Jerusalem, and the change was typified by the appearance of the new term "Christians," in the early 40's.[15] The distinctive word apparently was adopted by the Roman authorities in the city when they found it necessary to have an official designation for the new sect, which by now, in Antioch, was becoming distinct from Judaism.[16] Such a designation would be called for in Antioch where there were many cults of all kinds.

We have no evidence for the size of the Christian community at Antioch at this time. Concerning its organization we are told that there were "prophets" and "teachers," specified as Barnabas, Symeon Niger, Lucius of Cyrene, Manaen, and Paul.[17] It was these men and their comrades in the fellowship at Antioch who planned the systematic missionary campaigns of Paul and his colleagues; and the community

[13] See K. Lake, "The Chronology of Acts," in F. J. F. Jackson and K. Lake, *The Beginnings of Christianity*, London, 1920-33, v, pp. 445-474.

[14] On the chronology, see Knox, *op.cit.* (above, n. 4), p. 160, n. 1.

[15] Acts 11:26.

[16] R. Paribeni, "Sull'origine del nome Cristiano," *Nuovo bullettino di archeologia cristiana*, XIX, 1913, pp. 37-41; E. Peterson, "Christianus," *Miscellanea G. Mercati*, I, Vatican City, 1946, pp. 353-372 (*Studi e Testi*, No. 121); E. J. Bickerman, "The Name of Christians," *Harvard Theological Review*, XLII, 1949, pp. 109-124; J. Moreau, "Le nom des Chrétiens," *Nouvelle Clio*, I-II, 1949-50, pp. 190-192; H. Fuchs, "Tacitus über die Christen," *Vigiliae Christianae*, IV, 1950, p. 69, n. 5.

[17] Acts 13:1. On the organization of the early community at Antioch and its relation to the church at Jerusalem, see P. Gaechter, "Jerusalem und Antiochia: Ein Beitrag zur urkirchlichen Rechtsentwicklung," *Zeitschrift für katholische Theologie*, LXX, 1948, pp. 1-48.

provided the means by which the missionary journeys were started.

It is significant that in its organization the group at Antioch was different from that of Jerusalem, which was governed, in the manner of a synagogue, by a board of elders and presbyters, among whom James, the brother of the Lord, had a leading or presiding position. Since the community at Antioch had been started by refugees from Jerusalem, it is tempting to suppose that the difference in the organization at Antioch reflects deliberate choice, and that the refugees, not satisfied with conditions at Jerusalem, adopted in Antioch a form of fellowship more in keeping with their own views. This may be the earliest sign of the rift between Antioch and Jerusalem which later became of radical importance.[18]

Whether because of its numbers or because it included some well-to-do people, the community was strong enough by about the year A.D. 46 to send financial aid to the brethren in Jerusalem, by the hands of Barnabas and Paul, to relieve the distress caused by a famine which had occurred at that time.[19] It was apparently on this same visit to Jerusalem[20] that Barnabas and Paul had to bring up with the elders of the mother-church the question of the application of the Jewish ritual law in the case of Gentile converts.[21] Originally, when the converts had all been Jews, there had been no question as to their observance of the Law, although some of the Hellenist Jews, when the new faith began to take a distinct form, disputed the necessity of preserving the Law.[22]

[18] B. H. Streeter, *The Primitive Church*, New York, 1929, pp. 76-80.

[19] Acts 11:27-30. See K. S. Gapp, "The Universal Famine under Claudius," *Harvard Theological Review*, xxviii, 1935, p. 260.

[20] See Lake in *Beginnings of Christianity* (cited above, n. 13), v, p. 203, and C. H. Buck, Jr., "The Collection for the Saints," *Harvard Theological Review*, xliii, 1950, pp. 1-29.

[21] A clear summary of the question may be found in H. Lietzmann, *The Beginnings of the Christian Church*, transl. by B. L. Woolf, London, 1952, pp. 106-109.

[22] Acts 6:11-14.

However, when Gentiles began to be converted, the question became acute, in connection with circumcision and the prescriptions governing foods and the sharing of meals between Gentile and Jewish Christians. Paul maintained that it would not be practical to apply the Law to the Gentiles and that the converts must be exempted from the ceremony of circumcision, which, to the convert, would mean that he became a member of the Jewish nation or race, and gave up his Graeco-Roman heritage. In Jerusalem, Barnabas and Paul secured from James, Peter, and John, the leaders there, an agreement that the Gentile mission should be freed from the Law.[23] After this, Peter himself visited Antioch, evidently in order to give a visible token of the agreement and to demonstrate the unity of the followers of Christ; and he complied with the agreement to the extent of eating with Gentile Christians.[24] However, Judas and Silas were sent as emissaries to Antioch by James,[25] whether in connection with the agreement or for some other purpose; and these men, representing the traditional point of view which continued to maintain the necessity of the Law, sought to win over the Jewish members of the Christian community.[26] Peter and Barnabas appear to have been impressed by the argument that born Jews might not disregard the Law, and as born Jews they broke away from Paul.[27]

The chronology of this controversy is not clear. Likewise we cannot be sure of the dates of the missionary journeys that Paul and his colleagues carried out at about this time, using Antioch as their home base. The date of the first journey of Paul is difficult to fix. The second may have taken place in A.D. 47. On this, Paul did not travel with Barnabas,

---

[23] Galatians 2:1-10.   [24] Galatians 2:11-12.

[25] On James, see W. K. Prentice, "James the Brother of the Lord," *Studies in Roman Economic and Social History in Honor of A. C. Johnson,* Princeton, 1951, pp. 144-151.

[26] Acts 15:22; Galatians 2:12.   [27] Galatians 2:11ff.

as before, but took Silas with him.[28] Barnabas also set out on another journey, taking Mark as his companion.[29] After travelling in Asia Minor and Greece, he stayed at Corinth for eighteen months, after which he returned to Antioch, probably in A.D. 51 or 52.[30] In A.D. 52 he set out on his third journey, again through Asia Minor and Greece, from which he returned, not to Antioch, but to Jerusalem, in A.D. 55 or 56.[31] This was the end of his direct connection with the church at Antioch.

In later times Peter was sometimes spoken of as the "founder" of the church at Antioch and as its "first bishop."[32] This tradition has given rise to extensive debate, both in connection with the claims of the Roman see to primacy, based on the belief in the foundation of the church there by Peter, and in connection with the later question of the rank of the major churches (Rome, Jerusalem, Alexandria, Antioch). One of the essential difficulties is chronological. According to the Roman tradition, Peter was bishop in Rome for twenty-five years, until his martyrdom in A.D. 65, and it has seemed impossible to reconcile this account with the other evidence for Peter's activities elsewhere. An episcopate of this length in Rome would, for example, allow no opportunity for Peter's presence in Jerusalem when Paul consulted the elders there at the time of the famine, and it would not allow Peter to be in Antioch when his celebrated dispute with Paul occurred (Galatians 2:11). It now seems plain that the

[28] The chronology of the missionary journeys is not easy to settle; see the study of J. Jeremias, "Untersuchungen zum Quellenproblem der Apostelgeschichte: Die Datierung der ersten Missionsreise," *Zeitschrift für die Neutestamentliche Wissenschaft*, XXXVI, 1937, pp. 220f.

[29] Acts 15:36-41.

[30] Acts 15:41-18:22. On the chronology, see Lake in *Beginnings of Christianity* (cited above, n. 13), V, pp. 470f.

[31] Acts 18:23-21:18.

[32] A useful summary of the problem of Peter's episcopate in Antioch may be found in F. H. Chase, "Peter (Simon)," in J. Hastings, *Dictionary of the Bible*, III, p. 768.

tradition that Peter was in Rome for twenty-five years before his death cannot be maintained in its literal sense. The origin of this belief probably lies, not in papal claims, but in the effort of ancient scholars to draw up a complete sequence of bishops beginning with the Ascension.[33] The best interpretation of the sources indicates that Peter was in Rome on three occasions, in A.D. 42-45, 55-56 and 63-65.[34] Whether Peter visited Antioch in the early days of the mission there, as some sources claim,[35] we cannot now determine. The evidence for a very early visit is not good, but it is intrinsically likely that the surprising success of the early missionaries in a place as important as Antioch would have led Peter to visit the city in order to see and assist in the work. Peter was certainly in Antioch at the time of the dispute with Paul, which took place probably in A.D. 47, and it seems likely that he was active in the city, and made excursions from it for missionary work, between A.D. 47 and 54.

It is not difficult to understand how Peter came to be looked upon as the "founder" of the church at Antioch and as its "first bishop," regardless of the precise meaning attached to these terms. Peter was, according to all accounts, the first of the Twelve to visit the city, a fact that would have special importance when the major churches later laid claim to apostolic foundation (the church at Alexandria claimed to have been established by Mark, that at Rome by Peter and Paul, or Peter alone, that at Jerusalem by James the brother of the Lord).[36] The fact that Peter visited Antioch would by itself give rise to the inference that he (officially)

---

[33] C. H. Turner, "The Early Episcopal Lists," *Journal of Theological Studies*, XVIII, 1916-17, p. 115.

[34] This is the conclusion reached by G. Edmundson, *The Church at Rome in the First Century*, London, 1913, pp. 49-51, 71-78, cf. 239f.

[35] On the sources for Peter's work at Antioch and Rome, see J. T. Shotwell and Louise R. Loomis, *The See of Peter*, New York, 1927.

[36] C. H. Turner, "The Early Episcopal Lists," *Journal of Theological Studies*, I, 1900, pp. 181-200, 529-553; XVIII, 1916-17, pp. 103-134.

"founded" the church there. The church at Antioch indeed looked upon Peter and his teaching with special reverence.

So, whether or not Peter could be said to be literally the founder of the church at Antioch, it is plain that in local opinion he was the principal figure in the early history of the community. According to the "Pseudo-Clementine Romance," written in the early third century, one of the most prominent men in Antioch, named Theophilus, donated his "huge house" for use as a church, and the episcopal chair of Peter was placed in this.[37] Although it is known that private houses were used as places of worship at an early period, there is no way of determining whether the tradition of this early church in Antioch has any real basis.[38] It has been suggested that this Theophilus is the person to whom the Gospel according to St. Luke and the Acts of the Apostles were dedicated.[39]

After Peter, the head of the community was Evodius, who from his name seems to have been a Gentile Christian.[40] Evodius may have been elected by the local clergy, a practice presumably followed at this time.[41] During the time when he was head of the church at Antioch, the Christian community there may have been swelled by Jewish Christians who fled from Jerusalem during the persecution initiated by the high priest Ananus in A.D. 62, in which James the brother of the Lord was martyred.[42] We may believe that

[37] *Pseudo-Clementine Recognitiones*, 71 (*P.G.* I, col. 1453). The traveller Wilbrand of Oldenburg, who visited Antioch in November 1211, was shown the church in which Peter presided, which still contained his episcopal throne: *Peregrinationes Medii Aevi Quattuor*, ed. J. C. M. Laurent, Leipzig, 1864, p. 172, 13-16.

[38] On the early use of houses as churches, see J. Finegan, *Light from the Ancient Past*, 2d ed., Princeton, 1959, pp. 492f.

[39] Luke 1:3; Acts 1:1. See *Beginnings of Christianity* (cited above, n. 13), II, p. 507; IV, p. 2.

[40] Eusebius, *Hist. eccl.*, III, 22, 1; Malalas, p. 246, 20ff.

[41] Lietzmann, *Beginnings of the Christian Church* (cited above, n. 21), pp. 145, 193f, 247f.

[42] Eusebius, *Hist. eccl.*, II, 23.

any Jewish Christians who remained in Jerusalem at that time would have fled to Antioch, as the great center of Christianity, during the Jewish war of Vespasian and Titus in A.D. 67-70. These refugees, representing the Jewish element in Christianity rather than the Gentile point of view, would have strengthened the conservative party in Antioch, which had been opposed to the liberalism of Paul. Their transfer to Antioch would likewise have been important because they would have brought with them their books and their collections of the sayings of Jesus, so that the community at Antioch would now come to be more familiar with the tradition that had grown up in Jerusalem.

For the closing years of the first century, the meagerness of the sources makes it impossible to reconstruct any continuous narrative of the history of the Christian community at Antioch. However, during these years events of great importance for the future of Christianity took place.

According to some sources, Nicolaus of Antioch, who had been an early proselyte and one of the seven deacons in Jerusalem (Acts 6:5), became the author of an early heresy that was named for him. This Nicolaitan movement apparently sought to achieve a compromise between Christianity and the prevailing social usages by reconciling the observance of certain pagan practices with membership in the Christian community. This effort, however, involved the Nicolaitans in what seemed to some Christians to be sensual and idolatrous behavior (Apocalypse 2:6, 15). Whether the heresy actually originated with Nicolaus the proselyte of Antioch is doubtful; it seems more likely that the heresy, after it had come into being, falsely laid claim to Nicolaus as its author, hoping to win support through the prestige of his name.[43]

The Nicolaitan heresy was in some respects a forerunner

[43] A. von Harnack, "The Sect of the Nicolaitans and Nicolaus, the Deacon in Jerusalem," *Journal of Religion*, III, 1923, pp. 413-422.

of the much more prominent, and more important, Gnostic movement. This fantastic theosophy, which became a formidable rival to Christianity, possessed a powerful attraction for half-educated minds, and it flourished in an intellectual and religious atmosphere such as that of Antioch, where the mingling of diverse Greek and Oriental racial and religious groups provided ample opportunity for the study and propagation of new cults and philosophical systems.[44] As a syncretistic system of pagan philosophy and religion which, from Hellenic origins, adopted some Christian and some Jewish ideas, Gnosticism was in a position to offer competition to Christian doctrine. It promised knowledge (*gnosis*) of the divine scheme of the universe, and salvation, including security against evil forces on earth and a happy life in the hereafter. Starting in the East, Gnosticism spread throughout the Roman Empire. Its variations were innumerable, and the teaching of its individual leaders ranged all the way from systems that were definitely non-Christian to adaptations that took the form of Christian heresies.

Gnosticism as it reached Antioch was descended from the teaching of Simon Magus of Samaria, who in apostolic times preached that there was a supreme God who gave out powers or emanations, of which Simon himself was one. Simon claimed to be a rival of Jesus Christ, and gave displays of magic which attracted many followers.[45]

Simon's successor was Menander of Samaria, who went to Antioch and made many conversions by means of exhibitions of magic, in which he was as skilled as his master. There is no precise evidence for the date of Menander's activity at Antioch; but he worked there during the latter part of the first century, in the time of Bishop Evodius.[46]

[44] See R. M. Grant, *Gnosticism and Early Christianity*, New York, 1959.
[45] Acts 8:9-24; Irenaeus, *Adv. Haer.*, I, 23; Justin, *Apology*, I, 26; Eusebius, *Hist. eccl.*, II, 13f.
[46] Irenaeus, *loc.cit.*; Justin, *loc.cit.*; Eusebius, *Hist. eccl.*, III, 26.

Another Gnostic teacher was Satornilus (or Saturninus), a native of Antioch who became Menander's pupil and eventually his successor in the Syrian capital. In his hands the teaching was changed from a new religion which contained only some Christian elements into a real Christian heresy. Satornilus taught that Christ was sent to destroy the forces of evil, and that the Savior was unborn and incorporeal and without tangible human figure; and if he was thought to have been seen as a man, it was in appearance only.[47] Thus Gnosticism, instead of attacking the Church from without, began to attempt to corrupt it from within.

Another famous pupil of Menander's in Antioch was Basilides of Alexandria, who, after studying with the master, served as the transmitter of Gnosticism to his native city, in the time of Hadrian (A.D. 117-138).[48] One of the best known figures of this time was the Syrian Cerdo (Kerdon), a product of the Gnostic teaching in Antioch, who when he settled in Rome ca. A.D. 138-144 came into contact with Marcion, the founder of a new Gnostic sect that actually developed into a church and attained some importance. The Marcionite church became popular in Syria, as well as in other parts of the Roman Empire.[49]

Bishop Ignatius, whose personality and faith are familiar to us from his letters, is the first figure in the history of Christian Antioch at the close of the apostolic age who is at all well known.[50] Even so, details of his life are scanty. According to what was evidently a local source, Ignatius was arrested and condemned at the time of the earthquake which

[47] Irenaeus, *Adv. Haer.*, I, 24, 1f; Eusebius, *Hist. eccl.*, IV, 7, 3.

[48] Irenaeus, *Adv. Haer.*, I, 24, 3ff.

[49] *Ibid.*, I, 27; III, 4; Hippolytus, *Philosophumena*, VII, 37; Epiphanius, *Haer.*, XLI, 2. See John Knox, *Marcion and the New Testament*, Chicago, 1942, pp. 7f, 13, 17f; E. C. Blackman, *Marcion and his Influence*, London, 1948.

[50] See C. C. Richardson, *The Christianity of Ignatius of Antioch*, New York, 1935, and Virginia Corwin, *St. Ignatius and Christianity in Antioch*, New Haven, 1960.

took place on 13 December A.D. 115.[51] The local chronicler
Malalas states that Trajan was angry with Ignatius because
the bishop had used unsuitable language concerning him.
In addition, the people of Antioch held the Christians responsible for the earthquake, which was looked upon as a sign
of the anger of the pagan gods. If there was an outbreak of
anti-Christian feeling, the first victim would have been the
head of the Christian community. Ignatius was sent to Rome
by way of Asia Minor and was executed by being exposed
to wild beasts in the Coliseum. In the reign of Theodosius II
(A.D. 408-450) his remains were taken back to Antioch and
buried in the famous cemetery outside the Daphne Gate.[52]

Other martyrdoms took place in Antioch itself. According
to Ignatius' own letters, the outbreak lasted only a few weeks,
for the bishop refers to the election of his successor while he
himself was passing through Asia Minor.[53] The only other
victim whose name is preserved is Drosis or Drosina, mother
of three children, who is said to have been burned.[54] "Many
others" are reported to have been executed, or to have thrown
themselves into the flames, but no details of their martyrdoms
are preserved, and these victims may be imaginary.

On his journey to Rome through Asia Minor Ignatius
wrote to churches seven letters that give a remarkably vivid
picture of the popular faith of the early church and of the
eager religious life of the time. One of the major interests
of these letters is the light they throw on the contemporary
organization of the church.[55] Ignatius repeatedly discusses
the need for a threefold ministry, of bishops, presbyters, and
deacons, to whom the laity must give due obedience. The

[51] Malalas, p. 276, 10f.

[52] Jerome, *De viris illustribus*, 16.

[53] See J. Moffatt, "Ignatius of Antioch: A Study in Personal Religion,"
Journal of Religion, x, 1930, pp. 169, 173.

[54] Malalas, p. 277, 9f.

[55] C. C. Richardson, "The Church in Ignatius of Antioch," *Journal of
Religion*, xvii, 1937, pp. 428-443.

bishop is supreme, not because he represents the succession of the apostles, but because he is the representative of God on earth.[56] It is apparent from the way Ignatius writes that the threefold ministry has been a source of anxiety to him, and that its proper functioning is something for which he has had to struggle. A strong and ordered ministry of this sort was plainly necessary for the protection of Christians from heresy (notably Gnosticism) and from official persecution.

In addition to the need for a recognized and established organization of its communities, the church by the time of Ignatius was coming to appreciate the necessity and the value of the leadership of the larger communities. It would be only natural for the smaller congregations in Syria to look to Antioch for leadership and support, not only because of the historic role of the city in the growth of the early church and because of the prestige that attached to Peter's work there, but because Antioch was the capital of the province and the center of communications and information. It was in this sense that Ignatius in one of his letters spoke of himself as "bishop of Syria."[57]

Our knowledge of the period following Ignatius' death is scanty; for the most part we have only a bare list[58] of the bishops of Antioch—Heron (A.D. 116), Cornelius (A.D. 128), Eros (A.D. 142), Theophilus (A.D. 169). Theophilus was a Syrian by birth, and was well educated; he became a Christian only after he had grown to manhood.[59] Of his writings, only the apology for the Christian faith, *To Autolycus*, has survived. His exposition was unsystematic and betrays a

[56] On Ignatius' concept of the episcopate, see H. Chadwick, "The Silence of Bishops in Ignatius," *Harvard Theological Review*, XLIII, 1950, pp. 169-172.

[57] Romans 2:2.   [58] See above, n. 36.

[59] Eusebius, *Hist. eccl.*, IV, 24; R. M. Grant, "The Problem of Theophilus," *Harvard Theological Review*, XLIII, 1950, pp. 179-196; idem, "The Textual Criticism of Theophilus of Antioch," *Vigiliae Christianae*, VI, 1952, pp. 146-159.

confused sort of rationalism. His thought owes so much to Judaism, with which he was familiar because of the presence of the important Jewish community at Antioch, that he may be thought to give the appearance of being more Jewish than Christian, and the fact that a man of his views could become bishop of Antioch is suggestive of the rather unsettled condition of the Christian community there at the time. The distinctions between orthodoxy and heresy, and between Christianity and Judaism, were not yet perfectly clear on all points, and it is characteristic that the Christian services of worship at this time contain Jewish elements.[60] Theophilus' principal significance is that he represents an early attempt to formulate a learned theology. His doctrine reappears three generations later in one of his successors at the head of the church of Antioch, Paul of Samosata, who endeavored to reconcile Jewish and pagan teaching with the Christian doctrine; and his literal interpretations of scripture, relying on Jewish exegesis, mark Theophilus as a forerunner of the methods which later characterized the theological school of Antioch.

Theophilus was succeeded by Maximinus (A.D. 188-198), Maximinus by Serapion (A.D. 198 or 199), Asclepiades (A.D. 211-217), Philetus (A.D. 217-ca. 230) and Zabennus, bishop under Severus Alexander (A.D. 222-235). The "Syrian emperors" who occupied the throne at this period, and the members of their families, were much interested in religious matters. Elagabalus (A.D. 218-222) tried to establish a new syncretistic religion, which would include Christianity, and his cousin Severus Alexander (A.D. 222-235) was disposed to be tolerant of the Christians, having many of them at his court.[61] His mother, Julia Mamaea, possessed a wide educa-

---

[60] R. M. Grant, "Theophilus of Antioch to Autolycus," *Harvard Theological Review*, XL, 1947, p. 256; see also the same scholar's study "The Early Antiochene Anaphora," *Anglican Theological Review*, XXX, 1948, pp. 91-94.

[61] B. J. Kidd, *A History of the Church to A.D. 461*, Oxford, 1922, I, pp. 350f.

tion, like the other women of her family, and a philosophical mind; and if not actually a Christian, she was deeply interested in the religion. While she was living at Antioch between A.D. 231 and 233, she sent for Origen, whose fame as a teacher was then spreading, to come and instruct her in the Christian doctrine. Accompanied by a military escort which the empress had provided for his safety, Origen traveled to Antioch from Caesarea in Palestine, where he was living, and remained at the court, the church historian Eusebius says, "for some time," giving instruction to the empress, and doubtless to her friends. Since Julia Mamaea exercised a strong influence over her son, and was in fact the leading figure in the government, her interest in Christianity, and her invitation to Origen, must have given much encouragement to the Christians at Antioch. At about the same time the community was distinguished by the learned work of the scholarly presbyter Geminus.[62]

Under the Gordians (A.D. 238-244), the famous Babylas became bishop.[63] Babylas is well known because of his supposed encounter with the emperor Philip the Arab (A.D. 244-269) and because of the later adventures of his relics at Antioch under Gallus and Julian. A church dedicated to him, as his last resting-place, was found in the excavations, on the right bank of the Orontes, across from the city.

The widely circulated tale of Babylas and the emperor at the church door is fictitious. Babylas, the story goes, refused to allow Philip to attend a service in the church at Antioch, barring his way at the door, because the emperor had killed his predecessor (or, in some versions, because he had slain a Persian hostage who had been entrusted to him). This episode appears only in sources of a late date, and there is no contemporary reference to it; moreover, the versions are sometimes suspiciously different. It is unthinkable that the episode can have occurred as it is related. The bishop's com-

---

[62] Jerome, *De viris illustribus*, 64.   [63] Eusebius, *Hist. eccl.*, VI, 29, 5.

mand to the emperor would have been a blow to the imperial prestige which could not have been tolerated. Moreover, the sensation caused by Ambrose's excommunication of Theodosius I, which occurred after Christianity was the recognized state religion, makes it seem certain that if something similar had occurred in the mid third century, when Christianity was still an illicit sect, some trace of it would have been left in contemporary literature.[64] The story of the encounter of Ambrose and Theodosius, which is also legendary, appears in literature for the first time in the fifth century, some time after the incident was supposed to have happened, and it may not be impossible that the tale of the encounter of Ambrose and Theodosius was suggested by the apocryphal tale of Babylas and Philip.[65]

With Philip's successor Decius (A.D. 249-251) the position of the Christians was reversed. Wishing to undo the influence of his predecessor in every possible way, Decius instituted a persecution in the course of which Babylas died in prison in Antioch, and was succeeded by Fabius, in A.D. 250 or 251.[66]

Fabius was soon followed by Demetrianus, and not long after he became bishop, Antioch was captured by the Persians, in A.D. 253. As was their custom on such occasions, the conquerors, when they retired from the city, carried off into exile a number of skilled workmen whose services they desired. Among these there must have been a number of Christians, for one of the captives was Demetrianus; here we see the custom of the Persians of taking the leader of the Christian community so that he might reconcile his people to their fate and keep order among them.[67] When the exiles were

---

[64] *Ibid.*, vi, 34; see Kidd, *op.cit.*, i, p. 352.

[65] On the fictitious character and the political meaning of the encounter between Ambrose and Theodosius, see F. H. Dudden, *The Life and Times of St. Ambrose*, Oxford, 1925, pp. 387f.

[66] Eusebius, *Hist. eccl.*, vi, 39, 4.

[67] On the career of Demetrianus, see P. P(eeters), "Démétrianus, évêque d'Antioche?" *Analecta Bollandiana*, xlii, 1924, pp. 288-314.

settled in Persia, the bishop served as leader of the exiled community until he died. Evidently it was hoped in Antioch that Demetrianus might some day return, for no successor seems to have been elected before his death. Other Christians were among the captives transported by the Persians when they took the city for the second time in A.D. 260, and these were added to the community of the first exiles in Persia. While the see of Antioch was vacant, the neighboring bishop of Tarsus exercised a sort of protective supervision over it.

There is no record of the effect at Antioch of the persecution under Valerian (A.D. 253-260), which lasted from A.D. 257 to 260; but the emperor was either in Antioch himself, or made it the headquarters of his campaigns against the Persians for a large part of his reign, and where the emperor was, the measures decreed against the Christians would presumably have been faithfully carried out.

The persecution under Valerian was only one of the troubles from which Antioch suffered at this period. In A.D. 260 Valerian himself was captured by the Persians, and in the summer of the same year the forces of King Sapor again invaded Syria and once more captured Antioch. Roman power and prestige sank to a very low state, and the rulers of Palmyra took the opportunity to free their kingdom from Roman control. Antioch soon found itself within the spreading Palmyrene sphere of influence.

In this same year, A.D. 260, news finally came of the death of Demetrianus in Persia, and Paul of Samosata was elected bishop.[68] The political significance of Paul's appearance at this moment, and his activities as a worldly "political" bishop, have already been described (above, pp. 114ff.). The accounts of his career indicate that the Christian community at Antioch had by this time achieved a certain importance, for

[68] On the career of Paul, see F. Loofs, *Paulus von Samosata*, Leipzig, 1924; G. Bardy, *Paul de Samosate*, 2d ed., Louvain, 1929; H. de Riedmatten, *Les actes du procès de Paul de Samosate*, Fribourg en Suisse, 1952.

Paul's conduct suggests that the bishop of Antioch was re-garded as a figure of some consequence.

Theologically also, Paul of Samosata is a figure of signifi-cance. His teaching, which stressed the unity of God and the manhood of Christ, paved the way for Arianism and established a tradition in the doctrine of the theological school of Antioch.[69] Whether or not this simplified and, to many people, attractive teaching was put forward to please Zenobia the queen of Palmyra, who was supposed to have Jewish sympathies, cannot be demonstrated. Paul's view of the unity and power of God might have been influenced by the strict monotheism of the Jews. The denial or subordina-tion of the divinity of Christ was a concept that had arisen very early, as soon as the nature of Christ had become a subject for detailed study and debate, and Antioch by Paul's time was a place in which such a doctrine would find sup-port, just as, in the next century, the city became one of the strongholds of Arianism, which in essence held to the same interpretation.

While Paul's doctrine, to many of the clergy and the faith-ful, seemed blasphemous and perilous, his conduct as a civil official and his private life—or what his private life was rumored to be—likewise gave rise to scandal and alarm.[70] As fiscal officer he was accused of corruption and greed. In daily life, it is said, he behaved more like a civil official than a bishop, going about attended by secretaries and a guard. Apparently he conducted church services, and preached, in a theatrical fashion; and he put a stop to the singing of psalms and substituted hymns in honor of himself—and,

[69] On Paul's doctrine see R. V. Sellers, *Two Ancient Christologies: A Study in the Christological Thought of the Schools of Alexandria and Antioch in the Early History of Christian Doctrine*, London, 1940, pp. 118ff, and J. N. D. Kelly, *Early Christian Doctrines*, London, 1958, pp. 117-119, 158-160.

[70] See the extracts from the synodal letter quoted by Eusebius, *Hist. eccl.*, VII, 30.

what was almost more shocking in those days, had these sung by a chorus of women. He and the clergy of his suite were attended by handsome young women assistants, nominally deaconesses, and gossip followed.

In time the situation became such that action seemed necessary. Helenus, bishop of Tarsus, acting in his capacity as head of the nearest large church, called a synod, which met at Antioch in A.D. 264. In the presence of the synod, Paul was able to conceal and disguise his doctrines, and the bishops had to be content with a promise that he would change his teaching.

In a few years, however, it became plain that Paul was not going to emend his doctrine, and a new group of bishops were convoked for a council that met in A.D. 268. The occasion was looked upon as an important one, and a "large number" of bishops, perhaps eighty, attended.[71] This time the attack was successful. It was led by Malchion, a priest who was head of a school of rhetoric at Antioch.[72] Malchion possessed both the skill in dialectic and the superior learning that such a task demanded. He succeeded in forcing Paul to abandon the efforts to conceal his real beliefs which had saved him at the earlier synod; and so the heretical nature of Paul's teaching was definitely proved. Paul was excommunicated and in his place the synod elected Domnus, son of the old bishop Demetrianus, Paul's predecessor. The choice of a native of Antioch as the new bishop is significant in view of the trouble that had attended the career of the Syrian Paul.

The deposed Paul, relying on the support of the Palmyrene government and of his own followers, refused to accept the decision of the synod, and continued to exercise the functions of his office. Antioch thus possessed two rival bishops—one orthodox, one heterodox—a situation that was to recur during the Arian troubles of the fourth century. Paul's confidence

---

[71] *Ibid.*, vii, 28, 1.

[72] *Ibid.*, vii, 29, 2; Jerome, *De viris illustribus*, 71.

was justified, and he was able to maintain his position until Aurelian defeated Zenobia and drove her and her followers from Antioch in A.D. 272. He was then expelled, the church historian Eusebius writes, "with the utmost indignity."[73]

In the interval between the deposition of Paul of Samosata and the accession of Diocletian, three bishops of Antioch are recorded, but we know little more about them than their names. Diocletian's reign (A.D. 284-305) brought a period of persecution during which we hear of the sufferings of the church at Antioch. The bishop, Cyril, was arrested early in the persecution (February A.D. 303) and condemned to labor in the marble quarries in Pannonia, where he died three years later.[74] Another martyr of Antioch was a deacon named Romanus, who had his tongue cut out.[75] Romanus came to be venerated as one of the principal saints of Antioch, and a church was built in his honor. Some Christians were roasted over slow fires; others killed themselves before being taken. Domnina, a woman of wealth, fled from the city with her daughters Bernice and Prosdoce. When their flight became known, Domnina's husband, a pagan, was sent with a band of soldiers to capture them; but as the ladies were being taken back to Antioch they succeeded in drowning themselves in a river which they were crossing.[76] The maiden Pelagia, surprised alone in her house by the soldiers sent to fetch her, killed herself by leaping from the roof.[77] Other martyrs at

---

[73] *Hist. eccl.*, VII, 30, 18-20.

[74] See H. Delehaye, *Les passions des martyrs et les genres littéraires*, Brussels, 1921, pp. 328-344.

[75] H. D(elehaye), "St. Romain martyr d'Antioche," *Analecta Bollandiana*, L, 1932, pp. 241-283.

[76] Eusebius, *Hist. eccl.*, VIII, 12, 3f; Chrysostom, *Homilia de SS. Bernice et Prosdoce* (*P.G.*, L, cols. 629-640).

[77] Eusebius, *Hist. eccl.*, VIII, 12, 2; Chrysostom, *Homilia in S. mart. Pelagiam* (*P.G.*, L, cols. 579-584). This Pelagia is to be distinguished from a purported martyr of the same name, said to have been a penitent courtesan of Antioch. The courtesan Pelagia is not a historical figure, and the

Antioch at this period were Tyrannio, bishop of Tyre, and Zenobius, a physician-priest of Sidon.[78]

One of the most famous martyrs was Lucian of Antioch, the celebrated scholar, who died at Nicomedia in A.D. 312 after suffering many torments. As a priest famous for the sanctity of his life and as a celebrated scholar who edited the text of the Bible, Lucian played a prominent role in the history of Christianity.[79] His recension of the Bible came into general use in the patriarchates of Antioch and Constantinople and is the ancestor of the early printed versions. He was one of the earliest of the teachers whose work led to the development of the important and distinctive theology of the school of Antioch, with its careful training and meticulous Biblical scholarship; in fact the school that Lucian himself organized may be said to be the beginning of the theological school of Antioch, which rivalled that of Alexandria.[80]

Soon after the persecution began there occurred at Seleucia Pieria and Antioch a brief and abortive revolt of an army officer named Eugenius.[81] Such an episode at another time might have had little significance, but under the circumstances it had grave consequences for the people of Antioch and Seleucia.

In peace time, Roman troops were extensively employed for engineering operations, and about this time five hundred soldiers were occupied in deepening the harbor at Seleucia— the kind of task no soldier has ever enjoyed. The men claimed that they were inadequately fed and that they had to spend

---

accounts of her life and martyrdom are fictitious; see H. Delehaye, *Les légendes hagiographiques*, 4th ed., Brussels, 1955, pp. 186-195.

[78] Eusebius, *Hist. eccl.*, VIII, 13, 3f.

[79] G. Bardy, *Recherches sur Saint Lucien d'Antioche et son école*, Paris, 1936.

[80] Sellers, *op.cit.* (above, n. 69).

[81] The revolt is described by Libanius in three passages, *Antiochikos*, 158-162; *Orat.* XIX, 45f; *Orat.* XX, 18-20. See also Eusebius, *Hist. eccl.*, VIII, 6, 8.

their nights foraging for food. The grievance drove them to mutiny, and one morning they proclaimed their commander Eugenius emperor—against his will, it was said. The little band of revolutionaries set out for Antioch, knowing that there was no garrison in the city. On the way they plundered the farmhouses and made themselves drunk on the wine they found. At sunset they reached the city and attempted to seize the palace. The citizens collected what weapons they could and attacked the troops; even women joined in the fight. The soldiers, who were by this time both tired and intoxicated, were routed by the civilians; some were slain, some fled, the rest were captured. The revolution ended in the early part of the night.

Instead of thanking the people of Antioch for putting down the revolt and saving the city, the imperial authorities inflicted severe punishment on both Seleucia Pieria and Antioch; prominent men in both places were executed and their property was confiscated. Some punishment might have been due for laxity in supplying provisions for the troops, but the executions and confiscations seem to have been out of all proportion to the offence. The severity of the punishment can only mean that the imperial authorities believed that the rebellion had been instigated by the Christians.

During the persecution, the authorities had met with resistance from the Christians in the army, and this experience would lead the government to suspect that any military disorder had a religious basis. Whether the Christians really had any connection with the rising, we cannot now know; but the episode shows the state of anxiety to which the authorities had been brought, and likewise illustrates the danger to which a city such as Antioch, without a garrison or organized police force, was exposed.

CHAPTER VII

THE BEGINNING OF THE CHRISTIAN
ROMAN EMPIRE

THE conversion of Constantine the Great (A.D. 306-337) and
the triumph of Christianity marked a turning-point in the
history of the Roman Empire and introduced a new epoch
in the history of Europe.[1] With the establishment of Christianity, the Roman world entered an era of new creations;
the foundation of the new capital of the empire at Constantinople matched the military and administrative reforms that
transformed the Roman State.

During these years the history of Antioch, as we know it,
reflects the larger events in the empire, and here as well
begins a period during which the history of the city is better
known, thanks to an increase in the amount and the variety
of the sources which have been handed down to us.

Constantine's chief monument at Antioch, and one of the
most famous buildings in the city, was the octagonal Great
Church, often called the Golden Church, which was begun
by Constantine and completed by his son Constantius (Fig.
50, No. 18).[2] Of unusual size and beauty, the church was
appropriate for the principal city of the eastern provinces,
which was, in addition, an ancient center of Christianity.
It was an octagon surrounded by chambers and two-storied
side-aisles, the upper story reserved for the women members
of the congregation. Particularly impressive was the hemispherical dome, of great height, made of wood. The outer
covering of the roof was gilded, giving the church its epithet
of "golden." The interior contained statues, brilliant marbles

[1] See A. H. M. Jones, *Constantine and the Conversion of Europe*, London,
1948.
[2] The church was begun in A.D. 327 (Jerome, *Chronicle*, Olymp. 276, 3)
and completed in A.D. 341 (Philostorgius, *Hist. eccl.*, p. 212 ed. Bidez).

and columns, and decorations of brass and gold.[3] Since the church served as the prototype for the central, octagonal portion of the famous pilgrimage church of St. Symeon Stylites at Kalat Seman, an approximate idea of its appearance can be gained from the ruins of the shrine of St. Symeon.[4]

The church was built on the island near the palace, carrying out the pattern, which is found also at Constantinople, Salona, and Thessalonica, of close association of palace, principal church, and hippodrome. This juxtaposition of church and palace exemplified the role of the emperor in the church, and provided a "Great Church" which he could attend on the major festivals and state anniversaries.

The setting of the church matched its dignity. It stood in an open area surrounded by a portico, with an open square before it. In the enclosure were a guest-house for the accommodation of strangers; kitchens and dining rooms for feeding the poor and the widows and orphans, who were cared for by the church; schools for the instruction of converts and for the training of singers; and residences for the clergy.

Constantine's reign inaugurates the period of the great church councils, which guided the development of doctrine after the emancipation of the church. At Antioch, the history of the Christian community is largely concerned with the course of the Arian controversy over the nature of the divinity of Christ, which had divided the church in the eastern part of the empire into two camps. This dispute came to play a major part in the history of the church at Antioch under Constantine's son Constantius, and took on a political significance of the first importance in that it developed into an effort

---

[3] The building is described in chapter 9 of the panegyric composed by Eusebius for Constantine's thirtieth anniversary as emperor, as well as in Eusebius' *Life of Constantine*, iii, 50. Malalas, p. 419, 19ff relates that in the great earthquake of A.D. 526 the church remained standing for several days after the beginning of the shocks, but then caught fire and was destroyed.

[4] E. Baldwin Smith, *The Dome*, Princeton, 1950, pp. 34f.

on the part of the Arians to create an Arian state church under the control of the emperor. At first, however, this tendency did not appear. When he became sole emperor in A.D. 324, Constantine, who was chiefly anxious to secure peace and unity within the church, charged his counsellor Bishop Hosius (Ossius) with the mission of reconciling the quarrel. Hosius did not succeed; but toward the end of the year an opportunity arose for an attempt to settle the differences. Philogonius, bishop of Antioch since A.D. 319, died in December, A.D. 324, and a meeting of bishops was called (A.D. 325) for the election of a successor. Eustathius (bishop A.D. 325-326) was elected; and the meeting took the opportunity to condemn the heresy of Arius. At this meeting a great council to deal with the whole problem was proposed; and in an effort to forestall any chance of a mishap at the projected meeting, the synod of Antioch drew up and published a long and complicated anti-Arian creed, which is important as an early example of synodal creed-making.[5]

The council for which plans were made at Antioch was the Council of Nicaea (A.D. 325). Here a solution was adopted by which the *homoousion* or consubstantiality of the Father and the Son was inserted in the Creed. The Council also, among its other acts, settled the status of the dissident group called the Paulianists, some of whom remained in Antioch as followers of the teaching of Paul of Samosata; the Paulianists, by decision of the Council, were to be rebaptized, and their clergy were to be reordained.[6]

Eustathius did not enjoy his episcopal office for long.[7] While he was bishop, the Empress Helena, mother of Constantine the Great, made a pilgrimage to Jerusalem, and

[5] F. L. Cross, "The Council of Antioch in 325 A.D.," *Church Quarterly Review*, CXXVIII, 1939, pp. 49-76.

[6] See G. Bardy, *Paul de Samosate*, 2d ed., Louvain, 1929, pp. 385ff.

[7] The account given here of Eustathius' deposition follows the study of H. Chadwick, "The Fall of Eustathius of Antioch," *Journal of Theological Studies*, XLIX, 1948, pp. 27-35.

a sarcastic remark which Eustathius had the misfortune to make concerning her gave a final opportunity to the group he had opposed at Nicaea. With the emperor's approval, a council was called at Antioch under the presidency of Eusebius, bishop of Caesarea, the church historian and imperial adviser.[8] The council deposed Eustathius and Asclepas of Gaza, one of his chief supporters, and sent them into exile along with a number of their adherents. This action, and the conflicting opinions over the election of Eustathius' successor, provoked disorders among the Christians which soon involved the whole city, and Constantine had to dispatch troops under Strategius Musonianus (one of his advisers in theological matters) to restore order.

About A.D. 333 Antioch again appears in the Arian dispute, this time in connection with the attacks on Athanasius of Alexandria, who had become the principal champion of Nicene orthodoxy and the leading enemy of the Arians. Athanasius, in Egypt, was accused of magical practices, a serious crime, which was independent of the theological question; and the government was bound to take cognizance of the charges. Constantine ordered his relative Dalmatius, consul for A.D. 333, to take charge of the investigation. Dalmatius was at this time in Antioch. He summoned Athanasius to appear before him, but Athanasius was able to clear himself without coming to the city, and the emperor stopped the proceedings.[9]

In the latter years of Constantine's reign the growing expectation of war with Persia brought to Antioch a prominence as a military center that it was to retain until the reign of the Emperor Julian (A.D. 361-363). Rome and Persia had been at peace since a treaty made in A.D. 297, but when Sapor II came to the Persian throne in A.D. 310, he determined to

[8] The council is described in Eusebius' *Life of Constantine*, III, 59-61.
[9] Athanasius, *Apologia contra Arianos*, 65 (*P.G.*, xxv, col. 365); Socrates, *Hist. eccl.*, I, 27.

win back the portions of his empire which had been lost
to the Romans thirteen years before. The Romans on their
side resented Sapor's persecution of the Christians in Persia,
whom the Persian king looked upon as enemy agents.

Tension increased, and as the Romans pushed forward
their military preparations, Antioch must have felt the economic and social strains produced by the growing number
of troops for which the city served as headquarters. Then,
in the summer and autumn of A.D. 333, the whole of the
eastern part of the empire suffered a severe famine, which
is said to have been especially bad in Antioch and Cyrrhus
and their vicinity. The presence of the troops may have been
in part responsible for the shortage of food, as it was in the
famine and economic crisis at Antioch during the reign of
the Emperor Julian, when a crop failure ruined the city's
food supply just as preparations for a Persian campaign were
in progress. In any event, the mobilization of the forces must
have aggravated the shortage of food, and one can believe
that in any competition for food between soldiers and
civilians, the soldiers would secure what they considered to
be their share. There are said to have been many deaths, and
there may have been an epidemic of disease such as sometimes accompanied a famine. Constantine gave orders for the
churches in the various cities to serve as centers for the distribution of wheat.[10]

It was just about this time (probably about the year A.D.
333) that Constantine, judging the situation serious enough
to call for the presence of a member of the imperial house,
sent his second son, the Caesar Constantius, to Antioch. Constantius, who had been born in A.D. 317, was still too young to
take the active direction of the military preparations. However, his presence would be valuable for the morale of the
troops. The Persians promptly declared their intentions, and
began their operations with the occupation of Armenia in

[10] The famine is described by Theophanes, p. 29, 13-23, ed. De Boor.

A.D. 334. On this, the Romans began preparations in earnest for war.

One special measure adopted at this time was the creation of the office of Count of the East (*comes Orientis*). This official, who was unique in the administrative hierarchy of the empire, was a civilian administrator in charge of the "diocese of the Orient," a geographical division that embraced the provinces from Mesopotamia and Syria on the north to Egypt on the south. The Count of the East had the same administrative and judicial functions as the "vicars," who were in charge of the other dioceses of the empire; and like them he supervised the governors of the provinces that made up his diocese. He occupied a position in the hierarchy between the provincial governors and the praetorian prefect who was the chief administrator of the whole eastern portion of the empire. However, the Count of the East also had special powers and duties in connection with military matters (probably concerning the organization of supplies and the quartering of troops), which were evidently given him to facilitate the preparations for the Persian war.[11]

The first Count of the East was a Christian named Felicianus, appointed in A.D. 335; he was given as his headquarters the Temple of the Muses in Antioch.[12] The arrival of this new official meant that more civil servants were added to the already considerable number of officials and clerks who lived in the city.

Constantine became ill in the spring of A.D. 337, and Constantius set out from Antioch for Nicomedia, where he arrived before his father's death. Constantius was not yet twenty years old, but for four years he had been, as Caesar

[11] For a discussion of the office and its history, see G. Downey, *A Study of the Comites Orientis and the Consulares Syriae*, Diss., Princeton, 1939, pp. 7-11, also A. H. M. Jones, "The Roman Civil Service (Clerical and Sub-Clerical Grades)," *Journal of Roman Studies*, xxxix, 1949, p. 48, notes 112, 116.

[12] Malalas, p. 318, 23ff.

at Antioch, at least nominally in charge of the plans for war against Persia; he had received a careful education and became an excellent soldier and military organizer. Over a year after Constantine's death, a new partition of the empire took place, by which Constantius retained the East, where his capital would be Antioch. Immediately after this settlement with his brothers, Constantius returned to Antioch, where he spent the winter of A.D. 338-339 busy with military preparations. Special taxes were imposed to provide funds for the army.[13] The collecting of troops, supplies and equipment in and around Antioch, together with the presence in the city of the imperial court, must have had a marked effect upon the city's daily life and its business activities, and on the whole, although there were some strains on the economy, Antioch prospered under Constantius.[14] Since he made Antioch his headquarters and ordinary residence for a number of years during the Persian war, Constantius naturally took an interest in the city, and the future Emperor Julian, in his panegyric of Constantius, written at the end of A.D. 355, speaks of stoas, other buildings, and fountains which the emperor caused his governors to present to the city. In gratitude, Julian says, Antioch even called itself by the name of Constantius.[15]

During the time when Constantius was engaged in the recruitment and training of his army, and later while he was conducting almost annual campaigns against the Persians, he was also perpetually involved in the ecclesiastical quarrels concerning the Arian dogma and the creed of Nicaea which continued to split the church. Constantius himself, though

[13] Julian, *Orat.* I, 21d; *Cod. Theod.* XI, 1, 5.

[14] Constantius' preparation of the army and its equipment are described by Julian, *op.cit.*, 21f, and by Libanius, *Orat.* XVIII, 166-169, 205-207; *Orat.* LIX, 66-72, 89-93.

[15] Julian, *Orat.* I, 40d-41a. If Antioch took the name of Constantius, the name would have been something like *Antiochia Constantia*. There is no other evidence for the change of name, but there is no reason to doubt Julian's statement.

he was apparently not actually an Arian, disliked and distrusted those who adhered to the Nicene point of view, and
encouraged and favored the Arians, whose purpose it was
to build up an Arian state church dominated by the emperor.
Constantius' steady occupation with both military and ecclesiastical problems gives a special characteristic to the first
fifteen years or so of his reign at Antioch.

On the Feast of the Epiphany, 6 January A.D. 341, Constantine's Great Church was dedicated. The ceremony was of
a magnificence suitable to the importance of the building;
ninety bishops were present. On the church was placed a
metrical inscription of four lines in Greek:[16]

> For Christ Constantine made this lovely dwelling,
> Like in all respects to the vaults of heaven, bright-shining,
> With Constantius obeying the commands of the ruler.
> The Count Gorgonius carried out the work of chamberlain.

Gorgonius was a court chamberlain who had been placed
in charge of the work, succeeding Plutarchus who had supervised operations in the time of Constantine. Gorgonius later
appears as head chamberlain of the Caesar Gallus. Constantius presented costly liturgical vessels to the church, in
addition to those his father had already provided.[17]

The presence of the bishops provided an appropriate occasion for the holding of a council, just as had been done at
Jerusalem in A.D. 335 at the dedication of Constantine's new
Church of the Resurrection. As his father had done at Nicaea,
Constantius presided at the meeting, at which a further
effort was made to find a formula which might put an end
to the Arian dispute. Four creeds were drawn up and circulated, though only one, probably that of Lucian of Antioch,
was regarded as official.

[16] Malalas, p. 326, 1-4, also published in *I.G.L.S.*, no. 832, and by T.
Preger, *Inscriptiones Graecae metricae*, no. 111.
[17] Theodoret, *Hist. eccl.*, III, 12, 4.

The year A.D. 346 saw the completion of a new harbor at Seleucia Pieria, which improved the facilities there and greatly assisted the movement of military supplies. Aside from its military importance, this new harbor contributed to the economic prosperity of Antioch, by providing improved opportunities for travel and communications and for the movement of goods.[18]

In A.D. 351 Constantius advanced his nephew Gallus to the rank of Caesar and placed him in charge of the East, so that he himself might be free to deal with a revolt that had broken out in Gaul. Gallus was twenty-five or twenty-six years old. He enjoyed great prestige, not only as the son of Constantine's half-brother, but because he was married to Constantia, a daughter of Constantine. However, he soon showed himself a brute, and his wife was called a veritable Fury.[19] The four years he spent in Antioch were a time of continual trouble for the city, and they ended in disaster for the prince.

On his appointment, Gallus went at once to Antioch.[20] Here his naturally cruel disposition soon turned him into a tyrant. His wife's equally unpleasant character aided the process, and the court chamberlains, seeing opportunities for gain or personal revenge, took care to supply reports, often falsified or exaggerated, which brought prominent or wealthy persons under suspicion and usually led to their downfall.[21]

Not only were informers encouraged, but a regular spy system was organized, and men disguised as travelers went everywhere in Antioch, picking up remarks which they carried to the Caesar. Gallus himself, with a few attendants,

[18] Theophanes, p. 38, 6f, ed. De Boor; *Expositio totius mundi*, 28, p. 110 ed. Riese (*Geographi Latini minores*); Libanius, *Antiochikos*, 263f; Julian, *Orat.* I, 40d.

[19] Ammianus Marcellinus, XIV, 1. See E. A. Thompson, *The Historical Work of Ammianus Marcellinus*, Cambridge, Eng., 1947, pp. 56-71.

[20] Julian, *Letter to the Athenians*, 272; Socrates, *Hist. eccl.*, II, 28; Zonaras, XIII, 8, 4f; Chronicon Paschale, p. 540, 8-12.

[21] Ammianus Marcellinus, XIV, 1, 1ff; 11, 3; Julian, *loc.cit.*

would roam the streets at night, asking people what they thought of the Caesar; but he eventually had to give this up because, the streets being lit after nightfall, he was sometimes recognized.[22]

People were put to death on mere suspicion, and without trial, or had their property confiscated and were driven into exile or beggary; as the contemporary historian Ammianus Marcellinus writes, "wealthy and distinguished houses were being closed."[23] Accusations of magic and of plots to overthrow the government were common. The Caesar was fond of horse racing; he also took particular pleasure in bloody spectacles in the circus, and accused persons were savagely tortured.[24]

At the same time, Gallus thought of himself as a fervent Christian, and eagerly sought the company of holy men.[25] One of his favorite companions in Antioch was the well-known ultra-Arian apologist Aetius, whom Athanasius and his supporters called "the godless" because of his doctrines. After trying various callings as a young man, Aetius became distinguished as a theological disputant, and was ordained deacon in Antioch in A.D. 350 and licensed to teach in the churches. Gallus was at first persuaded to order his execution because of his teaching, but Aetius' protector, the bishop of Antioch Leontius, induced Gallus to rescind his order, and Aetius and the Caesar became close friends.[26]

In his religious zeal, Gallus was moved to conceive a striking device to combat paganism at Antioch. One of the most celebrated pagan shrines in the locality had long been the Temple of Apollo at Daphne, with which there was associated an ancient and famous oracle at the spring of

[22] Ammianus Marcellinus, xiv, 1, 9.
[23] Ammianus Marcellinus, xiv, 1, 4.
[24] Julian, *Misopogon*, 340a; Ammianus Marcellinus, xiv, 7, 3.
[25] Sozomen, *Hist. eccl.*, iii, 15.
[26] *Ibid.*; Philostorgius, *Hist. eccl.*, iii, 15-17 and 27.

Castalia. The temple and the oracle possessed great influence among pagans, while to Christians the whole of Daphne was abhorrent as a place of sinful pleasure. Gallus determined to counteract the influence of Apollo, and to give a holy atmosphere to Daphne as a whole, by transporting thither the relics of St. Babylas, one of the most celebrated local martyrs. The presence of such relics would spread sanctification through the whole of Daphne. A martyrium was built near the Temple of Apollo and the spring of Castalia, and the saint's body was taken there from its resting place in the Christian cemetery at Antioch. The oracle of Apollo was silenced. This event is notable as being the first translation of a martyr's relics recorded by the church historians.[27]

In A.D. 352 the rebel in the West, Magnentius, in an effort to cause trouble for Constantius and force him to come to a settlement, sent an agent to Antioch to assassinate Gallus. The agent enlisted the help of some of the troops stationed in the city, but he talked indiscreetly in the hearing of his hostess, an old woman who lived in a hut on the bank of the Orontes. The plot was revealed to the Caesar, and Magnentius' agent was taken and executed.[28]

The tyrannical behavior of Gallus reached a climax in the spring and early summer of A.D. 354. When he was about to set out for Hierapolis to take part in a campaign against the Persians, who were planning a raid into Mesopotamia, the people of Antioch appealed to Gallus to take measures to deal with the famine which was believed to be imminent.[29] In Syria, wheat and other cereal crops were planted after the November rains had fallen, and in the region of Antioch

---

[27] See G. Downey, "The Shrines of St. Babylas at Antioch and Daphne," *Antioch-on-the-Orontes*, ii, pp. 45-48, and H. Delehaye, *Les origines du culte des martyrs*, 2d ed., Brussels, 1933, p. 54.

[28] Zonaras, xiii, 8, 25-31; Ammianus Marcellinus, xiv, 7, 4.

[29] Ammianus Marcellinus, xiv, 7, 5ff; Libanius, *Orat.* i, 96-103; *Epist.* 394a ed. Wolf.

the harvest took place in May and June, before the dry summer set in.[30] Thus if the crops were to be deficient, the fact would be known by early spring, at about the time when Gallus would be preparing for a summer campaign. On the expectation of a scarcity of food, prices would rise, and landowners and merchants—including of course some of the prominent men of the city—would begin to hoard their stocks in anticipation of a further increase in prices. When the people appealed to Gallus for relief, he ordered a reduction in prices. This was opposed by the leaders of the local senate, who had an interest in the higher prices; and when the senators protested too vigorously against the Caesar's order, he decreed the execution of all of them. The men were put in prison and expected to lose their lives; but they were saved by the firm attitude of Honoratus, the Count of the East, who opposed the Caesar's order, and the senators were released on the day following their imprisonment. Evidently price control, if introduced at all, was unsuccessful, and popular demands for assistance continued. Gallus did not order a distribution of food or import supplies, as he might have done, but put the blame for the situation on Theophilus, the governor of Syria, saying that there would be no scarcity of food if the governor did not wish it. By this time actual hunger had set in. A mob collected and first set fire to the house of a wealthy merchant named Eubulus and then seized the governor Theophilus and dragged and beat him to death. The people were later punished for this lynching by Constantius.[31]

It was at this moment that Libanius, the celebrated teacher and orator, returned to Antioch, his native city. He had been pursuing a highly successful career as teacher and public speaker at Constantinople, but he was anxious to establish himself in his own home. After some difficulty he secured

[30] On the rainfall and climate, see Ammianus Marcellinus, XXII, 13, 4, and Libanius, *Antiochikos*, 31.

[31] Julian, *Misopogon*, 370c; Libanius, *Orat.* XIX, 47-49.

the consent of Constantius to the change, and so began the career which was to make him in his day the most distinguished citizen of Antioch.[32] Libanius happened to arrive just at the time when Gallus had condemned the recalcitrant senators to death, and he visited the senators in prison where they were awaiting execution.[33] On the next day they were released, and on the day following that, Libanius appeared before Gallus, by command, and delivered a discourse. In a short while, however, Libanius fell into disfavor with the Caesar, who had received false accusations against the sophist, and Gallus rather menacingly advised Libanius to leave Antioch. However, Libanius' old teacher Zenobius interceded for him, and he was allowed to remain.[34]

The career of Gallus was now rapidly drawing to a close. His conduct had been reported to Constantius unfavorably, and sometimes in exaggerated terms, by Thalassius, who had been appointed praetorian prefect of the East when Gallus was made Caesar, and so had served as the chief officer of the administration at Gallus' court. It was rumored that Gallus was plotting to make himself emperor; and in any case Constantius feared that his many victims might join forces and start a revolution. Thalassius died early in A.D. 354. Constantius then deprived Gallus of his command over all troops save his palace guards, and sent Domitianus to Antioch as praetorian prefect, with instructions to induce Gallus to leave Antioch and travel to the court of Constantius.[35]

Domitianus when he reached Antioch became arrogant and ordered Gallus to leave the city, threatening to cut off the supplies of his palace if he delayed. Gallus ordered the

---

[32] Libanius first came to Antioch on a four months' leave of absence from Constantinople; but he had to return to the capital and obtain permission for a permanent change.

[33] Libanius, *Orat.* I, 96f.

[34] *Ibid.*, 99f.

[35] Ammianus Marcellinus, XIV, 7, 9ff, gives the only detailed account of the following events.

prefect arrested. On this, Montius, Gallus' legal officer, intervened with the palace troops in an effort to prevent the prefect's arrest, which would have serious consequences. Gallus then assembled the troops and accused Montius of insubordination. The soldiers seized both Domitianus and Montius and dragged them through the streets until they were dead. The mutilated bodies were thrown into the Orontes.

All kinds of rumors and investigations followed.[36] It was said that some of the army officers in charge of the imperial arms factories at Antioch had promised weapons if a revolution were attempted. Domitianus' son-in-law was found to have made seditious remarks among the troops in Mesopotamia; and an imperial purple robe, made secretly, was discovered in a weaving establishment in Tyre. The trials were directed by Gallus with the utmost savagery and disregard for legal procedure.

Constantius was by now thoroughly alarmed, and once more tried to induce Gallus to come to him.[37] The emperor finally succeeded in persuading Gallus' wife Constantia to set out, and she did so, hoping to intercede with the emperor, her brother, on behalf of her husband. On the way, however, she died in Bithynia of a sudden attack of fever. Gallus himself hesitated for a long while, but finally yielded to the arguments of an officer named Scudilo who was sent especially to persuade him. He at last set out for Constantius' court, in the autumn of A.D. 354. On the journey he was summarily tried and executed.[38]

After the death of Gallus, Constantius proceeded to the punishment of the Caesar's friends and accomplices. The investigations did not take place in Antioch itself, where the proceedings might have stirred up popular feeling, but the

[36] Ammianus Marcellinus, XIV, 7, 18-21; 9, 1-9.
[37] Ammianus Marcellinus, XIV, 11, 1; Philostorgius, *Hist. eccl.*, IV, 1.
[38] Ammianus Marcellinus, XIV, 11, 23.

prisoners were taken to Aquileia and tried and punished there. It is recorded that punishment was also imposed upon the people of Antioch in general, though the precise details of this are not known.

For the next years Constantius was occupied in the West. The disputes in the Arian controversy in Antioch were renewed, and when a bishop had to be elected in A.D. 357, the choice of the new incumbent, Eudoxius, turned the city into a stronghold of Arianism. Three years later Eudoxius was translated to the see of Constantinople and a new struggle over the episcopal appointment took place. The Arian Euzoius was elected in A.D. 361 and remained bishop until A.D. 378.

At the same time the more prominent pagans in the city suddenly found themselves in great danger. The campaign against paganism which Constantius had instituted in A.D. 356 had lapsed when, in the spring of the following year, the emperor visited Rome for the first time and saw the full majesty of the pagan faith in the ancient capital.[39] However, in July A.D. 357, Constantius issued a decree designed to put an end to the consulting of oracles, augurs, interpreters of dreams and other diviners, by members of the imperial court. The decree provided, contrary to all precedent, that the officials could be questioned under torture if they were accused of such practices.[40] The measure was adopted largely because many high officials had been consulting the oracle of the god Bes at Abydos in Egypt, but it could be put into operation against anyone suspected of superstitious practices, and could be a powerful weapon where there was any suspicion of treason.

The imperial legal officer Paulus, a man famous for cruelty, and the Count of the East, Domitianus Modestus, were put in charge of carrying out the law. They established their

---

[39] A. Piganiol, *L'Empire chrétien, 325-395*, Paris, 1947, pp. 97f.
[40] *Cod. Theod.* IX, 16, 6.

headquarters at Scythopolis in Palestine because it was se-
cluded and was midway between Antioch and Alexandria,
where most of the accused persons were to be found. Many
prominent men were tortured and executed, and anyone who
gave any sign of magical practice, such as the wearing of an
amulet to guard against disease, became a victim. The alarm
and anxiety in Antioch were great, and a terrifying portent
appeared at Daphne in the birth of a monstrous infant reported to have two heads, two sets of teeth, a beard, four
eyes, and two very small ears. This was regarded as an omen
that the state was becoming deformed.[41]

All this while events were leading up to the renewal of
the Persian war. In A.D. 355 the praetorian prefect Strategius
Musonianus undertook diplomatic overtures which were designed to turn the truce with Persia into a permanent peace.
Antioch was the headquarters of the negotiations, and the
court orator Themistius speaks of seeing envoys from Susa
and Ecbatana in the city. Sapor, however, was falsely given
to understand that the Romans were weak and were being
constrained to sue for peace. On this basis he made excessive
territorial demands which were quite unacceptable, and he
threatened war if his conditions were not met (A.D. 358).
Alarm spread in Antioch.[42] In the next year King Sapor followed up his threats by invading Mesopotamia. On learning
of this, Constantius left Sirmium, where he had been making
his headquarters, and went to Constantinople, where he
spent the winter (A.D. 359-360) in order to be ready for
another invasion if it came. He chose Constantinople as his
headquarters not only because he wished to show favor to
the new capital but because Antioch was in a state of unrest
as a result of the inquisitions of Paulus and Domitianus
Modestus, begun the previous summer. Moreover, memories
of the tyranny of Gallus and of the disorders and punish-

---

[41] Ammianus Marcellinus, xix, 12, 19.
[42] Ammianus Marcellinus, xviii, 5, 10-15; Libanius, *Epist.* 47, ed. Wolf.

ments that had accompanied and followed his regime would not have made Antioch a comfortable place of residence for the emperor at this time.

Meanwhile the career of the Caesar Julian in Gaul was drawing toward a climax. The son of the half-brother of Constantine the Great, he was a half-brother of Gallus and a cousin of Constantius. Educated in seclusion, he had secretly become a pagan. After the execution of Gallus in A.D. 355, Constantius, in need of assistance in Gaul, appointed Julian to the rank of Caesar, and the young man quickly showed himself a capable soldier and administrator. In time, however, he came into conflict with the advisers and officers with whom Constantius had surrounded him, and it seemed possible that he might eventually meet the same fate as Gallus. Late in A.D. 359 Constantius took away Julian's best troops, ostensibly because they were needed for the Persian war. Julian began to fear for his life, and in February, A.D. 360, his troops, who were loyal to him and hostile to Constantius, proclaimed him emperor.

This news was brought to Constantius in March A.D. 360 in Cappadocia while he was en route for a campaign against the Persians. An attempt was made at negotiation; Constantius continued with his Persian campaign, Julian carried on his duties in Gaul. At the end of the year, after suffering severe losses in operations against the Persians, Constantius went to Antioch and spent the winter there.[43] While in the city he celebrated his marriage with Faustina, his third wife, his second wife Eusebia having died some time previously.[44] In May A.D. 361, Constantius went out against the Persians, but learned that they did not intend to take the field that year, for their omens had declared that a campaign should not be undertaken. In the mean time Julian, having discovered that Constantius was inciting a barbarian prince to

[43] Ammianus Marcellinus, xx, 11, 32; xxi, 6, 1; *Cod. Theod.*, xii, 2, 16.
[44] Ammianus Marcellinus, xxi, 6, 4.

attack him, saw that he must come to a settlement with the emperor. He set out from Gaul with his army, and marched toward Illyricum. When this news reached Constantius in the field, he returned to Antioch by forced marches,[45] made his preparations as quickly as possible, and set out in the autumn to march toward Julian and his forces. En route he fell ill of a fever. Before he died (November A.D. 361), he designated Julian as his successor for the sake of the empire and the dynasty.

[45] Ammianus Marcellinus, xxi, 13, 8; 15, 1.

CHAPTER VIII

THE PAGAN REACTION

At one time the reign (A.D. 361-363) of the Emperor Julian the Philosopher—or Julian the Apostate—was thought of as the last gallant struggle for a lost cause, and the youthful emperor, not yet thirty when he came to the throne, was portrayed as a romantic and melancholy figure. Modern research has given us a more just appreciation of the significance of this episode in the complex history of the fourth century, and Julian's reign is now seen as a natural and inevitable reaction against many of the policies of the Constantinian house, whose social and economic program had been causing hardship to many people. The pagans regarded the Christians as dangerous to the state because Christianity alienated the old gods on whose goodwill the prosperity and safety of the empire depended. In the eyes of the pagans, Christians were simply not good citizens. Thus, though the religious issue was the major cause of the reaction, it was not the sole cause.[1] It is of interest to see that of the three principal champions of paganism in the middle of the fourth century, Julian and the literary men Libanius and Themistius, the first two were closely associated with Antioch, and Themistius visited the city when he was in attendance at the imperial court.

After the death of Constantius (3 November A.D. 361), Julian proceeded to Constantinople, where he made a triumphal entry on 11 December. While spending the winter in the capital, he set in motion a purge of the advisers and

[1] On Julian's life and work, see J. Bidez, *La vie de l'empereur Julien,* Paris, 1930, with a revised edition in German, *Julian der Abtrünnige,* transl. by H. Rinn, Munich, 1940; A. Piganiol, *L'Empire chrétien, 325-395,* Paris, 1947, pp. 127ff; G. Downey, "The Emperor Julian and the Schools," *Classical Journal,* LIII, 1957-58, pp. 97-103; idem, "Julian and Justinian and the Unity of Faith and Culture," *Church History,* XXVIII, 1959, pp. 339-349.

close associates of Constantius, and began a series of measures for the reorganization of the government, the first of which was a substantial reduction in the number of the servants and officials of the court, notably the secret service. Julian's legislation at this period was not yet an attack on Christianity, but was primarily concerned with the establishment of freedom of worship and the restoration of their rights and property to pagans. He also recalled from exile the bishops who had been banished under Constantius. Julian's ultimate plans envisaged not only the revival of Hellenism for its own sake and the elimination of Christianity as an unworthy cult, but the substitution of Hellenism, as a "religion of good citizenship,"[2] for the Christian faith, which in the view of Julian and others had been discredited in a number of ways, notably by the attempt to set up an Arian state church dominated by the political ideas of Constantine and Constantius. The tensions within the church resulting from Arianism had shown that it was an impossible system, and the reaction against the Arians and their aims helped pave the way for Julian's reforms. However, it was not until he went to Antioch in the summer of A.D. 362 that Julian's plans were fully realized.[3]

Julian left Constantinople for Antioch after the middle of May and, travelling through Asia Minor, he reached the Syrian capital on 18 July. He was eager to be in the city,[4] and one indication of the importance he attached to his coming residence there is his appointment early in his reign of his uncle Julian to the influential post of Count of the East. This nomination would insure vitally needed support for the emperor's plans, and it is plain from the promptness

[2] The phrase is that of C. N. Cochrane, *Christianity and Classical Culture,* 2d ed., Oxford, 1944, p. 285.

[3] On Julian's program for the revival of Hellenism, see the study of Cochrane, *op.cit.,* pp. 261-291.

[4] Ammianus Marcellinus, xxii, 9, 14; Julian, *Misopogon,* 367c.

with which the appointment was made, and from the fact that the elder Julian was sent to his post at once, in advance of the emperor's coming, that Antioch was looked upon by the new regime as an important center for its program.

Evidently several motives were in Julian's mind when he made his plans to go to Antioch.[5] One consideration of a practical order was that Julian intended to carry on the war against Persia. After the death of Constantius, King Sapor had tried to make peace, but Julian was determined to administer a decisive check to the Persians and to reestablish the prestige of the Roman Empire; and although the Persians, desiring peace, would not invade Mesopotamia in the summer of A.D. 362, Julian wished to spend some time in Antioch to make even more careful preparations than usual for his campaign.[6]

Moreover, Julian seems to have looked upon Antioch as a more suitable headquarters for his religious program than Constantinople would be. Although Antioch was an important center of Christianity and most of its population, especially the common people, seem to have been Christians,[7] the Syrian capital was also an ancient center of Hellenism, with its famous temples, including the celebrated shrines of Daphne, and the local Olympic Games, which drew visitors and competitors from all over the Roman world. In addition, Julian's good friend, the famous pagan teacher Libanius, was now established in Antioch. These factors were potentially of great importance for Julian's program; and while the frivolous and unstable character of the population of Antioch eventually deceived his hopes for a Hellenic revival, the city at least in the beginning offered attractions that Constantinople did not possess.

A third motive may have influenced Julian in establishing

[5] On Julian's program at Antioch, see G. Downey, "Julian the Apostate at Antioch," *Church History*, VIII, 1939, pp. 303-315.

[6] Ammianus Marcellinus, XXII, 9, 2.   [7] Julian, *Misopogon*, 357d.

himself at Antioch, though this would have been a consideration of less importance. His program included an effort to
win the support of the Jews, in return for which he undertook—unsuccessfully, as it proved—the rebuilding of the
Temple at Jerusalem. Since Antioch possessed an important
Jewish community, it may well have been that Julian, in
going to the city, counted upon gaining the support of its
leaders.[8] Libanius, one of Julian's principal supporters, was
a friend of Gamaliel, son of the Jewish Patriarch Hillel II,
who himself was later to become patriarch as Gamaliel V.

Before Julian arrived at Antioch, a difficult and unpleasant
economic situation had developed, which, as it proved, was
to dominate the whole of his sojourn there.[9] Constantius' war
in the West with the usurper Magnentius, and the preparations for the Persian war, had brought about an inflation,
tolerated by the government, which must have affected most
of the people at Antioch.[10] In addition, the presence at Antioch of the soldiers and officials assembled for the Persian
campaigns must have had the inevitable effect of raising the
prices of foodstuffs, especially since the importation of food
was difficult and costly because of the cumbersome means of
transportation.[11] There had been a famine in similar circumstances in the time of Gallus; and in the summer of A.D. 360

[8] See Kraeling, "Jewish Community," pp. 156-158.

[9] This account of the city's economic condition is based on the writer's
earlier study, "The Economic Crisis at Antioch under Julian the Apostate,"
Studies in Roman Economic and Social History in Honor of A. C. Johnson,
Princeton, 1951, pp. 312-321. A treatment of the same subject has been
written by P. de Jonge, "Scarcity of Corn and Cornprices in Ammianus
Marcellinus," *Mnemosyne,* ser. 4, vol. 1, 1948, pp. 238-245, in which the
material is handled somewhat differently, although the results are substantially the same.

[10] Piganiol, *op.cit.* (above, n. 1), pp. 80, 297; A. H. M. Jones, "Inflation
under the Roman Empire," *Economic History Review,* ser. 2, vol. v, 1953,
p. 304.

[11] See A. H. M. Jones, *The Greek City from Alexander to Justinian,*
Oxford, 1940, p. 261.

the situation was repeated, when the city became crowded with troops and with visitors who had come to seek interviews with the emperor or to do business with officials of the court.[12] The troops themselves no doubt did little to mitigate the economic problems which their presence caused; Libanius describes the way in which a soldier could bully a market vendor.[13] When Julian became emperor late in A.D. 361, Antioch sent the customary delegation to offer congratulations, and the occasion was doubtless taken to describe the city's troubles to the emperor. Julian responded by remitting the arrears of the taxes, which had accumulated, and by increasing the membership in the local senate by two hundred, so that more of the wealthy men might be compelled to share the burdens of public service.[14] The seriousness of the situation may be gauged by the fact that Julian forgave the unpaid taxes in spite of his pressing need for money for his military preparations.

However, when Julian reached Antioch in July of A.D. 362, he found that the situation had become even worse; and the day of his arrival was ill-omened because it happened to be the second day of the annual festival of Adonis, when the death of the god was being lamented and cries of grief were heard on all sides. By particular bad luck, a drought at the beginning of the winter of A.D. 361-362 had caused the failure of the local wheat crop, which normally would have been harvested in May and June, A.D. 362.[15] Although it must have been known for some time that there would be a scarcity, nothing seems to have been done before Julian's arrival to relieve the shortage of wheat. Prices of course had risen. Thus

[12] Libanius, *Antiochikos*, 177f; Julian, *Misopogon*, 370b; Socrates, *Hist. eccl.*, III, 17.

[13] Libanius, *Orat.* XLVII, 33; see R. A. Pack, *Studies in Libanius and Antiochene Society under Theodosius*, Diss., Michigan, 1935, p. 16.

[14] Julian, *Misopogon*, 365b, 367d.

[15] Ammianus Marcellinus, XXII, 13, 4; Libanius, *Orat.* XVIII, 195; Julian, *Misopogon*, 369a.

when Julian came to Antioch the people at once greeted him in the hippodrome with the cry "Everything plentiful, everything dear!"[16] As a first step Julian on the following day called a conference of the leading citizens, farmers, retailers, and artisans, at which he attempted to persuade them to lower prices. They promised to correct the situation themselves,[17] and Julian proceeded to his other concerns.

It was well known to the people of Antioch, in advance of his visit, that one of the emperor's principal interests was the revival of Hellenism and the restoration of the full observance of the pagan festivals and sacrifices. The Count of the East, his uncle Julian, had once been a Christian and had held important posts in the civil administration, but he had been converted to Hellenism by his nephew and in his new post he was charged not only with his regular duties (which at this time included a part in the military preparations) but with the supervision of the maintenance and observance of the pagan cults and sacrifices. During the whole of the emperor's stay at Antioch his uncle appears as the chief official responsible for these matters, including an actual persecution of the Christians when that was undertaken.

The emperor also relied upon his old friend Libanius for support in his revival of Hellenism, and this was rendered in many ways. Libanius was now, in his late forties, one of the most distinguished teachers and prominent citizens of Antioch, and his influence was great, both in the city and, by means of his extensive correspondence, beyond it.

Julian himself, when he reached Antioch, at once began to visit the pagan temples and shrines on all the proper occasions, performing the fitting sacrifices. He frequented especially the temples of Zeus, Zeus Philios, Tyche, Demeter, Hermes, Pan, Ares, Calliope and Apollo, and also sacrificed

---

[16] Libanius, *Orat.* xviii, 195; Julian, *Misopogon*, 368c.
[17] Libanius, *Orat.* xviii, 195; Julian, *Misopogon*, 368d.

under the trees in the garden of the palace.[18] There was, however, one notable occasion on which he was severely disappointed. Soon after his arrival, the annual festival of Apollo was to be celebrated, and Julian went to the temple at Daphne, expecting to witness a rich procession provided by the municipal authorities. Instead, he found nothing but the chief priest, with a goose he had brought from his own home as a sacrifice.[19] This proof of public indifference to the old cults must have been a serious shock to the emperor.

By way of setting an example, Julian saw to it that the sacrifices to the gods throughout the city were performed with great splendor and with a generous provision of offerings—which to some people may not have seemed appropriate at a time of high prices and shortage of wheat. These spectacles made a bad impression because Julian's soldiers flocked to them and gorged themselves on the sacrificial meat; and when they had become stupefied by eating and drinking, they had to be carried back to their quarters by the passers-by. A particularly disagreeable impression was made by the rough Celtic soldiers whom Julian had brought with him from Gaul.[20]

Julian did not have the good fortune to find favor with the people of Antioch. He was small in stature, undignified and personally untidy, and addicted to philosophical study and conversation. With his ascetic and remote personality, he did not know how to make himself popular with the masses.[21] To the people of Antioch, one of his most remarkable peculi-

---

[18] Julian, *Misopogon*, 346b-d; Libanius, *Orat.* I, 121f; *Orat.* xv, 79. Julian also ascended Mt. Casius to sacrifice to Zeus (Ammianus Marcellinus, xxii, 14, 4).

[19] Julian, *Misopogon*, 361d.

[20] Ammianus Marcellinus, xxii, 12, 6-7.

[21] On Julian's personal appearance, see R. Jonas, "A Newly Discovered Portrait of the Emperor Julian," *A.J.A.*, L, 1946, pp. 277-282, and P. Lévêque, "Observations sur l'iconographie de Julien dit l'Apostat d'après une tête inédite de Thasos," *Monuments Piot*, LI, 1960, pp. 105-128.

arities was that he hated horse-racing, one of the city's favorite forms of entertainment, and he never attended races unless they were connected with the festivals of the gods.[22]

The famine and the high prices continued, but the emperor still hoped that the problem could be solved by the municipal authorities without intervention on his part. A month after his arrival in the city he did, however, take a helpful step by issuing a decree that rations were to be drawn only by those of the junior officers who were actually ordered to be on duty at the imperial court. Formerly officers in excess of the authorized strength had been allowed to be present at the court, but persons in this status were now to leave and return to their homes.[23]

Ten days later another decree was issued which should have had a more pronounced effect on the economic crisis. Julian's original order increasing the size of the local senate had not had the desired effect of helping to restore the city's financial situation. The senators had not elected men who ought to have served but had hitherto succeeded in escaping the burden of membership. Instead, they chose men who were not qualified by birth but had been engaging in speculation, with the result that the new members were able to use their membership in the senate to further their own and their colleagues' gains.[24] Julian now issued a decree which shows that the requirements for membership were being more strictly enforced and that everyone liable to serve as a senator was being forced to undertake his obligations.[25]

The situation still was not improved. As autumn approached, the hardships of the people increased. The winter weather would bring real suffering; and Julian's difficulties were now heightened by one of the most sensational events

[22] Julian, *Misopogon*, 340a-b; cf. Zosimus, III, 11.
[23] *Cod. Theod.* VI, 24, 1.   [24] Julian, *Misopogon*, 368a-b.
[25] *Cod. Theod.* XII, 1, 51; Zosimus, III, 11, 5; Libanius, *Orat.* XLVIII, 15.

of his stay in Antioch, the burning of the Temple of Apollo at Daphne.

The spring near the temple, in which the oracle resided, had been closed during the reorganization of the water supply at Daphne under Hadrian. The oracle, however, continued to operate, and we have seen how the Caesar Gallus, in order to nullify its influence and that of the cult of Apollo, had removed the remains of the famous local martyr Babylas from the Christian cemetery at Antioch to a shrine which he built near the temple. The oracle had been silenced. When Julian, on arriving at Antioch, had tried to consult the oracle, he was informed that the god was silent because of the presence of "bodies" in the neighborhood. This was interpreted as a reference to the relics of St. Babylas. Julian ordered the traditional ceremonies of purification to be performed and directed that the relics be returned to their former resting-place in Antioch. The stone coffin of the saint, when it was taken back to the city, was escorted by a large crowd of Christians singing psalms.[26]

Soon after this, on 22 October, the Temple of Apollo caught fire, and the roof and the great gold and ivory statue of Apollo, which reached to the ceiling, were burned.[27] The Christians were accused of setting the fire in retaliation for the removal of the body of St. Babylas. The Christians themselves maintained that the building had been struck by lightning. There was also a report that the fire was started, through the negligence of the temple attendants, by candles lighted by the philosopher Asclepiades, who had visited the temple to worship and make an offering. Although Julian himself later stated that the cause of the fire was not certain, a persecution of the Christians was begun, directed by the

---

[26] Philostorgius, *Hist. eccl.*, VII, 8; Socrates, *Hist. eccl.*, III, 18; Sozomen, *Hist. eccl.*, V, 19.

[27] Ammianus Marcellinus, XXII, 13, 1-5; Libanius, *Orat.* LX; Julian, *Misopogon*, 361b-c.

Count of the East and other officials. The Great Church was closed, and the liturgical vessels, which had been presented to it by Constantine and Constantius, were confiscated.[28]

At about this time, further troubles developed as the shortage of grain and the inflation of prices became critical. The prominent citizens had done nothing to help the situation, but were making handsome profits from speculation.[29] Julian now found it necessary to issue an edict fixing maximum prices. He also began to import grain. He first brought in a large quantity from the region of Chalcis and Hierapolis.[30] This must have been an expensive undertaking, attempted only as a last resort, for we hear that during a severe famine at Caesarea in Cappadocia at about this time grain could not be imported because of the prohibitive cost of land transportation.[31] When this first supply was used, Julian contributed grain from his own estates; and when this was not enough, he sent to Egypt for wheat. The grain was sold at a reduced price (15 measures at the price formerly charged for 10), and the price of bread was controlled.[32]

A further step was the reduction of the taxes by one fifth. Evidently the controlled prices were still high as compared with former prices, and the lowering of the taxes was undertaken in an effort to lighten the burden of the cost of living.[33]

Another expedient was the distribution of 3,000 units of municipally-owned land which had ceased to be cultivated. This land was made available, at popular request, as a means

[28] Theophanes, *Chronicle*, p. 50, 14ff, ed. De Boor; Theodoret, *Hist. eccl.*, III, 12, 4. The report in Philostorgius, *Hist. eccl.*, VII, 10, and in Sozomen, *Hist. eccl.*, V, 8, of the defiling of the church and the sacred vessels seems exaggerated.

[29] Julian, *Misopogan*, 350a. [30] *Ibid.*, 368d-369a.

[31] Gregory of Nazianzus, *Orat. in Praise of Basil the Great*, 34f, *P.G.*, XXXVI, cols. 541-544; cf. Jones, *loc.cit.* (above, n. 11).

[32] Julian, *Misopogon*, 369d-370a. The size of the units is not known. For a discussion of the prices, see the study of inflation by Jones cited above n. 10.

[33] Julian, *Misopogon*, 365d, 367a.

of assisting the small landowners and farmers, and increasing the food supply. While we do not know what the size of the units was, the sources indicate that this was a substantial amount of land.[34]

The special economic difficulties of Antioch were serious indeed, but they were in part, so far as the inflation was concerned, shared with the remainder of the empire. Constantius' war with the usurper Magnentius in the West, and the preparations for the Persian war had inflated prices, and the effects of a currency reform of Constantius (A.D. 342) had been offset when the new coins were later devalued.[35] Julian when he came to the throne found the resources of the government very straitened,[36] and he had in addition need of large sums for his military plans. An additional source of financial difficulty was that gold and silver for coins were scarce because the metals were being used for the manufacture of jewelry and silverware.[37] Consequently Julian in the autumn of A.D. 362 introduced a reform of the copper currency. This ought to have done something to alleviate the situation at Antioch, though the people of the city objected to the new coins.[38]

Julian's best efforts, however, were unsuccessful. All classes in the city failed to cooperate.[39] The imported wheat, sold at

[34] Julian, *Misopogon*, 362c, 370d.

[35] Piganiol, *op.cit.* (above, n. 1), pp. 133, 297f.

[36] Piganiol, *op.cit.*, p. 128; R. Andreotti, "L'opera legislativa ed amministrativa dell'Imperatore Giuliano," *Nuova rivista storica*, XIV, 1930, pp. 342-383.

[37] This is indicated by Themistius' address to Julian, extant only in an Arabic translation made from a lost Syriac version, which was in turn made from the lost Greek original; see lines 131-134 of the Latin paraphrase of M. Bouyges in *Archives de philosophie*, tome II, cahier 3, 1924, p. 22. A new edition of this oration, with translation, by Irfan Kawar will appear in the edition of Themistius' orations by H. Schenkl and G. Downey, now in press and to be published by B. G. Teubner, Leipzig.

[38] Julian, *Misopogon*, 355d; G. Elmer, "Die Kupfergeldreform unter Julianus Philosophus," *Numismatische Zeitschrift*, LXX, 1937, pp. 25-42.

[39] Libanius, *Orat.* xv, 23.

a fixed price, was bought by speculators and landowners who either held it in anticipation of a further advance in prices, or sold it in the country where price control could not be enforced.[40] Some of the merchants in the city, blaming the landowners for the high prices, simply ceased to do business, either because they could no longer make a profit, or because they hoped that Julian's program would collapse and that a "free economy" would be restored.[41] It was argued that the presence of the troops made hardship inevitable and that Julian had no right to try to reduce prices, but was only trying to gain popularity. The attempt to lower prices, it was claimed, would itself cause further scarcity.[42] Famine (people said) was caused by the weather, over which the authorities had no control. Nature must be allowed to take its course and the market must be allowed to regulate itself.[43] Moreover, the distribution of the municipal land was a failure, for the lots which were made available were promptly occupied by persons who did not need them.[44] Finally, the control of the price of bread failed to give relief to the urban populace, for the country people flocked to town to buy it.[45] The shortage of food was to continue even after Julian left Antioch. At least, however, Julian had not resorted to violent measures, as Gallus had done in a similar situation.[46]

Preparations for the Persian war continued. Toward the end of A.D. 362 King Sapor sent Julian a letter asking for a conference to settle their differences, but this overture was rejected, for Julian, confident of success, planned to put on the throne of Persia the prince Hormisdas, the younger

[40] Julian, *Misopogon*, 369c; Libanius, *Orat.* xviii, 195.

[41] Julian, *Misopogon*, 350a; Socrates, *Hist. eccl.*, iii, 17; Sozomen, *Hist. eccl.*, v, 19.

[42] Ammianus Marcellinus, xxii, 14, 1f; Socrates, *loc.cit.*; Libanius, *Orat.* i, 126.

[43] Libanius, *Orat.* i, 205; *Epist.* 1439, ed. Wolf.

[44] Julian, *Misopogon*, 370d.   [45] Julian, *Misopogon*, 369d.

[46] Libanius, *Orat.* xviii, 195.

brother of Sapor, who had fled from Persia in the time of Constantine the Great and, after serving as a cavalry officer under Constantius, was now in Antioch with Julian, waiting to accompany him on his campaign.[47] Julian did, however, accept an offer of assistance from Arsaces, king of Armenia.[48]

On 1 January A.D. 363, Julian entered upon the consulship at Antioch, taking as his colleague a private individual (an unusual thing at this time), Sallustius, the former praetorian prefect of Gaul. Libanius wrote an address to the emperor for the occasion, and during the ceremonies the consuls visited the Temple of the Genius of the Roman People.[49]

In the final stages of the preparations for the coming campaign there developed serious disaffection in the army, partly because of the measures taken against the Christians in the service, partly because the campaign itself was unpopular and the emperor's plans were thought too optimistic. Julian knew of the complaints and criticisms, but was unmoved by them.[50] One incident occurred in late December or early January, when two Christian soldiers named Bonosus and Maximilianus, who were standard bearers, refused to remove the Christian symbols from their standards, and likewise declined to perform the ritual sacrifice to the pagan gods. They were examined by Julian the Count of the East and were condemned to death, and a large crowd, including Bishop Meletius, accompanied them to the military training ground across the river, where they were beheaded.[51]

Even more serious were ideas circulating in the imperial guard itself. Two officers, Romanus and Vincentius, were

[47] Libanius, *Orat.* xviii, 164, 258; *Epist.* 1457, ed. Wolf; *Acta Sanctorum*, 21 August, tome iv, p. 431.

[48] Ammianus Marcellinus, xxiii, 2, 1f.

[49] Idem, xxiii, 1, 1-4; cf. Libanius, *Orat.* xii.

[50] Ammianus Marcellinus, xxii, 12, 3f.

[51] *Acta Sanctorum*, 21 August, tome iv, pp. 430-432. One of the hearings took place "in the old bath," evidently a public bath that had been converted into a military headquarters.

convicted of "making plans beyond their station" and were punished by exile.[52] Then, late in January, two other officers of the guard, Juventinus and Maximinus, were reported to the emperor for seditious talk, and it was said that there was a plot to assassinate Julian.[53] The emperor examined the men himself, and they were condemned and executed; according to one report, the executions took place secretly, in the middle of the night.

All this while, shortage of food continued, and this must have added to the emperor's unpopularity. Julian on his part was saddened and discouraged by the deaths of two of his principal assistants, Felix and his uncle Julian, the latter after a long and painful illness.[54] Scurrilous verses about the emperor were posted in the city.[55] After the middle of February, when he had only a short time to remain in Antioch, Julian brought his efforts in the city to a fitting close by publishing the *Misopogon* ("Beard-hater"), the famous satire in which, by pretending to mock himself and his philosopher's beard, he set down his feelings about Antioch and its people. Julian, as a bookish person, had already written a number of treatises and satires, many of them designed to play a part in his revival of Hellenism. This new satire was published by being posted outside the palace, at the Tetrapylon of the Elephants, near the Royal Street which served as an entrance to the palace.[56]

Before his departure, Julian found a singularly appropriate

[52] Ammianus Marcellinus, xxii, 11, 2.

[53] Theodoret, *Hist. eccl.*, 15, 4-9; Malalas, p. 327, 15-21; Libanius, *Orat.* xv, 43; *Orat.* xviii, 199, cf. *Orat.* xii, 84-90; P. P(eeters), "La date de la fête de SS. Juventin et Maximin," *Analecta Bollandiana*, xlii, 1924, pp. 77-82.

[54] Ammianus Marcellinus, xxiii, 1, 4f; Philostorgius, *Hist. eccl.*, vii, 10 and 12; Sozomen, *Hist. eccl.*, v, 8. Felix died of a hemorrhage, Julian of a mysterious and unpleasant disease. Their deaths were thought by the Christians to have been punishment for their impious deeds.

[55] Libanius, *Orat.* xvi, 30.

[56] Malalas, p. 328, 2-4.

means of expressing his displeasure. This was the appointment to the post of governor of Syria of Alexander of Heliopolis, a man noted for his bad temper and cruelty. Alexander, Julian said, was not worthy of the post, but was the kind of man fit to govern the rebellious and avaricious people of Antioch. When the emperor left the city, on 5 March, he announced that when the summer campaign was completed, he would not return to Antioch, but would make his winter headquarters at Tarsus in Cilicia.

A large crowd accompanied the emperor as he left the city, wishing him success and attempting to placate his anger.[57] After Julian had departed, Libanius sent an address to the emperor in an effort to mollify him, and also delivered an oration to the people of Antioch upbraiding them for their behavior. After this the citizens passed through an uncomfortable period. The shortage of food continued, and the new governor of Syria, a zealous pagan, performed his duties with the utmost rigor and harshness; the administration of the city was quite transformed, and the surprised and terrified people paid their taxes even before they were due.[58] Among other things, Alexander saw to it that as many young men as possible from all over Syria enrolled as students of Libanius.[59]

Julian never returned from his campaign. He was killed in Persia in June, and with him there came to an end the dynasty of Constantine. The news of his death was greeted with rejoicing by the majority of the people of Antioch,[60] though the pagans mourned him, and Libanius wrote a Monody and a Funeral Oration on the emperor.

No record is preserved of any public buildings constructed by Julian at Antioch. He did, however, found a new library

[57] Ammianus Marcellinus, XXIII, 2, 3-6.
[58] Libanius, *Orat.* xv, 74; *Epistles* 722, 1053, 1057, 1450, ed. Wolf.
[59] Libanius, *Epist.* 758, ed. Wolf.
[60] Theodoret, *Hist. eccl.*, III, 28; Libanius, *Epist.* 1186, ed. Wolf.

in the city. George, bishop of Alexandria from A.D. 357 to 361, had formed an excellent collection of books, including philosophy of every school, history, and Christian writings, and Julian had become familiar with the collection before he became emperor. Having been installed as bishop of Alexandria by the government of Constantius, George was unpopular with many of the people in the city, and when the news came of the death of Constantius, the bishop was lynched by a mob on Christmas eve, A.D. 361. Julian when he was at Antioch secured the dead bishop's library and had it brought to the city and installed in the temple which had been built by Hadrian in honor of the deified Trajan.[61] The temple and all the books were burned by a mob a short time later during the reign of Julian's successor Jovian.

The history of the church at Antioch under Julian is soon told. When Julian became emperor, the Christian community at Antioch was divided into three groups, (1) the Arians composing the "official" church under Bishop Euzoius (A.D. 361-378); and the orthodox or followers of the doctrine of Nicaea, divided into two groups (2) the Eustathians, led by the priest Paulinus, who later became bishop, and (3) the Meletians, whose leader Bishop Meletius soon returned from exile under the recall of banished bishops proclaimed by Julian. Euzoius, as the official incumbent, occupied the Great Church. The Meletians worshiped at different times, according to their status at the moment, either in the ancient "apostolic" church in the old part of the city, or in a church outside the city. Euzoius (no doubt glad to keep his opponents divided) allowed the Eustathians to use one of the smaller churches in the city.[62]

[61] Julian, *Epistles* 106f ed. Bidez-Cumont; Suidas, *s.v.* Iobianos. See C. Callmer, "Die antiken Bibliotheken," *Opuscula archaeologica*, III, 1944, p. 184.

[62] The Arian church historian in Philostorgius, p. 230, 14, ed. Bidez; Theodoret, *Hist. eccl.*, II, 31, 11; III, 4, 3; Socrates, *Hist. eccl.*, III, 9.

In permitting the exiled bishops to return, Julian hoped that they would resume their quarrels and thus weaken the opposition to his revival of Hellenism.[63] In reality, the Christians closed up their ranks in the face of the common foe and attempted to settle their differences, a process made easier by the decline of the strength of Arianism at this time. In the case of Antioch, however, the effort at consolidation failed. Soon after Athanasius returned from exile, early in A.D. 362, a council was held at Alexandria which dealt, among other things, with the situation at Antioch. An effort was made to unite Paulinus and Meletius and their followers. This plan, however, failed, for Lucifer of Calaris, who had not waited for the council of Alexandria to propose the reconciliation, had himself gone to Antioch, and had there seen fit to consecrate Paulinus as bishop.[64] This action, creating two "Nicene" bishops in Antioch, put an end to all hope of healing the local dissension, and created a schism that lasted for fifty years.

[63] Ammianus Marcellinus, xxii, 5, 3f.

[64] Socrates, *loc.cit.*; Sozomen, *Hist. eccl.*, v, 13; Theodoret, *Hist. eccl.*, iii, 5, 1.

CHAPTER IX

PAGAN AND CHRISTIAN TRADITIONS

JULIAN's program for the revival of Hellenism collapsed with his death and his successor was a Christian, an army officer named Jovian. It seemed plain that paganism no longer had the strength to displace Christianity; yet paganism was still enough of a force for Jovian to think it politic to show tolerance toward the pagans.[1]

Jovian died after a reign of less than nine months (A.D. 363-364) and was succeeded by Valentinian, another Christian army officer who had served at Antioch under Julian.[2] Valentinian divided the empire with his brother Valens (A.D. 364-378), Valens taking the East, Valentinian the West. Freedom of worship was still the announced policy of the government.[3]

Valens had a morbid dread of magic, and he made the practice of it a capital offense.[4] His fears were fulfilled when it was discovered that a number of persons at Antioch, Valens' headquarters, had been engaging in efforts to discover the name of the person who would succeed him. The letters of the alphabet were written around the rim of a wooden tripod, like that used by the oracle at Delphi, and a ring suspended on a thread above the tripod, when set in motion, swayed in different directions; its motions indicated the letters THEOD. The same result was reached by Libanius and a friend by using a fowl as a medium. The alphabet was written on the ground and a grain of wheat was placed on each letter. The fowl was then set free and allowed to peck at the grains of wheat. As the fowl went from one grain to another,

---

[1] A. Piganiol, *L'Empire chrétien,* 325-395, Paris, 1947, pp. 147f.

[2] Theophanes, p. 51, 7-11, ed. De Boor; Philostorgius, *Hist. eccl.,* VII, 7; Socrates, *Hist. eccl.,* IV, 1; Sozomen, *Hist. eccl.,* VI, 6; Theodoret, *Hist. eccl.,* III, 16; Zonaras, XIII, 15, 4f.

[3] *Cod. Theod.* IX, 16, 9.   [4] *Ibid.,* 8.

the watchers recorded the letters of the alphabet at which it stopped, and again the message was the same, THEOD.

These activities were betrayed to the authorities, and the discovery resulted in a veritable reign of terror at Antioch, which eventually spread to Asia Minor. It developed that one of the imperial secretaries, named Theodorus, had been privy to the consultations. He and many others whose names also happened to begin with the fatal letters were executed. The investigations were carried on with the utmost ferocity, and the tortures and executions, the contemporary historian Ammianus Marcellinus wrote, resembled the slaughtering of animals. It appeared that Valens had been in real danger; proper judicial procedures were suspended and many innocent persons perished or were exiled, and the confiscation of their estates, which brought a large increase of wealth to the emperor, came to be regarded as one of the major factors in the persecution. Ultimately the investigation was extended to all persons who could be accused or suspected of any magical practice, and a number of philosophers lost their lives. Books dealing with magic were seized and burned, and many people as a precaution burned their entire libraries even though the books were innocent.[5]

Valens' stay in Antioch ended in the spring of A.D. 378, when he left the city hurriedly to deal with the invasion of the Goths in Thrace. After a brief visit to Constantinople he took the field and was killed in the disastrous battle of Adrianople.[6]

Building was a special interest of Valens, and from the beginning of his reign he took care that the cities in his part of the empire should have the use of some of the taxes reserved for public building purposes. At Antioch—which, the chronicler Malalas says, the emperor liked because of its

[5] Ammianus Marcellinus, XXIX, 1, 5ff.

[6] Ammianus Marcellinus, XXXI, 7, 1 and 11, 1; Philostorgius, *Hist. eccl.*, IX, 17; Socrates, *Hist. eccl.*, IV, 35.

site, its air, and its water—Valens carried out important building operations, the most notable of which was the construction of a new market-place called the Forum of Valens (Fig. 5).[7] This was situated at the eastern end of the short colonnaded street which ran between the mountain and the river, crossing the principal colonnaded street of the city; in part, it was built over the course of the winter torrent Parmenius. There had already existed in this part of the city a number of notable public buildings. The oldest of which we know was the Temple of Ares, probably Hellenistic in origin. Opposite this Julius Caesar had built his Kaisarion, a basilica with an open court and a vaulted apse, in front of which stood statues of Caesar and of the Tyche of Rome. At the eastern end of the street, near the Temple of Ares, Trajan had erected the Middle Gate, a monumental arch. In the same neighborhood Commodus had constructed the Xystos for use in the Olympic Games, with a temple to Olympian Zeus. The same emperor had also erected here a public bath named for himself, and had restored the Temple of Athene, which was probably of the Seleucid period. At the same time or a little later the Plethrion, another structure for use in the Olympic Games, was built near the Xystos and the Bath of Commodus.[8] In the same neighborhood stood the Horologion or public clock, which may be identical with the Tower of the Winds built by Vespasian.[9]

The literary evidence enables us to reconstruct the principal features of the new forum, which seems to have resembled that of Trajan at Rome. Space for the main area of the forum was obtained by demolishing part of the Kaisarion, and by building heavy stone vaults over the Parmenius, with marble paving laid on top of them. Some of these vaults, and part of the paving, were found in the excavations.[10] The vaulted

---

[7] Malalas, p. 338, 19ff.   [8] *Ibid.*

[9] Malalas, pp. 262, 3f; 338, 22.

[10] See the reports of the trial excavations in this area, *Antioch-on-the-*

apse of the Kaisarion was rebuilt or restored and became a prominent feature of the new forum. The open area of the forum was surrounded by four porticos, decorated with coffered ceilings, paintings, variegated marbles, and mosaic work. The columns were of marble from Salona, and the covered walks were ornamented with statues.

When the forum was completed, it was surrounded by important public buildings, structures already existing and new ones given by Valens. The literary texts enable us to determine with some degree of accuracy the positions of some of the buildings and their relations with one another. The Plethrion had adjoined the demolished part of the Kaisarion and so stood on one side of the forum, with the apse of the Kaisarion on another side. On still another side was the Bath of Commodus, which later became the headquarters of the governor of Syria. This bath was flanked by the Xystos. Opposite the bath and the Xystos, on the other side of the forum, Valens erected a new basilica.

Near the forum, but apparently not on it, was a new *macellum* or provisions market, which Valens installed on the site of the former Temple of Ares. The temple had stood in a very large open enclosure such as would provide a suit-able site for a market. This was close to the Middle Gate of Trajan, behind the apse of the Kaisarion. The open area of the market was surrounded by porticos and shops, with a fountain in the center of the open space.

Three statues of Valentinian I were set up, one on a column in the middle of the open space of the forum, two others in the apse of the Kaisarion. One of these was a seated statue made of "costly stone."

Another operation was the rebuilding of an amphitheater for the hunting and slaughtering of animals.[11] This had formerly been a gladiatorial amphitheater, but when gladiatorial

---

Orontes, ii, p. 4; iii, pp. 17f. See also the report in *A.J.A.,* xliv, 1940, p. 418.

[11] Malalas, p. 339, 15-17.

shows were forbidden, as repugnant to Christianity, combats of animals were substituted. The conversion of the building was effected by the construction of two curved ends containing rows of seats carried on arches, and by the installation of the cages necessary for keeping the animals.

Under Valens the history of the church at Antioch was once more troubled, for the emperor favored Arianism, and in the spring of A.D. 365 he began a veritable persecution of the orthodox. The Christian community was still divided among the followers of Euzoius, Meletius, and Paulinus respectively. The effect of Valens' attitude was to restore the situation to what it had been at the end of the reign of Constantius. Meletius went into exile once more, and Euzoius again became the "official" bishop of the city. The Meletians held their services in the open air, first on the slope of the mountain, then, when they were driven thence, on the banks of the river; finally they had to meet on the military training ground across the river.[12] The Arians in fact were now the majority of the Christian population of the city.[13] The Meletians, however, managed to maintain themselves, under the leadership of the priest Flavian (later bishop of Antioch) and of Diodorus and the famous ascetics Aphraates and Julian, who came into the city from their retreats to help support the flock.[14]

The persecution continued with such severity that in A.D. 375 or 376 the court orator Themistius, who was a pagan, thought it necessary to deliver before Valens, in Antioch, an oration in which he advised the emperor to cease the persecution. This advice had some effect, and the persecution was made less rigorous.[15]

[12] Theodoret, *Hist. eccl.*, IV, 24f; *Relig. hist.*, II.

[13] Sozomen, *Hist. eccl.*, VI, 21.

[14] Theodoret, *Hist. eccl.*, II, 24; *Relig. hist.*, II and VIII; Theophanes, p. 62, 26-32, ed. De Boor.

[15] Socrates, *Hist. eccl.*, IV, 32; Sozomen, *Hist. eccl.*, VI, 36f.

St. Jerome's visit to Antioch in A.D. 374-375 is known in some detail thanks to his letters.[16] His host, the wealthy priest Evagrius, provided him with admirable facilities for work. Many religious visitors and pilgrims on their way to and from Jerusalem passed through Antioch, and we hear much of their visits and their discussions. In A.D. 375 Jerome decided to retire to the desert of Chalcis, east of Antioch, but in A.D. 379 he returned to the city and was ordained to the priesthood by Paulinus, the Eustathian bishop.

The reign of Theodosius I, the Great (A.D. 379-395), is in many ways the most characteristic period in the history of Antioch because it brought out, in the persons of two great protagonists, Libanius and John Chrysostom, the pagan and Christian traditions the interaction of which gave Antioch its special importance in the history of Greek Christian civilization. Thanks to the voluminous writings of Libanius and Chrysostom we know more about Antioch at this period than we do about any other city of the eastern part of the Roman Empire at this epoch.

As the Arian controversy was dying out, a measure of peace was restored to the church at Antioch. Bishop Meletius returned from exile and came to an understanding with Bishop Paulinus.[17] To signalize the restoration of orthodoxy, Meletius began the construction of a cruciform church, designed as a martyr's shrine for St. Babylas, the foundations of which have been excavated across the Orontes from the city.[18] The relics of the saint were removed from the cemetery outside the city and buried in the church. The crossing of the church, when excavated, revealed a monolithic sarcoph-

[16] For a detailed study of Jerome's sojourn in Antioch and its vicinity, see F. Cavallera, *Saint Jérôme, sa vie et son œuvre*, Louvain-Paris, 1922, I, pp. 26ff.

[17] Theodoret, *Hist. eccl.*, v, 3f.

[18] J. Lassus, "L'église cruciforme," *Antioch-on-the-Orontes*, II, pp. 5-44; G. Downey, "The Shrines of St. Babylas at Antioch and Daphne," *ibid.*, pp. 45-48.

agus designed for the reception of two bodies, one placed above the other. This can only have been intended for the reception of the relics of Babylas and the body of Meletius which, the contemporary sources relate, were buried in the same receptacle.

Local developments were now further affected by the religious program of Theodosius. The famous decree of 27 February A.D. 380[19] established orthodoxy as the religion of the empire and condemned heretics to both divine and earthly penalties. Thus the Arian disorders were brought to an end, and at Antioch, as elsewhere, the final measures could be taken for the full restoration of the orthodox faith. The Arians were expelled and the custody of the Great Church was given to Meletius.

In material matters, the opening of Theodosius' reign was not an easy time for the Roman Empire, for military troubles and economic distress were felt everywhere. In addition, Antioch had to suffer from a famine caused by unfavorable weather which began in A.D. 382 and continued intermittently until A.D. 384. The inhabitants of other cities traveled to Antioch hoping to find food there, only to be disappointed, and the farmers from the region of Antioch whose crops had failed also crowded into the city looking for help.[20] A limited supply of bread was available, but it was difficult to control its distribution. Guards were posted at the gates of the city to prevent travelers from carrying out more than two loaves of bread at once.[21] The bakers, fearing to be blamed for the situation, fled from the city.[22]

Side by side with the history of the famine, Libanius' speeches give us a detailed picture of the municipal administration of Antioch at this period.[23] The policies that had been

[19] *Cod. Theod.* XVI, I, 2.   [20] Libanius, *Orat.* XXVII, 6.
[21] *Ibid.*, 14.   [22] Libanius, *Orat.* I, 226.
[23] On this see the masterly study of P. Petit, *Libanius et la vie municipale à Antioche au IV* siècle, Paris, 1955.

followed for some years by the imperial government were tending to weaken the local municipal governments and to discourage and impoverish the middle classes; and the farmers and the lower classes, who had never found life easy under the prevailing economic system, continued to suffer from their usual troubles, especially from the tax burden and the obligation to lend their pack animals to the government and to work on the public roads. We hear of all this from Libanius, who gives us, in addition, special information on certain problems in the "reform speeches" which begin in A.D. 381.[24]

Libanius, himself a member of the senatorial class, was constantly troubled by the way in which both the property and the energy of the senators was being used up in the public services that they were required to perform, such as heating the public baths and providing animals for shows. Eligible men were avoiding service in every possible way, and Libanius advised the emperor that it was urgently necessary to increase the membership in the local senate in order to distribute the burdens more equitably. There was also an almost chronic state of warfare between the imperial governors and the senators, as the governors sought to realize the financial profits that were a perquisite of their office.

The farmers, who, along with the senators, formed one of the important elements in the local economy, were also suffering, not only from the natural hazards of weather and insects to which their occupation was subject, but from other evils. The governors compelled them to perform public services to which they should not have been liable, and their farms were damaged by swarms of wandering monks, who considered themselves entitled to take whatever food they could secure. Independent farmers were also, as a result of the imperial policies of the time, in danger of falling under the control

[24] R. A. Pack, *Studies in Libanius and Antiochene Society under Theodosius*, Diss., Michigan, 1935.

of the large landowners who used their financial capital and their political influence to dominate or absorb the small cultivators. The small tradesmen in the city suffered from similar oppression.

All these conditions, as Libanius portrays them, are inevitably associated with his own protracted series of personal quarrels with the successive Counts of the East and governors of Syria. These enmities form the theme of something like eleven of his extant orations. Among the Counts of the East, Proculus (A.D. 383-384) was attacked because of his cruelty and maladministration, though he honored Libanius. His attempt to enlarge the Plethrion was bitterly criticized because it would have changed the sacred character of a part of the Olympic Games.[25] Proculus' successor Icarius (A.D. 384-385) was greeted with an open letter warning him not to follow in his predecessor's footsteps. Libanius later had to write three more pieces reproaching Icarius for his lack of friendship for Libanius and for his cruelty and misgovernment.

Of the governors of Syria, practically all those who held office between A.D. 384 and 395 became the subjects of attacks by Libanius. Eumolpius (A.D. 384), a relative of Libanius, earned the orator's praise for his mildness during the famine, but Libanius eventually turned against him for advising his pupils to go to Rome to study Latin.[26] Tisamenus (A.D. 386) drew upon himself a variety of accusations of oppression and neglect of duty. Timocrates is criticized for being influenced by the manifestations of approval or disapproval of his actions which came from the claque in the theater. Celsus (A.D. 387) is noteworthy in that his conduct is praised and never blamed. Lucianus (A.D. 388) was bitterly criticized for his severity toward the senators and was removed from office as a result of the complaints made about him.

[25] Libanius, *Orat.* x.
[26] Libanius, *Orat.* xxvii, 6 and 18; *Orat.* xl, *passim.*

It is not always easy to know the rights and wrongs involved in the difficulties between Libanius and the governors. It does, however, seem true that the administration of justice at Antioch at this time was far from what it should have been; and Libanius wrote an address to the emperor on this subject in which we get what appears to be a not too distorted view of the problem.[27] Owing to a venal and inefficient judiciary, many men were committed to prison, but few left it. The judges often forgot or neglected the accused, and the senators did not dare interfere; and the deplorable living conditions in the prisons made confinement for even a short time a harsh experience. Libanius petitioned the emperor to compel the unwilling judges to observe the provisions of an existing law[28] which forbade the holding in prison either of convicted prisoners who had not yet been punished, or of guiltless persons who ought to be freed.

This is the background of the insurrection of A.D. 387, one of the best known episodes in the history of Antioch.[29] General economic discontent existed not only at Antioch but throughout the eastern part of the empire, coupled with dissatisfaction with Theodosius' policy toward the barbarians. There were disorders at Constantinople, at Alexandria, and at Thessalonica (when the famous massacre took place), as well as rioting at Berytus just before the outbreak at

[27] Cf. *Orat.* XLV, *On the Prisoners.* A translation, commentary and study of this oration, with an essay on the contemporary interest in penal reform, may be found in Pack, *op.cit.* (above, n. 24).

[28] *Cod. Theod.* IX, 3, 6.

[29] On this insurrection, see A. Hug, *Antiochia und der Aufstand im Jahre 387 n. Chr.,* Winterthur, 1863; R. Sievers, *Das Leben des Libanius,* Berlin, 1868, pp. 172-187 (the best account); R. Browning, "The Riot of A.D. 387 in Antioch: The Role of the Theatrical Claques in the Later Empire," *Journal of Roman Studies,* XLII, 1952, pp. 13-20. The principal sources are Libanius' five speeches concerned with the insurrection (*Orat.* XIX-XXIII) and Chrysostom's twenty-one *Homilies on the Statues* (*P.G.* XLIX).

Antioch.[30] Taxation had to be increased in order to pay for
the rebuilding of the army after the disaster at Adrianople
in A.D. 378, and for Theodosius' defensive operations against
the barbarians, also in order to compensate for the loss of
income from land ruined by the wars. Thus when an imperial
edict providing for heavier taxation arrived at Antioch in
the early part of A.D. 387, there was immediate resistance to
what was considered to be an insupportable burden. When
the decree was read at the law court to the assembled senators,
who filled the building, there was immediate complaint.
The senators, along with other prominent citizens, went
to ask the governor of Syria to have the tax reduced. Getting
no satisfaction from the governor, they went to the residence
of Bishop Flavian; but not finding him, they returned to
the law court. At this point the crowd was taken in charge
by the theatrical claque, an organized and paid body which
is encountered elsewhere in the history of Antioch.[31] This
claque, originally a group of dubious characters paid to
applaud the dancers and actors in the theater, had come to
take on a political role as well, by applauding or censuring
the measures of the local governor, the demonstrations taking
place when the governor paid his quasi-official visits to the
theater. Skilled in stirring up the crowd, these claques had
come to be powerful leaders of mobs, and could be hired
for political purposes. At Antioch and elsewhere they had
come to be feared by the governors.

On the present occasion, the mob was led by a man who
was known to have been responsible for creating disorders
in Berytus. Gathering reinforcements from the crowd that
had collected outside the law court, the mob went to the

[30] Browning, *op.cit.*, p. 13.

[31] It is the merit of R. Browning, in the study cited above, to have
called attention to the importance of the part played in the uprising by
this claque, and to have assembled valuable comparative material on the
activities of such claques elsewhere in the Empire.

headquarters of the governor of Syria and fell upon the balustrade and the door behind it with such violence that the governor's servants feared that he would be killed. Fortunately the crowd could not break into the residence, and had to be content with shouting abuse. Next the mob rushed along the portico which stood in front of the law court and came to a public bath, where the rioters cut the ropes by which the hanging lamps of the bath were suspended.

After this came the attack on the imperial images and statues which was the climax of the riot. The mob first stoned the wooden panels bearing painted portraits of the imperial family, and jeered as they broke into pieces. This was a crime against the sovereign power, for these official portraits, made at Constantinople after the accession of new emperor and distributed to the cities of the empire, had a constitutional and legal significance as embodiments of the imperial dignity. The power of the emperor was thought of as residing in his portrait, so that the sovereign was present, in the form of an image, everywhere in the empire.[32] To damage such an image was to offer violence to the emperor himself. Thus the mob's action now passed from disorder into revolution.

From the wooden portraits the mob turned to the bronze statues of the emperor, his wife and the prince Arcadius. The statues were pulled from their pedestals with ropes and dragged about; some were broken up. At this point, messengers set out to take the news of the rebellion to Constantinople. Leaving the remains of the statues to the children to play with, the mob now set fire to the house of a prominent citizen who had spoken in favor of paying the tax. There was also talk of setting fire to the palace. At this point the commander of the archers who acted as police appeared

[32] On the contemporary understanding of the nature of the images, see A. Grabar, *L'empereur dans l'art byzantin*, Paris, 1936, pp. 4-10; and the chapter "Imperial Images" in K. M. Setton, *Christian Attitude towards the Emperor in the Fourth Century*, New York, 1941, pp. 196-211.

with his men to put out the fire, and the Count of the East, who had not yet taken any action, now came up with his military guard and arrested the leading rioters, who were sent off to the law court. Order was restored by midday. The authorities at once set about to separate the prisoners according to their crimes. Apparently the trials were conducted with the utmost dispatch. Some of the prisoners were beheaded, others burned alive, still others executed by being thrown to wild animals in the amphitheater. Children were not spared on account of their age.

Libanius gives us a vivid picture of the way rumors spread as to the punishments the emperor might be expected to inflict on the city. The city was to be devastated and plundered by soldiers; the senators were to be executed; property was to be confiscated; and so on. Many people fled and took refuge in the mountains or the fields, and the governor of Syria had to order the senators to remain in Antioch. The city was quiet and filled with apprehension. John Chrysostom, beginning his career as a preacher, took this opportunity to deliver the twenty-one *Homilies on the Statues*, which were designed to bolster the spirits of the people and at the same time to show them how they could take advantage of the occasion for spiritual self-examination and renewal.[33]

Bishop Flavian had carried out his duty as leader of the Christian community, and a few days after the riot he had undertaken the journey to Constantinople, in spite of his advanced age, in order to intercede with the emperor. Meanwhile the original report of the uprising had reached the capital and Theodosius had dispatched two commissioners, Caesarius and Hellebichus, to make an investigation. In addition to the order for an inquiry, an imperial decree embodied a preliminary and comprehensive punishment of

[33] A study of the homilies has been made by Sister Mary Albania Burns, *St. John Chrysostom's Homilies on the Statues: A Study of their Rhetorical Qualities and Form*, Washington, 1930.

the whole city. Antioch was deprived of its rank as metropolis and made subordinate to its ancient rival Laodicea, a punishment repeating that which had been given to the city by the Emperor Septimius Severus. The city was deprived of its military status, the hippodromes, theaters and baths were all closed, and the free distribution of bread to poor persons was suspended. Also it was made known that the emperor held the senators responsible for what had happened. This was a relatively mild sentence, in comparison with what the emperor might have decreed.

During the investigation which Caesarius and Hellebichus conducted, Libanius sat with the commissioners by virtue of the dignity of honorary praetorian prefect bestowed on him several years earlier. The meetings were held in Hellebichus' regular military headquarters. John Chrysostom stood first with the silent crowd outside the building, then entered the courtyard, from which he could hear the proceedings. The first day was devoted to questioning the members of the local senate and other persons of prominence, and the people were relieved by the mildness of the commissioners' deportment. On the next day began the trials of accused persons. Again the commissioners were inclined to be moderate, but they were also firm. In the end, no one was condemned to death, but it was announced that all the members of the senate were to be imprisoned until the emperor's decision, based on the commissioners' report, was made known. Chrysostom watched as the senators in chains were led to prison through the market place.

The senators were at first confined in an unroofed building next to the council chamber. The confinement was rigorous and visitors were not allowed. Permission was finally obtained to break a passage through the wall between the prison and the council chamber. This gave the senators more room, and also proper shelter, for they could use the auditorium of the council house, as well as the colonnaded courtyard, in the middle of which was a garden containing vines, figs, trees, and vegetables. Even so the detention was a hardship.

During the trials, a number of the ascetics who lived in the caves of the mountain above Antioch left their dwellings and came down into the city to intercede with the commissioners, advising them to urge the emperor to put aside his anger and pardon the city. One of these holy men, named Macedonius, is reported to have made a particularly eloquent appeal to Hellebichus. In the end, the commissioners decided to recommend clemency to the emperor, and Caesarius set out for Constantinople, traveling at top speed, so that he reached the capital on the sixth day after leaving Antioch.[34] He found the emperor inclined to listen to the official recommendations, for Bishop Flavian had been in Constantinople for some time, interceding with the emperor, and the senate and people of the capital had expressed a hope that Theodosius would pardon their sister city. The emperor decided to grant clemency to Antioch, and wrote a detailed letter in which the existing penalties and restrictions were rescinded, privileges were restored, and poor relief was reinstated. This message was given to a courier who could travel at top speed, and when it reached Antioch there was great rejoicing, with illuminations and banquets in the streets, and all the other pleasures to which the city was so devoted. The news arrived about Palm Sunday, and by Easter Bishop Flavian was back in the city and could officiate at the festal service. One result of the episode was that a number of pagans were so impressed by the part played by Bishop Flavian and by his discourses, which were addressed to the public at large, that they were converted to Christianity.[35]

All during this time, the pagan Libanius was the leading public figure at Antioch. In spite of the failure of Julian's program the city was still part pagan, and its importance as

[34] Libanius, *Orat.* XXI, 15.
[35] Chrysostom, *De Anna sermo*, I, I (*P.G.* LIV, col. 634).

a center of classical Greek culture had a deep influence on the development of the Greek Christian intellectual and literary tradition. The strength of the pagan and Christian heritages is strikingly exemplified by the two outstanding figures of Libanius and John Chrysostom. The programs of these two leaders show us what was involved in the relationships of paganism and Christianity and what each culture was striving to accomplish.[36]

Libanius was born in A.D. 314 in a wealthy and prominent family of Antioch. He was educated under the foremost pagan man of letters in Antioch at that time, Zenobius, and when he was twenty-two he went to Athens to complete his education in the famous schools of literature and philosophy there. When he was twenty-six, having spent four years in Athens, he opened his own school in Constantinople and had an immediate success as a teacher of classical literature and oratory. Driven from Constantinople by the jealousy of his rivals, he transferred his school to Nicomedia in A.D. 346, when he was thirty-two. After a brief return to Constantinople, he finally settled in Antioch when he was forty, in A.D. 354. There he spent the remainder of his long career.

In Antioch his success as a teacher continued and grew until at one time he had four assistant teachers and eighty students. Among his pupils were a number of Christians, including John Chrysostom, Theodore of Mopsuestia, Basil the Great, and Gregory of Nazianzen.[37]

Libanius was always primarily a teacher, absorbed in studies of style and declamation, and he was continually preoccupied for the welfare and success of his pupils. But the exhibition of his powers as a writer and orator quickly won him the respect of the whole city and he soon became one of

[36] See a recent study of this by A. J. Festugière, *Antioche païenne et chrétienne: Libanius, Chrysostome et les moines de Syrie*, Paris, 1959.

[37] On Libanius' school, see J. W. H. Walden, *The Universities of Ancient Greece*, New York, 1909, and Paul Petit, *Les étudiants de Libanius*, Paris, 1956.

the chief citizens of Antioch. An early success was his encomium of Antioch, the *Antiochikos* (*Oration* xi), written for delivery at the local Olympic Games in A.D. 356 or 360. This splendid panegyric of his native city, with its review of the city's history and its account of its beauty, became one of the most famous encomia of ancient cities, and it immediately established the reputation of Libanius in Antioch.

It is plain that Libanius felt called upon to concern himself with all the public affairs of the city. He made himself a spokesman for the city as a whole, in its relations with the imperial government and with the local officials sent out from Constantinople. Many times, especially during the investigation of the riot of A.D. 387, his counsel carried weight and he was able to make successful intercession for his fellow-citizens. Governors of Syria and Counts of the East had to take his opinions into account. But this was by no means all. Libanius was by nature a humanitarian and was deeply concerned for the welfare of people who needed help, beginning with his own students. He spoke as the champion of the farmers, the small tradesmen, and the prisoners—of any who by their station or situation in life were exposed to the exploitation and oppression of the more powerful. He saw where reform was needed—as for example in the administration of justice and the management of the prisons—and he spoke out freely and boldly to everyone, including the emperor himself; he succeeded in making such a position for himself that he could not fail to command attention and respect. His achievement was a tribute to the power which literary style and skill in oratory could command in those times. As a leading public figure he was still an outstanding teacher.

It was Libanius' purpose to teach and to keep alive the old classical culture, which he regarded as the essential foundation of civilization. In his view, classical literature and the worship of the pagan gods were inseparable,[38] and the two together were what had given Greek civilization its unique power. The traditional educational system, based on the study of the great writers of the classical period, had come to be recognized as the best means of preparing the individual for life, as a member of a family, a member of society, and a member of the state. The formation of character was best achieved by study of the depiction of character by the great writers, beginning with Homer; and Homer was still the basic textbook in the schools. This educational system, coupled with the proper worship of the gods, was what had made the Greek people great and it was what distinguished them from the barbarians who surrounded the empire. The system was essential for training for public life, especially for careers in law and the public service, for here the ability to speak effectively was a fundamental requirement, and a distinguished literary style was necessary for advancement in the civil service.[39] A cultivated style of writing and speaking were the accepted marks of mental competence, for it was plain that a man who could not express himself clearly and elegantly was not capable of thinking correctly. Libanius thought with pride of the numbers of his pupils who were prominent in public life.

This pedagogical program had been in operation for a long time and its value was well established. If the curriculum was based on the study and imitation of the classics, this did not mean that contemporary writers and thinkers were sterile, but rather that the classical masters were considered to have reached the highest peak of human achievement; and since they could not be surpassed, the best thing to do was to study them closely and imitate them.

[38] Libanius, *Orat.* XVIII, 157.

[39] See further G. Downey, "The Emperor Julian and the Schools," *Classical Journal,* LIII, 1956-57, pp. 97-103; "Education in the Christian Roman Empire: Christian and Pagan Theories under Constantine and his Successors," *Speculum,* XXXII, 1957, pp. 48-61.

To Libanius and his peers, this was the only possible way of life; and it was being threatened by Christian doctrine, which did away with the old gods and with the literature that had been created by men who worshipped the old gods. The political danger resulting from the neglect of the worship of the traditional deities and powers was bad enough; but if Christians turned their backs on classical literature, Hellenic civilization would cease to exist. It was true that some Christian writers advocated the salvaging of some of the classical literary tradition, to be reworked and transformed in the new Christian spirit; but to Libanius and the other pagans this could never be the same thing. In Libanius' eyes, the decline of classical teaching had set in under Constantius and was progressing. There had been a moment of hope in the time of Julian, but this hope had died.

Classical civilization had been nurtured by the city-state and it was the Greek *polis*, the city, which was looked upon as the ideal center in which Hellenic culture could develop. The Graeco-Roman-oriental city of Libanius' day was different in many ways, of course, from the Greek city such as Athens had been in the fifth century before Christ; but in Libanius' time the city of Antioch was still a city, socially if not politically, and it was here that Libanius saw the one hope of being able to preserve something of the ancient ideal. Hence came Libanius' extraordinary devotion to his native city and his constant effort to serve it and to keep alive the classical ideals in it, both by his teaching and by his public activity. His encomium, the *Antiochikos*, is remarkable testimony to this devotion, and it must have called forth a warm response from the people of Antioch. Antioch was a great city, Libanius insisted, because of the virtue of its citizens, and it was his task to teach and indeed to exemplify in himself this virtue. How far Libanius thought such a program could stand up against Christianity, we have no way of knowing;

but he devoted his life to the preservation of the ancient ideal as he knew it.

Libanius' views had wide influence through his numerous pupils. One of the most distinguished of his students was John Chrysostom. Chrysostom was born in Antioch in A.D. 344 or 347 of well-to-do parents. His father, a prominent official of the imperial civil service stationed in Antioch, died when Chrysostom was small and the boy was brought up by his mother. He had under Libanius a thorough training in Greek literature and rhetoric, and originally intended to study law—his Christian vocation only came later. After a career in the church in Antioch (A.D. 386-397) he was made Patriarch of Constantinople.

Chrysostom's greatest success in Antioch was as a preacher and pastor. His literary output was enormous—sermons, essays, and letters all attested his singular homiletic gift which, added to his original rhetorical and classical training, made him one of the greatest preachers the Greek church produced and one of the most respected members of the Christian community in Antioch.

If Antioch was becoming a Christian city, its Christian leaders were still having to obtain at least the fundamentals of their education in the classical tradition. This might have either of two results. One is illustrated by Basil the Great, another pupil of Libanius', who was older than Chrysostom. Basil came to believe that there was some good in parts of classical literature, viewed as material for educational use and as a means of forming the moral character, in addition of course to the new Christian instruction. Here of course Basil viewed classical literature much as the pagans themselves did. While some of pagan writing was by reason of its subject matter and point of view obviously unsuitable for Christians, Basil felt that this did not mean that the whole body of classical literature had to be discarded. It could be adapted and used with profit within the new Christian framework. Basil, with the help of others of like mind, was able to make his view prevail and thus a new theory of Christian education was founded which has lasted to the present day.

On the other hand Chrysostom did not follow Basil in holding openly to the best parts of the pagan educational tradition. Instead he devoted the results of his classical training to the service of Christian eloquence alone. In this we can see a conscious reaction to pagan culture different from Basil's.

With Christian and pagan living side by side, each was constrained to form a strong opinion concerning the other's religion and culture. To a certain extent Christians and pagans did in fact share the same culture, but this common possession would itself serve to accentuate the differences between them. And when a Christian had been educated in the pagan tradition, his later reaction against the pagan world might be all the stronger. So it was, outwardly, with John Chrysostom. In his sermons he made disparaging remarks about Plato, and compared him unfavorably with St. Paul. But in spite of this Chrysostom could not escape his classical heritage. He might think that he was reacting against classical culture but he could never free himself from it completely. His treatise *On the Priesthood*, one of his most important works, is cast in the dialogue form, long popular as a literary device in classical literature. And in a city such as Antioch Chrysostom was unable to escape the influence of the classical concept of the *polis*, the city as the organism built up of the individual citizens. Repeatedly in the *Homilies on the Statues*, delivered at the time of the riot in A.D. 387, Chrysostom appeals to his congregation's pride in its membership in so distinguished a *polis* as Antioch, and reminds his hearers of the noble history of the city, of which they must prove themselves worthy. The greatness of the city, he reminds his flock, is made up of the virtue of the citizens. This is in the pure Hellenic tradition. Whether Chrysostom was conscious that the ideal to which he was appealing might be considered un-Christian, we do not know. Christians indeed here have no lasting city, but seek the city which is to come— the city which has foundations, whose builder and maker is God.[40] This was surely the antithesis of the classical ideal of the man-made city as the center of civilization, but in a place such as Antioch, it would seem, loyalty to the city was so compelling, pride in its history so strong, that even the Christian might admit this old and cherished ideal alongside his own new loyalty to the heavenly citizenship.

Thus Libanius and Chrysostom, each in his own characteristic way, show the results of the interaction of Christianity and paganism in a city such as Antioch. If Christianity triumphed, as it was inevitably destined to do, men such as Libanius were able to assure the preservation, in the new Christian culture, of the best elements of the classical heritage.

[40] Hebrews 11:10, 12:22, 13:14.

CHAPTER X

"FAIR CROWN OF THE ORIENT"

THROUGHOUT its history Antioch was considered one of the most beautiful cities in the Graeco-Roman world. For its appearance in the Hellenistic epoch we have only the literary records of some of its buildings, but beginning with the Roman imperial period we have a measure of direct testimony, both literary and archaeological, and this suggests that the historian Ammianus Marcellinus, writing in the latter part of the fourth century of our era, was abundantly justified in calling his native city the "fair crown of the Orient," *orientis apicem pulcrum*.[1]

The appearance of the city in imperial times and the style of the buildings is known both from the encomium of Libanius, the *Antiochikos* (written A.D. 356 or 360),[2] and from the results of the excavations; here of course we have notable evidence in the famous series of mosaic floors which were recovered in the excavations. These floors, discovered both in private houses and in public buildings, especially baths, show the artistic history of the city from the first century of our era to the sixth, and likewise give us unique evidence for the intellectual interests and the daily life of the people of Antioch.[3] The mosaics were the major discovery of the excavations and they provided, for the artistic and intellectual history of Antioch, a body of material equaled elsewhere in the ancient world only at Pompeii.

The mosaics, recovered in unexpected quantities, immedi-

[1] Ammianus Marcellinus, XXII, 9, 14.

[2] See the English translation, with commentary and map, by G. Downey, *Proceedings of the American Philosophical Society*, CIII, No. 5, 1959, pp. 652-686.

[3] The mosaics, originally published in the excavation reports, *Antioch-on-the-Orontes*, I-III, have been assembled in a corpus by Doro Levi, *Antioch Mosaic Pavements*, Princeton, 1947.

ately supplied one of the missing chapters in the history of ancient painting. From the frescoes at Pompeii we knew painting at the beginning of our era, and the earliest illuminated manuscripts and the famous mosaics preserved in churches in Italy showed the way in which this art had developed in the fifth and sixth centuries, but the evidence for painting in the second, third, and fourth centuries remained very scanty. From the splendid collection of floors recovered at Antioch we learned how the "Alexandrian" style, as it had previously been known, must have been common to the great cities founded in the Near East by Alexander the Great and his successors. C. R. Morey, the organizer of the excavations and the pioneer in the interpretation of the new material, showed how the early "Alexandrian" manner, now attested for the first time at Antioch, followed a line of development there under the influence of the Neo-Attic school characteristic of Asia Minor.[4] At the same time, the Antioch floors showed the influence of Persia, with which Antioch, of all the great cities in the Graeco-Roman world, was naturally in closest contact.

The technique of mosaic had been brought by the Roman imperial period to a high degree of perfection. An almost infinite range of colors and shades could be achieved by the use of the marble cubes, and greens and blues could be supplied by glass cubes. The practical purpose of the art was to supply a permanent floor that would be cool in summer and could be easily washed; in hot weather the floors were sprinkled with water to make them cooler. In winter the floors could be covered with rugs if this were desirable for warmth.

The decorative possibilities were almost limitless. Any

[4] Morey's first evaluation of the new evidence was published in preliminary form in his *The Mosaics of Antioch*, New York, 1938, to be followed by more detailed studies represented in his comprehensive work *Early Christian Art*, 2d ed., Princeton, 1953.

type of geometric pattern could be effectively used, and here the designers and artists showed great ingenuity and resourcefulness (Figs. 24, 25, 65). Floral patterns and compositions of birds and animals were also popular (Figs. 27, 32, 36, 43, 45, 67-69). The highest stage of the craft was of course the figure mosaics, showing either single figures, heads, busts, or elaborate compositions. The subjects were narration, allegory, literary themes, or mythology. These floors were often copies of "old masters," and by their accomplished technique in the selection and arrangement of marble cubes the mosaic artists could come very close to the distinguished paintings they were reproducing. Mosaics imitated carpets (Fig. 32), and were used as a setting for inscriptions in churches and baths, where they recorded details of the construction of the buildings. The mosaic technique lent itself with great distinction to lettering. One characteristic example is an inscription of welcome placed at the entrance to an inn (Fig. 44).

Mosaics increasingly showed the influence of Iranian art in Antioch.[5] This appears both in the style of ornament, and in the choice of subjects, such as the heraldic rams' heads, which were a Persian symbol of royalty, in the border of the Phoenix floor (Fig. 32). The floor itself, with its use of an over-all ornamental pattern, shows the influence of the oriental decorative scheme, which makes the composition of this vast surface (over 30 x 40 feet) an easy matter.

The floors found at Antioch show that mosaic work played an important part in the planning and decoration of houses of all kinds, both relatively modest dwellings and the mansions of the wealthy.[6] Even the less affluent could still afford

[5] See D. N. Wilber, "Iranian Motifs in Syrian Art," *Bulletin of the American Institute for Iranian Art and Archaeology*, v, 1937, pp. 22-26.

[6] A study of domestic architecture at Antioch has been published by Richard Stillwell, "Houses of Antioch," *Dumbarton Oaks Papers*, xv, 1961, pp. 45-47.

decorative geometrical or floral pavements, which provided central points of interest in the rooms or corridors in which they were placed. In more elaborate houses, each room and each corridor had its special floor or floors (Figs. 22, 23). Often a figure panel would be surrounded and set off by geometric designs, or a figure panel would have an elaborate floral border (Figs. 25, 37). A large open court would be paved with a mosaic such as the famous Phoenix floor, already mentioned (Fig. 32).

Everywhere the placing and content of the mosaics was carefully planned as a part of the architecture of the building. In a dining room, the central panel would be chosen and placed so as to provide a focus of interest, in view of all the diners as they reclined at the table which extended around the three sides of the room (Fig. 23). Where the end of the dining room was open, showing a view of mountain or valley across a colonnaded corridor, the corridor was paved with mosaic panels to add interest to the vista. When a house was situated so that its individual rooms commanded several views of different kinds, the mosaics in the various rooms were adapted to their architectural settings.

Mosaics often formed the floors of pools and the background of fountains, both in private houses and in monumental public buildings. Libanius[7] describes the apsidal Nymphaeum or fountain that stood at the central point in the main colonnaded street, "high as heaven and turning every eye with the dazzling light of its stones and the color of its columns and the gleam of its pictures [i.e. mosaics] and the wealth of its flowing water." Such mosaics often depicted marine deities and fish, which were shown with shadows beneath them as though they were swimming in the water. In private houses one would see pools, fountains, and fish ponds with this type of decoration.

A favorite architectural composition was a view from the

[7] Libanius, *Antiochikos*, 202.

open end of a dining room looking across a colonnaded corridor to a pool built in the form of a semi-circular apse. Sometimes, when the location of the house permitted, the pool was combined with a view of the Orontes valley.[8]

By chance most of the Antioch mosaics that we have came from private houses and villas, but public buildings shared in the use of this type of decoration. The chronicler Malalas[9] speaks of the mosaics and paintings that decorated the colonnades about the Forum of Valens, and a number of fine floors were recovered from large public baths (Figs. 24, 41). Here the special architectural requirements, such as the paving and decorating of large areas, meant both a lavish use of geometric designs and a possibility of large figure compositions, more elaborate than most houses could accommodate. The architectural setting made it possible to combine the mosaics with decorative marble slabs in the pavement.

Originally the figure mosaic had been a picture set in a floor, the picture itself being a copy or adaptation of a famous painting. The remainder of the floor was filled with geometric or floral ornament that served to fill the space and to set off the chief figure panel. In time, however, there is a significant change. As M. Jean Lassus has put it, "the craftsmen leave off putting pictures in a floor and begin to compose the floor itself."[10] In the splendid villa of the period of Constantine the Great (A.D. 306-337) found at Daphne this new scheme is worked out in magnificent fashion. Here the floor is composed according to the characteristic technique of ceiling decoration which came into prominence in Rome in the second century after Christ and became a standard type for many years. The center of the floor was occupied by an octagonal fountain. From this to the four corners of the room radiated four diagonal panels, each showing a personification

---

[8] Morey, *Mosaics of Antioch* (cited above, n. 4), p. 31.
[9] Malalas, p. 339, 6f.   [10] Morey, *op.cit.*, pp. 37f.

of one of the seasons of the year. Each figure was appropriately depicted with the attributes of a particular period of the annual cycle. In the trapezoids which radiated from the octagonal fountain between the Seasons there were hunting scenes (Fig. 66), always a favorite theme of the mosaic maker. Around the edges of the floor were smaller rectangular panels showing a variety of small scenes, including vignettes of pastoral life. A maeander pattern fills the intermediate spaces (Fig. 67). In all, the pavement was made up of over forty separately composed panels.

Another special type of composition appears in the great mosaic of the personification of *Megalopsychia* ("Greatness of Soul") from a villa at Daphne (Fig. 45). Here the square floor had at its center a medallion of *Megalopsychia* which faces the spectator as he enters the room. Grouped about the medallion are a series of hunting scenes forming a commentary on the idea of *Megalopsychia* (which will be discussed below). Around the outer edge of the room runs the famous topographical border (Figs. 46-59) providing a series of scenes of contemporary Antioch which, when read in sequence, form an imaginary tour of the city (to be examined in detail below). Here the artist combined in one floor the central medallion, the open field with the hunting scenes, and the continuous strip of scenes forming the border. This was in fact the best way in which the topographical scenes constituting a tour of the city could be presented in a continuous sequence.

The endless diversity of the floors reflects the varied interest that the mosaics have for the student, illustrating as they do all aspects of life in ancient Antioch. The largest single group of figured mosaics are those showing scenes of mythology. Here all the rich resources of the Greek world of myth are employed for decorative purposes. Outstanding in this group is the mosaic of the Judgment of Paris, now in the Louvre (Fig. 28). Found in a house dating in the early part of the second century after Christ, this composition illustrates a theme that must have been popular at Antioch, since the local legend was that the judgment took place in Daphne.[11] Associated with this were two floors showing the drinking contest of Herakles and Dionysos and a dialogue of Aphrodite and Adonis. Another floor of the same epoch depicts the idyl of Polyphemus and Galatea. The Bacchic revel is a favorite subject, and scenes of the life of Dionysos are common; one shows the intoxicated god supported by a young satyr. Narcissus was a popular subject, appearing in three different floors. Ganymede is depicted giving water to the eagle of Zeus.

One of the most popular themes is that of Oceanus and Thetis, who are portrayed, singly or together, a number of times. Erotes are depicted fishing, and another floor shows an old peddler catching Erotes and putting them in a cage for sale. A striking floor illustrates Hermes carrying the infant Dionysos to the nymphs of Nysa, who will care for him.

Another local legend appears in a floor showing Apollo pursuing the maiden Daphne, who is being transformed into a laurel tree to save her from the god (Fig. 31). This episode was supposed to have occurred at Daphne, and it was one of the reasons why the suburb was sacred to Apollo.[12] Another floor depicted Europa being carried off by Zeus in the form of a bull. Another amorous adventure of Zeus was illustrated in a floor of Leda and the swan.

The winged horse Pegasus was shown being groomed and watered by the nymphs. Another floor portrayed Lycurgus entangled in the vine, telling the story of the Thracian king

[11] Libanius, *Antiochikos*, 241. The Judgment of Paris is shown on a painted bowl which the owner, Ray Winfield Smith, suggests may have been made in Antioch; see G. M. A. Hanfmann, "A Masterpiece of Late Roman Glass Painting," *Archaeology*, IX, 1956, pp. 3-7.

[12] Libanius, *Antiochikos*, 94-96.

who was driven mad in punishment for having scorned Dionysos and his suite. A floor of Eros and Psyche depicted Psyche stealing the weapons of the sleeping god of Love.

Another important group is formed of the floors which exhibit scenes from Greek tragedy. Homer and Euripides were the two Greek authors most often illustrated in the Byzantine period, and the popularity of Euripides is well exemplified at Antioch.[13] A scene from the *Iphigeneia at Aulis* illustrates the moment (vv. 1098ff.) when Clytemnestra summons Iphigeneia to move Agamemnon to pity and make him alter his resolution to sacrifice his daughter in order to make the Trojan expedition possible (Fig. 27). Another floor records a scene from the *Helen* (vv. 865-872) in which the seer Theonoë speaks to her attendant. But the most remarkable floor with dramatic scenes is one with five panels containing scenes from five plays of Euripides which depicted passionate love that was at the same time destructive. Episodes are taken from the *Hippolytus*, showing the love letter which Phaedra's nurse has handed to Hippolytus (Fig. 26); from the *Meleager* (a lost play), showing the scene which follows the killing of the boar as Meleager and Atalanta are hunting; from the *Stheneboea*, another lost play, showing the wife of King Proitos in love with the chaste youth Bellerophon; from the *Trojan Women*, in which Helen tells of the Judgment of Paris; and from the *Medea*, in which Medea and Jason are shown conversing (vv. 866ff.). These panels are all scenes of actual dramatic productions, depicting the actors in their costumes on the stage.

Comedy is represented by two mosaics of Menander, one of which is the first representation to be found of the poet's mistress Glykera.[14] One of the mosaics (Fig. 25) shows

[13] K. Weitzmann, "Illustrations of Euripides and Homer in the Mosaics of Antioch," *Antioch-on-the-Orontes*, III, pp. 233-247; idem, "Euripides Scenes in Byzantine Art," *Hesperia*, XVIII, 1949, pp. 159-210.

[14] A. M. Friend, Jr., "Menander and Glykera in the Mosaics of Antioch," *Antioch-on-the-Orontes*, III, pp. 248-251.

Menander and Glykera discussing the letter of King Ptolemy with its summons that forces the lovers to separate.

Scenes from Homer must have been popular, although only one, showing the farewell of Briseis (*Iliad*, I, 345ff.), was found.

Mosaics based upon scenes from literature were of special interest. Two of these were found in the same house, which the excavators called the "House of the Man of Letters," because of the mosaics which were discovered in it. One panel depicting the lovers Metiochus and Parthenope was the first representation of the pair to be found; previously they had been known only from three meager references in ancient papyri. This mosaic may give evidence for the performance of a mime about Metiochus and Parthenope in the theater at Antioch. The companion floor was a scene from a Hellenistic novel concerning Ninus and Semiramis.[15]

The mosaics also attest contemporary religious cults and philosophical ideas. In the former category the most interesting are a group of floors concerned with Isis, the Egyptian goddess whose worship became highly popular in a Hellenized form. She was famous for her virtues, her miracles, and her accomplishments; and it has been said that she "came more and more to mean all things to all men."[16] In Antioch, several floors exhibiting scenes from the rites in honor of the goddess were found in a house whose owner had apparently held her in particular reverence.[17] One shows a part of the initiation rite, described by Apuleius, *Metamorphoses,* Book XI, and another depicts part of the spring festival of Isis celebrated in March at the annual opening of navigation in

[15] G. M. A. Hanfmann, "Notes on the Mosaics from Antioch," *A.J.A.,* XLIII, 1939, pp. 242-246; Doro Levi, "The Novel of Ninus and Semiramis," *Proceedings of the American Philosophical Society,* LXXXVII, 1944, pp. 420-428.

[16] T. A. Brady, "Isis," *Oxford Classical Dictionary,* Oxford, 1949, p. 459.

[17] Doro Levi, "Mors Voluntaria: Mystery Cults on Mosaics from Antioch," *Berytus,* VII, 1942, pp. 19-55.

the Mediterranean, also described by Apuleius. A similar floor from another house helps to demonstrate the popularity of the cult at Antioch.

Other floors bring us testimony of the most valuable kind to the growing interest in philosophical abstractions and personifications of abstract ideas in the later imperial period. One remarkable floor contains the figure of a deity labeled Aion, the personification of time in the absolute sense, who is accompanied by figures representing other "Times," Past, Present, and Future.[18] Aion became a deity, connected with concepts of the creation and government of the world, and philosophers continued to try to determine the nature of absolute time. Here we have a glimpse of the interests of intellectual circles at Antioch. Such subjects were doubtless discussed at the banquets in the city.

A number of abstractions, virtues, and other qualities are illustrated,[19] mostly as female figures, usually busts. Power (*Dynamis*) and Renewal (*Ananeosis*) are illustrated, as are Acquisition of Wealth (*Ktisis*) and Use of Wealth (*Chresis*). Pleasure (*Tryphe*) and Life (*Bios*) are linked in one pair of floors, Pleasure being to the owner of this floor the object of Life. A bath shows figures of Salvation (*Soteria*) and Enjoyment (*Apolausis*); as Libanius wrote, all those who used them knew that baths brought healing as well as pleasure.[20]

Such abstractions and expressions are found elsewhere in the Graeco-Roman world, both in the form of lists of virtues and moral qualities incorporated in honorific inscriptions, and in mosaics and frescoes in which abstractions are represented, such as the paintings at Saqqara in Egypt showing

---

[18] Doro Levi, "Aion," *Hesperia*, XIII, 1944, pp. 269-314.

[19] G. Downey, "Personifications of Abstract Ideas in the Antioch Mosaics," *T.A.P.A.*, LXIX, 1938, pp. 349-363.

[20] Libanius, *Antiochikos*, 134, 237, 242.

figures labeled (in Greek) Faith, Hope, Charity, Prudence, Patience, Fortitude.

One personification of remarkable interest is Greatness of Soul (*Megalopsychia*), a concept that had been studied by a number of Greek philosophers (Fig. 45).[21] Aristotle defined greatness of soul as the quality which makes a man worthy of great things, and conscious that he is worthy of them, while the Stoics employed the term to describe "the knowledge or habit of mind which makes one superior to anything that happens, whether good or bad equally."[22]

Finally, a personification of Freedom from Care (*Amerimnia*) adorned a tomb in the suburbs of Antioch. This seated female figure was shown in a panel of the floor of the central tomb chamber, facing the entrance. A similar figure of Memory (*Mnemosyne*) was found elsewhere in connection with a tomb.

A special interest is attested by a series of scenes of Friendship (*Philia*), in which are shown, in peaceful mood, pairs of animals which are not normally friendly toward each other, a lion with a humped ox, a tigress with a boar, a leopard with a goat, a lioness with a stag. These scenes might be an illustration of the verses of Isaiah, 11:6ff, "And the wolf shall dwell with the lamb. . . ."

This collection of abstractions, found in one place, is almost unique in the Graeco-Roman world, and it brings before us, in a way literature could not, the interests of the people of Antioch and their curiosities and their speculations. Before the excavations took place, the preoccupation with abstractions in the late imperial period had been known from other sources, but our knowledge was immeasurably increased by the discovery of the floors at Antioch; and so the excava-

[21] G. Downey, "Ethical Themes in the Antioch Mosaics," *Church History,* x, 1941, pp. 367-376; idem, "The Pagan Virtue of Megalopsychia in Byzantine Syria," *T.A.P.A.,* lxxvi, 1945, pp. 279-286.

[22] Aristotle, *Nicomachean Ethics,* 1123b; Diogenes Laertius, vii, 93 (cf. 128).

tions in this way made a contribution of capital importance to the intellectual history of late antiquity. Men must have had a real interest in these concepts if they had them represented so freely in their houses.

Turning from philosophical ideas to daily life, we find many floors that show us the houses, public buildings, streets, occupations and diversions, superstitions, costumes, and even the food of the people of Antioch. One of the most exciting discoveries of the excavations was the large and handsome floor from a villa in Daphne, already mentioned, containing a medallion of *Megalopsychia* surrounded by hunting scenes, with a series of topographical pictures as border (Fig. 45). The topographical border is unique at Antioch, and, in fact, unparalleled among the archaeological discoveries thus far made in the Graeco-Roman world. Nothing exists to match this itinerary of Antioch in the latter part of the fifth century of our era; yet it may not have been exceptional at Antioch, for the route through the city followed in the border exactly matches the imaginary tour adopted by Libanius in his encomium of Antioch in the middle of the fourth century, and there may easily have been other visual counterparts to Libanius' famous description, which became a model for the praise of a city, and was copied throughout the Byzantine period.

The tour begins in the lower left hand corner of the room and unfolds along the edge of the wall, from left to right. This means that more than a quarter of the itinerary has been lost at the back of the room, where the floor is missing, and along part of the right-hand wall; but enough has been preserved to show the route clearly.

As in Libanius' tour, the imaginary visitor arrives by the road from Beroea and passes through the massive city gate (Fig. 46, No. 1; cf. Figs. 10-11). Like Libanius, who brings his description of Antioch to a climax with praise of the springs of Daphne, the itinerary in the mosaic ends with two of the springs at Daphne: the semicircular colonnaded reservoir of Castalia (Fig. 59, No. 51) and Pallas (Fig. 59, No. 52), with a tiny figure swimming in the water to represent the deity who dwelt there.

This mosaic is one of the most precious documents of ancient life ever recovered by archaeologists, and with its companion piece, the encomium of Libanius, it gives us an enchanting view of ancient Antioch. It is fascinating to find that so many of the scenes depicted on the mosaic can be duplicated in the streets of modern Antioch. Snapshots (Fig. 60) taken after the mosaic was found offer a delightful commentary on the unchanging character of daily existence in Antioch.[23] The modern costumes are Arabic and Turkish, or European, rather than Graeco-Roman, but many of the pastimes and occupations are the same, and donkeys are still to be seen everywhere.

After this introduction to the life of Antioch we are in a better position to appreciate other mosaics illustrating themes of daily life. One of these, a floor found in one of the public baths, shows a group of three jugglers and entertainers, purveyors of popular amusement in the streets (Fig. 41). One remarkable floor shows a buffet supper laid out in order on a horseshoe-shaped table (Figs. 37-40). The courses are shown in sequence, beginning at the right. The food is served on the silver dishes which were common in the houses of the well-to-do, and the table is decorated with garlands of flowers. Round flat rolls of bread are scattered about. First in order come the hors d'œuvres, two boiled eggs in egg cups with spoons, two cold salted pig's feet, and two artichokes. There were doubtless other vegetables as well—Antioch was famous for its cucumbers—but the mosaic has suffered damage at the point at which they would be shown. Next,

[23] See J. Lassus, "Dans les rues d'Antioche," *Bulletin d'études orientales* (*Institut Français de Damas*), v, 1935, pp. 121-124. Only one of M. Lassus' perceptive snapshots is reproduced here (Fig. 60).

on a rectangular plate, is a fish which looks like a sculpin or porgy. Then there is a ham, with a wine cup. Next we can make out what look like two birds, which are not perfectly preserved in the mosaic. There follows a gap in the mosaic, at the point at which the menu called for fruit. The last dish at the end of the table is the sweet—a layer-cake of cylindrical shape with a convex top. The layers are of different colors. This is not a regular banquet with its succession of hot dishes, but rather a series of cold dishes designed to form a buffet meal. At either end of the table rest two silver ladles and the wreaths that were given to the guests when the meal was finished and the libations began. Libanius tells us that Antioch was famous for its food, and we have here an example of what was eaten in the great houses of the city. Was the buffet meal laid out for two people who wished to dine in privacy, without being served by attendants?

Other floors show pastoral occupations, commonly depicted in mosaics all over the Graeco-Roman world, and their companion pieces, allegorical personifications of the months, each with its labors, allegories, and attributes.[24]

Among the occupations and diversions of the men of Antioch, hunting was one of the most characteristic and the most popular, and a number of floors show hunts, both mythological and contemporary. One of the finest is the large floor now in the Museum at Worcester (Fig. 36), with its central figure representing the triumph of man in the hunt.

Finally, another link between the past and the present is provided by the mosaics illustrating the superstition of the Evil Eye, still prevalent in Mediterranean countries.[25] In one mosaic the eye is shown being attacked by various animals and weapons (Fig. 63), as a means of averting the

[24] Doro Levi, "The Allegories of the Months in Classical Art," *Art Bulletin*, XXIII, 1941, pp. 251-291.

[25] Doro Levi, "The Evil Eye and the Lucky Hunchback," *Antioch-on-the-Orontes*, III, pp. 220-232.

assaults of the Evil Eye itself. Allied with these floors is a mosaic which shows the Lucky Hunchback (Fig. 62), the first such representation to be found in the classical world.

Antioch had other arts, including a special tradition of fine craftsmanship in gold and silver work dating back to the Hellenistic period. Examples have just been seen in the dishes and ladles shown in the mosaic of the buffet supper. Work of this kind is notoriously subject to destruction, but some notable examples of it have been recovered from sites near Antioch. This is church silver, buried by its owners to save it from the Persian invasions of the sixth and seventh centuries; sometimes the silver has been preserved for us because the owners never came back to recover it. Antioch and Constantinople were the two great centers for the manufacture of this liturgical silver in the eastern part of the empire.[26] A small number of pieces were found at Antioch (Fig. 73), so that we know that they were used there, if not made there.[27] Other pieces found elsewhere in Syria likewise can be taken as illustrating the work done at Antioch (Figs. 71, 72, 74-80).[28] Sometimes these pieces are inscribed with the names of the donors, and it is possible to trace a family and its offerings through several generations. Some churches were apparently well equipped with liturgical silver, though the largest churches, such as Constantine's Great Church at Antioch, would have had liturgical vessels of gold encrusted with jewels.

One of the most famous pieces of liturgical silver from

[26] Marvin C. Ross is preparing a comprehensive study of the Syrian silver. See *Dumbarton Oaks Papers*, xv, 1961, p. 250.

[27] See M. C. Ross, "A Small Byzantine Treasure Found at Antioch-on-the-Orontes," *Archaeology*, v, 1952, pp. 30-32; idem, "A Silver Treasure from Daphne-Harbie," *ibid.*, vi, 1953, pp. 39-41.

[28] Two treasures were found at Hama, a third at Riha, and a fourth at Stouma. For the extensive bibliography of the publications on these treasures see L. Jalabert, R. Mouterde, and C. Mondésert, *Inscriptions grecques et latines de la Syrie*, ii, nos. 694-698; v, nos. 2027-2049.

the neighborhood is the celebrated Chalice of Antioch, which is said to have been found near Antioch in 1910 (Fig. 70). Study by art historians has shown that although this cannot be the actual chalice used at the Last Supper, as was at one time claimed,[29] it is not a modern forgery. The best evidence indicates that it was made in the fourth or fifth century. Whether it was made in Antioch, or was used there, cannot be demonstrated.

Another piece of unusual interest is the Helmet of Emesa, found at Emesa and now in the Museum at Damascus (Figs. 79-80).[30] The helmet includes a face mask covered with silver, while the rest of the head piece has ornaments of silver. This is not a parade helmet but one designed for combat. It is dated at the beginning of the first century of our era. The richness of the work indicates that it belonged to a distinguished personage, and the style shows that it came from Syria. The owner appears to have been a general and a close associate of the Hellenized Arab king of Emesa, and he was probably a member of the ruling dynasty. Very likely the mask reproduces certain individual features of the owner's face. In view of the exceptional quality of the work, it seems safe to attribute it to the workshops of Antioch, for it was there that a personage of Emesa would naturally order such an object.

It is to the accidents of preservation and the chances of archaeology that we owe our knowledge of the art of Antioch, and there are areas in which the excavators' hopes were disappointed. Nothing of the Hellenistic period was recovered, and Christian objects were not numerous. Yet

[29] J. J. Rorimer, "The Authenticity of the Chalice of Antioch," *Studies in Art and Literature for Belle Da Costa Greene*, Princeton, 1954, pp. 161-168. This study is also available as a separate publication of The Cloisters of the Metropolitan Museum of Art in New York.

[30] H. Seyrig, "Le casque d'Emèse," *Annales archéologiques de Syrie*, II, 1952, pp. 101-108; idem, "A Helmet from Emisa," *Archaeology*, V, 1952, pp. 66-69.

the richness of what was found will perhaps compensate for such lacunae. If our picture of Antioch in the Seleucid period is not wholly satisfactory, what we know of it in the later imperial era brings us a precious insight into the life of the times, and we can see that Ammianus Marcellinus was not unjustified in his description of his native city.

CHAPTER XI

THE EAST ROMAN EMPIRE

AN IMPERIAL visit is the best-known event in the life of Antioch during the reign of Theodosius II (A.D. 408-450).[1] In A.D. 438 the Empress Eudocia made the arduous journey from Constantinople to Jerusalem in fulfillment of a vow, accompanied by the Patriarch Cyril of Alexandria as spiritual adviser. Eudocia, who was the daughter of a pagan professor of literature at Athens and herself an accomplished author, delivered an encomium of Antioch in the traditional style before the local senate in the senate-chamber. The empress spoke from a portable throne which she took with her on her travels, a golden chair set with precious stones. In closing, she complimented the audience by paraphrasing a line of Homer,[2] "Of your lineage and race I declare myself to be," alluding to the way in which her own Athenian origin united her in kinship to the people of Antioch, who were always proud of the tradition that their city had been colonized in part by settlers from Athens. No courtesy could have been more warmly appreciated, and the senate of Antioch in gratitude voted a gilded bronze statue of the empress, to be set up in the chamber in which she had pronounced her encomium, and a bronze statue outside the Museum. As was proper on such an occasion, the empress added material benefits to her literary praises, by giving funds for a distribution of grain and for the restoration of the Bath of Valens, which had been partly burned.

[1] The principal sources are Malalas, *Tusculan fragments*, in *Spicilegium Romanum*, ed. A. Mai, II, pt. 2, Rome, 1839, p. 15; Chronicon Paschale, pp. 584f, Bonn ed.; Evagrius, *Hist. eccl.*, I, 20; Socrates, *Hist. eccl.*, VII, 47; Theophanes, p. 92, 25-29 ed. De Boor. Some fragments of Eudocia's writings have been preserved and are published by A. Ludwich, *Eudociae Augustae Procli Lycii Claudiani . . . reliquiae*, Leipzig, 1897.
[2] *Iliad* VI, 211.

One major event in the history of the city which is also associated with Eudocia's visit is the enlargement of the city wall.[3] According to the tradition, the empress requested Theodosius to make this enlargement, and the work was carried out under the supervision of Antiochus Chuzon, a former praetorian prefect. The city walls had been repaired (but not enlarged) in A.D. 395-396, and there had evidently been an increase in the population of the city, resulting in settlement outside the existing walls.

The wall was extended for one mile at the south of the city (Fig. 5), along the road that led to Daphne, and a new "Daphne Gate" was built, which was gilded and named the "Golden Gate," the gilding being carried out by an official named Nymphidianus. The new walls started from the Philonauta Gate, which stood on the Orontes, and ascended the mountain, joining the old wall of Tiberius at the source of the mountain stream called Phyrminus, at a place called Rhodion ("The Roses"), doubtless a rose garden on the side of the mountain. Traces of the old wall, which Theodosius' work replaced, were still visible in the latter part of the sixth century.

A number of other building operations are recorded during this period. The emperor, as has been noted, granted two hundred gold pounds for the repair of the Bath of Valens. Theodosius then sent to Antioch three officials, Memnonius, Zoilus and Callistus, who each presented the city with a building known by his name.[4] Memnonius built a structure called the Psephion, which contained an inner court open to the sky. As its name indicates that it was connected with voting, this building appears to have been a law court. Zoilus built a basilica south of the Stoa of Rufinus, which had been

---

[3] The evidence (Malalas, p. 346, 5ff., Evagrius, *loc.cit.*), is conflicting; see the study of G. Downey, "The Wall of Theodosius at Antioch," *American Journal of Philology*, LXII, 1941, pp. 207-213.

[4] Evagrius, *Hist. eccl.*, I, 18.

constructed in the time of Theodosius I. The third official, Callistus, erected a handsome stoa which stood before the law courts; this may have been near the Forum of Valens.

Then, in A.D. 439, Theodosius ordered Anatolius, who was commander of the troops in the Diocese of the East, to construct a basilica in the city, and the emperor provided the funds for the work.[5] This is described as a "large illuminated basilica," splendidly adorned, bearing an inscription in gold mosaic giving the emperor's name. It also contained representations, in sculpture or mosaic, of Theodosius II and of the emperor in the West, Valentinian III.

Regarding the churches of the city, we hear that two rooms were added to the cruciform Church of St. Babylas across the Orontes. A mosaic inscription found in one of the chambers records that the room was built, and the mosaic floor laid, during the episcopate of Theodotus (bishop of Antioch A.D. 420-429), under the supervision of Athanasius, priest and administrator of the church, and of Akkiba, deacon and custodian of the edifice.[6]

The Olympic Games of Antioch still suffered from financial difficulties which had begun during the reign of Theodosius I. Under Theodosius II, an imperial decree had to be issued preventing the Alytarch, the presiding official of the games, from trying to reimburse himself for his expenses by cutting down trees in the sacred grove in Daphne.[7] A little later the financial burden of giving the Olympic Games must have been somewhat eased when Antiochus Chuzon of Antioch, the former praetorian prefect, gave an endowment for the support of the hippodrome spectacles, the Olympic Games, and the Maiouma.[8]

---

[5] Malalas, p. 360, 7-15; Evagrius, *loc.cit.*

[6] J. Lassus, "L'église cruciforme," *Antioch-on-the-Orontes*, II, p. 33, with plan 4 on pp. 218f, on which the rooms are nos. 2 and 3, in the north-east angle of the crossing of the arms of the church. The inscription is published and discussed by Lassus, pp. 41-43.

[7] *Cod. Just.*, XI, 78, 2.   [8] Malalas, p. 362, 18-21.

The popular religious interest in Antioch, in the early part of the reign of Theodosius II, centered about a famous local figure, St. Symeon Stylites the Elder, the first and most famous of the pillar saints, who passed their lives on the tops of columns high above the ground.[9] Symeon won such veneration for his surpassing holiness, evidenced by his extreme self-mortification, that he gained enormous influence not only in Antioch itself, the city which always claimed him as its own, but throughout the Christian world. Monasticism, with its striving for spirituality through ascetic discipline, had become an important and well-developed movement within the church, and its power was increased and extended by the remarkable examples of men like Symeon. Symeon lived on a series of pillars, each higher than the last, for forty-two years, spending the last thirty years of his life on his tallest column, about sixty feet high, in the mountains east of Antioch. As his fame grew, numerous pilgrims came from all over the Christian world to see Symeon, and many of these must have passed through Antioch. Likewise many citizens of Antioch, of all ranks, made the journey to the saint's pillar to consult him, or ask for his prayers, or receive his blessing. The commander-in-chief of the troops in the Diocese of the Orient, while stationed in Antioch, was cured by the saint after having suffered a heart attack. Symeon became so powerful that on occasion he sent advice to the emperor, and his advice was followed.

Theodosius II left no male heir; and on his death his sister Pulcheria, a lady already past fifty, chose the experienced military officer Marcianus, a man almost sixty, to become emperor as her nominal husband. Marcianus proved to be a good ruler, and he was later looked upon as an emperor to be imitated by those who followed him. During his reign (A.D. 450-457) the eastern part of the empire en-

[9] A Syriac biography of Symeon is translated by F. Lent, *Journal of the American Oriental Society*, xxxv, 1915-17, pp. 103-198.

joyed peace, and he made a serious effort to relieve the financial burdens of his people.

In these years we hear of the career at Antioch of the commander-in-chief of the troops of the Diocese of the East, Ardaburius, a typical figure of the times. Son and grandson of powerful figures in the government, Ardaburius was born not much later than A.D. 425. As a young man he distinguished himself by his military successes against the barbarian invaders of Thrace, and was appointed consul for the year A.D. 447. Marcianus, before he became emperor, had served under Ardaburius' father and grandfather, and as a reward for his work in Thrace the emperor appointed the young man to the command of the troops in the East. In this capacity he was called upon to repel an invasion of some Arab tribes near Damascus. The remainder of his tenure of command being peaceful, the young man gave himself up to the pleasures of life in Antioch and Daphne, indulging himself in "woman-like luxuriousness," and devoting himself to "mimes and magicians and all the delights of the stage."[10] Apparently in the course of these activities he built himself in Daphne a private bath which appears on the topographical border of the mosaic of *Megalopsychia* at Daphne. It has been suggested that the building in which the mosaic was found was itself Ardaburius' villa.

In the reign of Marcianus' successor Leo I (A.D. 457-474) the chief event in the life of Antioch was the severe earthquake, one of the most serious in the city's history, which occurred in mid-September, A.D. 458. The damage must have been considerable. The local historian Evagrius, whose account is the fullest preserved description of the disaster, states that the destruction occurred primarily in what was still called the "new quarter" of the city, that is, the island, where "nearly all" the buildings were thrown down, and in the

---

[10] Priscus, frag. 20, *F.H.G.*, IV, p. 100, preserved in part in Suidas, *s.v.* Ardabourios. Priscus was a friend of Ardaburius.

quarter called Ostrakine in the main part of the city.[11] The chronicler Theophanes, writing much later, records that "nearly the whole city fell."[12] Probably the truth lies somewhere between these accounts. Some idea of the severity of the shocks can be gained from the fact that the Syriac biography of St. Symeon Stylites states that the walls of the city were shaken down.

Locally the earthquake, which occurred at night, was considered the most severe since the disaster in the reign of Trajan. On the island, half the palace was thrown down, with the bath which stood beside it. The arches and columns of the tetrapylon before the palace, at the crossing of the main streets of the island, were destroyed, along with the colonnades that flanked the approach to the palace from the tetrapylon. The twin towers that flanked the entrance to the hippodrome were destroyed, as well as the colonnades which adjoined this entrance.

Alongside the palace another bath remained standing. This, Evagrius says, had previously fallen into disuse; but it was the only bath on the island which had not suffered damage, and it was now put back into operation and must have rendered important service for the health and comfort of the survivors of the catastrophe.

In the "old city," on the mainland, Evagrius goes on, "there was no harm at all to the colonnades or the buildings, but the baths of Trajan, Severus, and Hadrian were somewhat damaged." In the quarter of Ostrakine the earthquake threw down certain buildings along with the Nymphaeum and "the colonnades" along the streets.

A late account of the earthquake adds that, as often happened, it was followed by a fire. The same source relates that the bishop of Antioch, Acacius, rendered notable service

---

[11] Evagrius, *Hist. eccl.*, II, 12.
[12] Theophanes, p. 110, 22f, ed. De Boor.

in rescuing and caring for the survivors.[13] The people of the city, fearing the successive shocks which often followed the initial earthquake, made a pilgrimage to the column of Symeon Stylites and remained there for fifty-one days. Isaac of Antioch, a theologian and poet who wrote in Syriac, composed a monody on the city, lamenting its destruction in the disaster.

Whenever possible, when cities were visited by similar catastrophes, the imperial government granted relief from taxation in order to facilitate the rebuilding of the city. On this occasion the emperor remitted a substantial sum from the regular tribute paid by the people of Antioch, and citizens were excused from paying taxes on buildings that had been destroyed. The imperial government in addition took the responsibility for the restoration of the public buildings.

Just a year later, when the city was still recovering from the earthquake, it suffered another calamity, the death of Symeon Stylites. This must have seemed to the people of Antioch in those days nearly as great an affliction as any earthquake could be, for Symeon was regarded as the special patron and protector of the city. Symeon's death would seem to leave Antioch deprived of a precious source of counsel and spiritual strength.

After the saint's death everyone, among his immediate followers and the people of that part of Syria, would think at once of the question of where Symeon's relics should be preserved. The saint had been a powerful wonder-worker and healer, and his body, or any part of it, would, in those times, be expected to continue his miracles. As soon as Symeon's death became known, General Ardaburius went to the saint's pillar accompanied by members of his staff and by a considerable body of troops, both in order to do honor to the saint and to prevent disorder in connection

---

[13] *Chronicon miscellaneum ad A.D. 724 pertinens* (*Corp. Scr. Christ. Orient., Scr. Syri*, ser. 3, tome IV, *Chronica minora*, pt. 2), pp. 108-110.

with the disposition of the relics. The people of Antioch made a special request to be allowed to receive the body so that it might serve as a protection for their city, which had lost its walls in the recent earthquake.[14] How or by whom the question was decided, we are not told. Ardaburius was the imperial representative on the ground, with a strong military force. He was fond of Antioch, where he had enjoyed all the pleasures the city could offer; and no doubt Antioch had promised that Symeon's body would be buried with exceptional honor. It was decided that the remains should be given to Antioch, and the festal procession escorting the coffin took five days for the journey of fifty miles, reaching Antioch on Friday, 25 September.[15]

After passing the suburb Meroë, five miles from the city, the procession was greeted by a great crowd who came out on the road to meet the body. The coffin was taken first to the Church of Cassianus.[16] Thirty days later it was removed to the Great Church of Constantine—the first time, it was said, that a body had rested there—and finally a church was built for the permanent reception of the remains.[17] The Emperor Leo wrote to request that the body be sent to Constantinople, so that it might lend its spiritual strength to the whole empire, but the people of Antioch begged to keep their saint, and they were successful in their petition.[18] The saint's relics were treated with the greatest veneration and Martyrius, the bishop of Antioch, and his clergy held services

[14] See the Syriac biography of Symeon edited by H. Lietzmann with a German translation by H. Hilgenfeld, *Das Leben des hl. Symeon Stylites* (*Texte u. Untersuchungen*, XXXII, 4, 1908), ch. 133, p. 177.

[15] *Ibid.*, ch. 137, p. 180. Symeon's death, and the taking of the body to Antioch, are described by Malalas, p. 369, 10-16; the Chronicon Paschale, I, p. 593, 17ff; and Evagrius, *Hist. eccl.*, I, 13.

[16] The temporary sojourn of the body at the Church of Cassianus is described in the Greek biography of Symeon by Antonius (Lietzmann, *op.cit.*), ch. 32, p. 76.

[17] Antonius, Malalas, Chronicon Paschale, *loc.cit.*

[18] Syriac biography of Symeon, ch. 136, p. 179.

before the coffin every day. As had been hoped, the relics worked many miracles, and the corpse was still well preserved when the local historian Evagrius saw it at the end of the sixth century.[19]

Like his predecessor Marcianus, Leo found it necessary to deal with economic difficulties throughout the empire, and we possess laws of his designed to enforce economy and to keep the revenue from taxes up to its former levels. At the same time, Leo was anxious to lighten the fiscal burdens of his subjects. The senatorial class at Antioch continued to find it difficult to meet its obligations for many public services, notably in connection with the presentation of the Olympic Games. In A.D. 465 an imperial decree was issued providing that in future the function of Alytarch in presenting the games should be borne by the Count of the East, and the function of the Syriarch, another important official of the games, by the governor of Syria; and it was further stipulated that the members of the local senatorial order should not be allowed to assume these burdens even if they wished to do so.[20]

A remarkable glimpse of the survival of paganism at this time has been preserved by the reports of the trial of the pagan teacher Isocasius of Antioch. This trial seems to have attracted wide attention, and it is recorded in a number of sources. We first hear of Isocasius in the time of Domnus, bishop of Antioch A.D. 441/2-449, in connection with the claim, made by the bishop's enemies, that Domnus had been consecrated as bishop in an irregular manner, and that he had had the support of the "pagan" Isocasius and of other "disreputable" persons.[21] Isocasius was a friend and correspondent of Bishop Theodoret of Cyrrhus, and from the

---

[19] Evagrius, *Hist. eccl.*, I, 13.   [20] *Cod. Just.*, I, 36, 1.

[21] "Akten des Ephesinischen Synode vom Jahre 449," ed. J. Flemming, *Abhandlungen der k. Gesellschaft d. Wissenschaften zu Göttingen, philol. histor. Kl.*, N. F., xv, pt. I, 1917, p. 127, 16.

bishop's letters we learn that Isocasius kept a school at Antioch, and also that he was concerned in some way with the
law.[22] Isocasius always remained a pagan, and became a man
of wealth and property in Antioch, holding many public
offices. In the reign of Leo I, when he was a law official,
an accusation against him for various offences, including
paganism, was laid before the emperor. His property was
confiscated and he was arrested and brought to trial in Constantinople, in the year A.D. 468.[23] Isocasius defended himself
with a philosophical speech which seems to have made a
great impression, and the trial was brought to an end when he
agreed to receive Christian baptism.[24] The episode is instruc-
tive as an example of the survival of paganism among the
highly placed and wealthy persons at Antioch at this time.

A number of Germans had been serving in the army and
at court for some years, and during Leo's reign their influence
was rising. Indeed, this development became one of Leo's
chief problems. In order to offset the German influence, the
emperor had sought the support of the Isaurian mountaineers
who lived in the wild regions of the Taurus Mountains at
no great distance from Antioch; and in order to consolidate
this support, he had married his elder daughter Ariadne to
an Isaurian chieftain named Tarasicodissa, who took the
Greek name of Zeno.[25] Zeno was named consul for the year
A.D. 469, three or four years after his marriage, and toward
the end of that year he was appointed commander of the
troops in the Diocese of the Orient, an office he held until
A.D. 471. After his appointment he took with him to his
headquarters in Antioch a priest named Peter the Fuller,
who had attracted Zeno's attention and held views congenial

[22] Theodoret, *Epistles* 27, 28, 38, 44, 52, ed. Azéma (*Sources chrétiennes*).
[23] Theophanes, p. 115, 9-18, ed. De Boor.
[24] Malalas, p. 369, 17ff; Chronicon Paschale, 1, p. 595, 6ff.
[25] On Leo's relations with the Isaurians, and the career of Zeno, see
E. W. Brooks, "The Emperor Zenon and the Isaurians," *English Historical Review*, VIII, 1893, pp. 209-238.

to his heretical inclinations. When Zeno and Peter arrived at Antioch, the bishop was Martyrius, a strictly orthodox leader, who had been bishop when Symeon Stylites died. Apparently Peter found in Antioch conditions which suggested to him that he could, with Zeno's support, make himself bishop of the city, and he set to work toward that end. Probably he found that there were dissident elements in the city which thus far had lacked leadership, though with proper guidance they would, Peter thought, be strong enough to overthrow the orthodox regime. Peter the Fuller's career at Antioch was the first occasion when the monophysite heresy played a major role in the affairs of Antioch. This heresy was the belief that Christ when he was on earth existed in a single, divine, nature, rather than in two natures, human and divine, as the orthodox believed. The Monophysites became powerful in Egypt and Syria, especially among the indigenous, non-Greek-speaking elements in the population, and under the leadership of Peter the Fuller they held control over the church at Antioch for some years.

Understanding very well the way to organize popular support, Peter provided a slogan that was instantly successful. This was the phrase "Who was crucified for us," added to the Trisagion ("Thrice-Holy") which formed an important part of the communion service, "Holy God, Holy and Strong, Holy and Immortal, have mercy on us." Peter's phrase was added between the third invocation and the refrain. If it was taken as an address to our Lord, there could be no objection to it. But some people—and we know that this was true at Constantinople—considered the Trisagion as an address to the Trinity rather than as an address to our Lord; and in this case Peter's phrase represented the patripassian or theopaschite heresy, according to which it was God himself who was crucified.[26] The phrase, then, was capable of two interpretations, one orthodox, one heretical. As Peter in-

---

[26] Theophanes, p. 113, 27f, ed. De Boor.

tended it should, the slogan split the population of Antioch. Every religious service became an occasion for a demonstration of the monophysite party. Not only was the authority of the bishop threatened, but the Monophysites had gained a powerful rallying point.[27] Martyrius was so alarmed by this unexpected consolidation of the local monophysite feeling that he went to Constantinople to appeal to the emperor for help. By the good offices of Gennadius, patriarch of Constantinople, Martyrius was received with great honor by the emperor, who was strongly orthodox; but while Martyrius was away from Antioch, Peter the Fuller, with the support of Zeno—and, it was said, by the use of force—got himself consecrated as bishop of Antioch by some bishops at Seleucia Pieria, and exercised the office for a time while Martyrius was still in Constantinople.

Martyrius, then, returned and found Peter acting as bishop. Severe disorders were taking place in the city. Martyrius concluded that opposition was hopeless, and resigned his episcopate.[28] This placed Peter in power for a time as nominal bishop, but a synod was called at Antioch, presumably on the emperor's orders, which deposed Peter and elected Julian in his place. At the instance of the Patriarch Gennadius, the emperor ordered Peter into exile. The exile was, however, commuted to internment with the *Acoemetae*, the "Sleepless Monks," in Constantinople, and thus Peter remained in a position to take advantage of any future opportunities.

When the Emperor Leo I died (3 February A.D. 474), he left, as Augustus, his grandson Leo the Younger, son of Zeno. The younger Leo being a child of six years, his father became regent. It was decided that the child Augustus should confer the imperial dignity on his father, and when the child Leo

---

[27] On the epigraphical evidence for the local popularity in Syria of Peter's formula, see W. K. Prentice, "Fragments of an Early Christian Liturgy in Syrian Inscriptions," *T.A.P.A.*, XXXIII, 1902, pp. 81-86.

[28] Theodore Lector, *Hist. eccl.*, I, 21 (*P.G.* LXXXVI, pt. I, col. 176); Theophanes, p. 113, 30-34, ed. De Boor.

died, later in the same year, Zeno became sole emperor. Zeno's reign was to be a troubled one. The empire was beset by external difficulties and the emperor discovered that he was surrounded by a court which was bitterly hostile to him and to his supporters because they were Isaurians. At Antioch, after what seems to have been an extended period of peace, these years were turbulent, and the city served as the headquarters of the various rebels who set themselves up against Zeno. Religious strife did not cease, as Peter the Fuller returned to the city and the disorders connected with the monophysite movement continued.

The first of the plots against Zeno was formed by his mother-in-law the Augusta Verina, widow of Leo I, with the cooperation of her brother Basiliscus. She persuaded Zeno that his position was insecure and that he was in such danger that he ought to leave Constantinople (January A.D. 475). Zeno, realizing his unpopularity as an Isaurian, believed her and took refuge in Isauria. Verina's plan, however, miscarried, for Basiliscus proceeded to put his sister aside and had himself crowned as Augustus.

Basiliscus favored the monophysite party and sought to strengthen his position by appointing monophysite patriarchs in Alexandria and Antioch, so as to secure the support of the monophysite elements in Syria and Egypt. In Antioch, it was Peter the Fuller who was appointed. When he arrived to take over the patriarchal throne for the third time, the orthodox patriarch was so strongly affected that he died, it was said, "of vexation."[29] Peter proceeded to institute harsh measures against the orthodox in Antioch, and his insistence on his monophysite addition to the Trisagion caused riots in which people were killed.[30]

After Zeno fled to Isauria, Basiliscus sent two military

[29] Theodore Lector, op.cit., 1, 31 (col. 181); Theophanes, p. 121, 1-23 ed. De Boor; Malalas, p. 377, 2-5.
[30] Theophanes, p. 121, 22-26, ed. De Boor.

officers, the Isaurian brothers Illus and Trocundus, with a force of troops, to keep Zeno shut up in the stronghold in which he had taken refuge. However, Basiliscus failed to keep his promises to Illus and Trocundus, and they decided to join forces with Zeno and restore him to the throne. Zeno and Illus, with a large body of Isaurian troops, set out for Constantinople. Zeno was successful in reestablishing himself, and a detachment of Isaurians, commanded by Trocundus, was sent to Antioch to depose Peter the Fuller.[31] An imperial order was issued exiling Peter to the Caucasus, but he managed to escape and find concealment in a monastery in Helenopontus.[32] The diocesan synod met in Antioch and elected John Codonatus to succeed Peter, but this appointment was not acceptable to the government, for John was a Monophysite and a protégé of Peter the Fuller's, and he attempted to carry on Peter's policies. John was removed from office after three months and was replaced by an orthodox priest, Stephen. The partisans of Peter the Fuller, as might be expected, attacked Stephen and brought an accusation before Zeno; but a synod which the emperor summoned to meet at Laodicea vindicated the patriarch and restored him to his throne. However, in the first part of A.D. 479 Stephen was murdered by the Monophysites, who found a convenient occasion when the patriarch had gone outside the city to the church of the local martyr St. Barlaam, to celebrate the festival of the Forty Martyrs of Sebaste, which occurred on 9 March. Stephen was set upon by some monophysite priests in the baptistry of the church, and was stabbed to death with sharpened reeds; his body was thrown into the Orontes.[33] This brutal murder must have touched off new disorders in the city.

[31] Theophanes, p. 124, 10ff, ed. De Boor; Malalas, p. 378, 17ff.

[32] Theophanes, p. 125, 17-19, ed. De Boor; Malalas, p. 380, 21ff.

[33] Theophanes, p. 128, 17-22, ed. De Boor; Evagrius, *op.cit.*, III, 10; Malalas, p. 381, 2-6. The location of the Church of St. Barlaam is not

At about this time, a rupture occurred at Constantinople between Zeno and Illus, and two attempts were made to assassinate Illus. He then asked the emperor to be given an assignment outside of Constantinople, and he was made commander of the troops in the Diocese of the East.[34] Thus, at the end of A.D. 481 or the beginning of 482, Illus arrived at Antioch, his headquarters, accompanied by several officials he had chosen to assist him in his new post. There was also a substantial military escort. Illus' companions had no doubt been selected on the basis of the support they might be expected to render to his ambitions. We know the names of several. Leontius was a Syrian, distinguished both for his education and his military experience, whom Illus had attached to himself. The neoplatonist Pamprepius was a prominent pagan, born in Egypt, who had served as a law officer in Constantinople. Marsus was an Isaurian military officer. Justinian was an ex-prefect of the city of Constantinople. Matronianus, a military officer, was Illus' brother-in-law. Aelianus had recently been praetorian prefect of the East.

Illus spent the next two years in Antioch making careful plans for the rebellion which would be the inevitable outcome of recent events. He adopted a favorite means to make himself popular and presented the city with a number of buildings.

One of the plans for the rebellion appears to have been an effort to bring together the forces of orthodoxy (now on the defensive in the eastern part of the empire) and of paganism, in an effort to create stronger opposition to the monophysite party, which Zeno had supported before he came to the throne. It had not been very long since the pagan teacher Isocasius had been a prominent figure in

---

known; it may be conjectured, from the fate of the bishop's body, that it was somewhere convenient to the Orontes.

[34] Malalas in *Excerpta de insidiis*, pp. 164f, ed. De Boor; Theophanes, p. 127, 13ff, ed. De Boor; Evagrius, *op.cit.*, III, 27.

Antioch, and Illus' plans suggest that he and his advisers considered that there was enough pagan sentiment remaining in Antioch and Asia Minor to make it worth while to seek backing there. It would be easy, in any case, to appeal to the Hellenic heritage as a means of rallying pagans and Christians with classical education, and to call upon them to oppose the Monophysites on a patriotic and cultural basis. We hear of a trip by Pamprepius to his native Egypt, evidently in order to build up support for Zeno among the Greeks there.

It was at this time that the Patriarch Calandio arranged to have brought back to Antioch the relics of Eustathius "the Great," the famous bishop of the city in the fourth century who had defended the orthodox cause against the Arians and was finally deprived of office and exiled to Philippi in Thrace, where he died and was buried. When Calandio brought the relics back, more than one hundred years after Eustathius' death, the joyful people went ten miles outside the city to meet the procession, and those who were still separated from the local church, through loyalty to Eustathius' principles, were reunited.[35] Calandio's undertaking thus not only restored peace among the local orthodox Christians, but also served to give them a stronger front against the Monophysites.

Late in A.D. 483 or early in 484, after Illus had been in Antioch for two years, both Zeno and Illus took steps which could only lead to war between them.[36] Knowing that as an Isaurian he would suffer from the same popular enmity Zeno had felt, Illus did not attempt to make himself emperor, but instead decided to put forward Leontius, not an Isaurian but a Syrian by birth, who had been one of Illus' companions when he went to Antioch. To secure a legal basis for his

[35] Theodore Lector, op.cit., II, 1, (col. 184); Theophanes, p. 133, 3-7, ed. De Boor.
[36] The most detailed study of this episode is that of Brooks, op.cit. (above, n. 25), pp. 223-228.

action, Illus released the Augusta Verina from the fortress in Isauria in which she had been imprisoned, and he had no difficulty in enlisting her services against her son-in-law Zeno, through whom she had suffered so much. As Augusta, Verina crowned Leontius emperor on 19 July A.D. 484, in the Church of St. Peter, outside Tarsus. The customary proclamation announcing the coronation was read in Antioch outside the headquarters of the commander of the troops in the Diocese of the East and was well received, and Leontius thereupon entered the city on 27 July and made it his headquarters.

Leontius maintained his regime in Antioch for about sixty or seventy days.[37] He had time to strike coins and to set up a government with Aelianus as praetorian prefect, Pamprepius as Master of the Offices and Justinian as treasurer, while Illus himself remained the guiding spirit of the whole enterprise. The Patriarch Calandio joined the rebels. The only opposition in Syria was at Edessa and Chalcis.

Zeno, when the news of the rebellion reached him, sent a strong force of troops under John the Scythian, and Leontius' soldiers were defeated.[38] Leontius, Illus, Verina and their supporters fled from Antioch to the stronghold of Papyrion in Isauria. They withstood a siege for four years, but in the end were captured by treachery and executed (A.D. 488).

After the suppression of the regime of Illus and Leontius, the Patriarch Calandio was removed from office and exiled, on the emperor's orders, because of his adherence to the rebels. Zeno then sent Peter the Fuller back to Antioch to be

---

[37] John of Antioch, frag. 98, p. 136 *Excerpta de insidiis*, ed. De Boor; cf. Brooks, *op.cit.*, pp. 227-231.

[38] Malalas, *loc.cit.* (above, n. 33). The location of the battle is not specified, but the accounts seem to indicate that it did not take place in or near Antioch. According to Malalas, Leontius and Pamprepius were in Antioch when Leontius' troops were defeated. Joshua the Stylite, *Chronicle*, ch. 16, relates that when the people of Antioch heard of the imperial force that had been dispatched against them, they "tumultuously" called upon Illus and Leontius to leave the city.

patriarch for the fourth time. A synod met and recognized Peter. Hostile writers describe the "many evil things" he did and the trouble he stirred up.[39]

At about this time, in the last years of the reign of Zeno, we have fairly detailed reports of factional disorders at Antioch, accompanied by an anti-Jewish outbreak. The first incident recorded was a clash in the hippodrome between the Greens and the Blues, the two principal circus factions which had originally been formed to support rival charioteers but had come to constitute political and religious parties. In Antioch at this time the Greens represented the Monophysites and the local Syrian element in the population, while the Blues, traditionally the conservative and aristocratic party, supported orthodoxy and thus represented the interests of the central government. In the hippodromes of the various cities, the two factions occupied fixed locations, and their cheering and applause (or invective) were regulated by their leaders, as were the traditional acclamations with which the emperor and other officials were greeted when they appeared in public on ceremonial occasions. In this outbreak at Antioch, the Greens began to attack the Blues in the hippodrome by throwing stones at them.[40] One hit the governor of Syria, Thalassius, on the head and he left the hippodrome. Thalassius had identified the thrower of the stone as one Olympius, an attendant in one of the baths—he must have been a well-known ringleader for Thalassius to have recognized him—and when he reached the safety of his headquarters, on the Forum of Valens, the governor sent police to arrest Olympius and bring him to the headquarters. When Olympius was brought, Thalassius began to conduct the customary examination in which the prisoner was flogged in order to elicit reliable testimony.

[39] Zachariah of Mitylene, *Chronicle*, v, 9f; Theophanes, p. 133, 32ff, ed. De Boor.

[40] Malalas in *Excerpta de insidiis*, pp. 166f, ed. De Boor; Church Slavonic version of Malalas, pp. 109-112.

When the Greens heard of Olympius' arrest and examination, they hurried to the governor's headquarters, attacked the building and set it on fire and rescued the prisoner. The fire spread into the colonnade with which the Forum of Valens was surrounded, and reached the Xystos, which stood on one side of the forum, and burned it. Thalassius fled to Hippocephalus, a place several miles outside the city. He resigned his office and was replaced by Quadratus, and the disorder was brought to an end.

Six months later there was a new outbreak of fighting between the factions, this time involving the Jews, who had made common cause with the Blue party. The Greens attacked the Blues and their Jewish allies in the hippodrome and killed a number of them, and then plundered and burned the synagogue named for Asabinus. For failing to keep order, Theodorus, the Count of the East, was relieved of his office, and the fighting ceased.

The third episode reported is a further outbreak of anti-Semitism. It is related that a monk walled himself up in one of the towers in the southern wall of the city—an extraordinary act of mortification characteristic of the times—leaving a small opening through which he harangued the people. He preached an attack on the Jews, who had one of their principal synagogues near by, in the southern quarter of the city. The Greens fell upon the synagogue and burned it, and dug up and burned on a pyre the bodies of the Jews who were buried there. They also burned other buildings in this area, which was called the Distadion because it occupied the interval of two stadia (about two-fifths of a mile) between the older wall of Tiberius and the new wall built by Theodosius II. The chronicler Malalas reports that when Zeno, who was favorable to the Greens, was told of this incident, he was angry with the factionists because they had burned only dead Jews and had not thrown living ones on the fire.

Our final information concerning Antioch during the

reign of Zeno comes from the record of public buildings put up by Mammianus, who, having started life as an artisan, became a senator.[41] In Daphne, he built the Antiphorus, on a site formerly planted by vines, opposite a public bath. From its name, this would appear to be a building which served "in place of a forum." The citizens in gratitude set up a bronze statue inscribed to "Mammianus the benefactor of the city." In Antioch he built two colonnades, described as being "very seemly in their construction and adorned with striking and brilliant stone work," and paved with stone from Proconnesus. These colonnades were named for Mammianus. Between them he erected a tetrapylon, an ornamental structure of four columns supporting a roof, "very finely adorned with columns and bronze work." The colonnades, rebuilt after suffering damage on various occasions, were still visible in the time of the local historian Evagrius, who saw them in the latter part of the sixth century, but the tetrapylon had by that time disappeared.

[41] Evagrius, *Hist. eccl.*, III, 28.

CHAPTER XII

THE LAST YEARS

ALTHOUGH the history of Antioch in its final chapters is a chronicle of troubles and disorders, it was also a time of real economic prosperity. All through the reigns of Zeno (A.D. 474-491) and Anastasius (A.D. 491-518), and into the beginning of the succeeding epoch of Justin I and Justinian, the city shared the increasing wealth of the region of the Belus Mountains which lay to the east of Antioch. This area had become an important center for the production of olive oil, one of the major items in the ancient economy. Many of the great farms were owned by citizens of Antioch, who sometimes passed the summers there on their estates. The sale of the oil, both for consumption in Antioch and for export to other parts of the empire, brought wealth which was reflected in the notable increase in building activity throughout the Belus region.[1] This must have been matched by similar building at Antioch.

Throughout the empire the history of Anastasius' rule was colored by his position in the religious situation, and, later, by his financial policy in restoring the resources of the state, which Zeno's reign had seriously depleted. Both his support of the Monophysites, and his energetic measures for financial reform and recoupment, made Anastasius unpopular in many quarters. The emperor possessed admirable personal qualities. He was a deeply religious man, and his long experience as an official in the imperial administration gave him qualifications for his office not always found in the emperors of those days; but at the same time, the unpopularity of some

[1] The history of the Belus region has recently been illuminated by the archaeological explorations of G. Tchalenko, *Villages antiques de la Syrie du Nord: La région du Bélus à l'époque romaine*, 3 vols., Paris, 1953-58. See also the more general work of J. Mattern, *Villes mortes de Haute Syrie*, 2d ed., Beirut, 1944.

of his measures actually produced an increase in the public disorders and clashes between the circus factions throughout his reign.[2]

A series of riots began in A.D. 507 with the arrival at Antioch of Porphyrius Calliopas, the most celebrated charioteer of the day, who was then at the height of his career. He had been a popular and powerful figure among the factions at Constantinople, where he had been acclaimed in a number of epigrams (which were considered worthy of inclusion in the *Greek Anthology*), and had been honored by a monument, still partly preserved, erected in the hippodrome about the year A.D. 500.[3] After some victories of the new charioteer in the hippodrome at Antioch, violence broke out during the celebration of the Olympic Games in July and August of A.D. 507, beginning with an assault on the Jews, who had already been attacked, as associates of the Blue party, during the reign of Zeno. Waiting for a time when most of the people of Antioch were at Daphne for the games, Calliopas and the Greens attacked the Jewish synagogue there and burned it, and killed many people. The cross was planted on the site of the synagogue, and later a church of the martyr St. Leontius was erected on the spot.

When this outbreak was reported to the emperor, he dismissed the Count of the East, Basilius of Edessa, and appointed in his stead Procopius of Antioch. The emperor also sent to Antioch, along with Procopius, a new chief of police, Menas of Byzantium. When the next outbreak of

[2] On the factional disorders, see G. Manojlović, "Le peuple de Constantinople," *Byzantion*, xi, 1936, pp. 617-716, and F. Dvornik, "The Circus Parties in Byzantium: Their Evolution and their Suppression," *Byzantina Metabyzantina*, i, 1946, pp. 119-133.

[3] Malalas, p. 395, 20ff; *Excerpta de insidiis*, p. 168, frag. 40; John of Nikiu, *Chronicle*, LXXXIX, 23-30. A detailed study of the career of Porphyrius, based on both the archaeological and the literary evidence, has been written by A. A. Vasiliev, "The Monument of Porphyrius in the Hippodrome at Constantinople," *Dumbarton Oaks Papers*, iv, 1948, pp. 29-49.

violence occurred, Menas set about seizing some of the rioters. Having had advance information of his intention, they fled to the Church of St. John, outside the city, to seek sanctuary there. The chief of police discovered where they had gone, and went to St. John's with a force of Gothic troops, choosing the noon hour when the rioters might be expected to be off their guard. One of the factionists, Eleutherios by name, was found hiding under the holy table, and was killed and beheaded on the spot. Menas took the head back to Antioch and threw it into the Orontes from the principal bridge. In the afternoon the Greens went to the church, and finding the body of their comrade, they placed it on a stretcher and bore it back to the city. When they came opposite the Basilica of Rufinus, at the Bath of Olbia, they encountered the police, along with the Blues, in the Street of the Thalassioi. In the fight that followed, the Greens won. They then seized the Basilica of Rufinus and the Basilica of Zenodotus and set them afire. The fire destroyed the Basilica of Rufinus together with the two tetrapylons on either side of it and the headquarters of the Count of the East. Procopius himself fled the city and the Greens then seized Menas, cut off his head, mutilated the body, and dragged it through the streets to the Antiphorus, where they hung it on a bronze statue. Later they took down the body, dragged it outside the city, and burned it. The emperor, when the outbreak was reported to him, appointed as Count of the East Irenaeus Pentadiastes, who as a citizen of Antioch was well acquainted with local conditions. Irenaeus held an investigation and, as the chronicler Malalas writes, "caused terror in the city." Order was restored, and the emperor rebuilt the structures that had been burned.

The religious situation in Syria presented Anastasius with a difficult problem. Feeling between the orthodox and the Monophysites was becoming very bitter and the monophysite cause had now become associated with the nationalistic emotions of the Syrian element in the population, as the Syriac-speaking people of indigenous stock became increasingly alienated from the Greek-speaking ruling classes.[4] The combination of religious passion and local patriotism inevitably became a powerful force. When Anastasius came to the throne, monophysite sentiment was gathering strength in Antioch under the powerful influence of Philoxenus, bishop of Hierapolis, a protégé of Peter the Fuller. The emperor himself inclined toward monophysite views and took what opportunities he could to favor the party.

The patriarch of Antioch at this time, the orthodox Flavian II, found himself constantly under attack by the Monophysites. Finally the bands of monophysite monks who lived in the vicinity of the city invaded Antioch, under the leadership of Bishop Philoxenus, and staged organized demonstrations against the patriarch. The citizens resisted the invaders by force and killed a number of them, and threw their bodies into the Orontes.[5] Further disorders then occurred when the orthodox monks of Syria, among whom Flavian had lived before becoming patriarch, came to the city en masse to defend him. To give an opportunity for the disorders to quiet down, Flavian left Antioch and stayed at the suburb Platanon (modern Beilan), on the road from Antioch to Tarsus. He was later deposed and exiled.

The new patriarch was the monophysite champion Severus, consecrated by twelve bishops in the Great Church on 16

[4] On the policy of Anastasius, see P. Charanis, *Church and State in the Later Roman Empire: The Religious Policy of Anastasius the First, 491-518*, Madison, Wisconsin, 1939. On monophysitism and the nationalist tendencies in Syria and Egypt, see E. L. Woodward, *Christianity and Nationalism in the Later Roman Empire*, London, 1916, pp. 41ff, and A. H. M. Jones, "Were Ancient Heresies National or Social Movements in Disguise?" *Journal of Theological Studies*, new series, x, 1959, pp. 280-298.

[5] Zachariah of Mitylene, *Chronicle*, vii, 10; Evagrius, *Hist. eccl.*, iii, 32; Theophanes, pp. 153, 29ff ed. De Boor.

November, A.D. 512.[6] Severus' statement of faith, read on this occasion, was repeated two days later at a festival service held in the Church of St. Romanus, and was read a third time in the Church of St. Euphemia in Daphne.

Concerning Severus' ecclesiastical activities we have a considerable amount of information in his preserved writings, notably his letters, and these illustrate the difficulties he encountered in controlling the bishops and clergy in his jurisdiction, who were in many cases hostile to him. Antioch can hardly have been a peaceful place during Severus' patriarchate, and there was such intense activity that Severus found it necessary to keep a permanent synod of bishops regularly resident in Antioch, on the model of the similar synod maintained by the patriarch of Constantinople. Severus continued as patriarch until the death of Anastasius, when the new emperor Justin, who was orthodox, issued an order for his arrest.

When Justin I (A.D. 518-527) became emperor, the advent of a new and exceptionally able dynasty opened an important era in the history of the Later Roman Empire, which was to bring many changes to Antioch as well as to the other great cities of the empire.[7] The period is also one of more than ordinary interest in local history. Beginning with the time of Justin, Malalas' *Chronicle* becomes much more detailed than it had been for previous reigns. Malalas himself lived at Antioch during at least part of this period and was an eye witness of some of the events he recorded; and after he settled in Constantinople (probably after the earthquake of A.D. 526) he and his continuator show a special interest in events connected with Antioch. Further information of special value comes from the work of the historian Procopius

---

[6] Malalas, p. 400, 7-10; Evagrius, *op.cit.*, III, 33. See Charanis, *op.cit.*, pp. 47ff.

[7] On the reign of Justin, see the monograph of A. A. Vasiliev, *Justin the First*, Cambridge, Mass., 1950.

of Caesarea, who devoted two major passages in different works to the sack of Antioch by the Persians in A.D. 540 and its rebuilding following that disaster. The capture of the city by the Persians, coming soon after a fire in A.D. 525 and earthquakes in A.D. 526 and 528, marked the beginning of the end of the prosperity and importance of ancient Antioch, and the history of the city as a Graeco-Roman metropolis comes to a close not long after, with the invasion of Syria in the seventh century first by the Persians and then by the Moslems.

The accession of the orthodox Justin as successor to the monophysite Anastasius was bound to provoke disorders between the circus factions, for it would now be the Blue party— the party of the orthodox—which would represent the interests of the government, rather than the Green faction, which had been the party of the Monophysites. The Olympic Games of Antioch were discontinued by imperial decree in A.D. 520, and the ancient report connects the suppression of the games with fighting between the Blues and the Greens in the city.[8] There had been financial difficulties in the past, and the government had had to take over the support of the games, through the official participation of the Count of the East and the governor of Syria, when it became impossible for private persons to bear the expense. At the same time, however, the festival was of great economic importance because it attracted throngs of visitors to the city, and it also carried great prestige by reason of its antiquity. However, there was such an increase in factional fighting at this time that the suppression of the games was decided upon as a measure of public order. A few years later it was found necessary, for the same reason, to forbid theatrical shows and performances by dancers throughout the empire.[9]

The first of the disasters that inaugurated the decline of

[8] Malalas, p. 417, 5-8; cf. the Church Slavonic version, pp. 123f.
[9] Malalas, p. 416, 20ff.

the city was a great fire which broke out in October A.D. 525.[10]
The city was burned from the Church of St. Stephen the
Protomartyr to the headquarters of the Master of the Soldiers,
near the Forum of Valens. According to one account, the
fire was started by lightning; there was also a report that it
was set by members of the warring factions. Following the
initial great fire, a series of smaller fires broke out in other
parts of the city for a period of six months. Some of these
were said to have started in the roofs of the buildings. Many
buildings were destroyed and there was considerable loss of
life. On the representations of the Patriarch Euphrasius, the
emperor granted the city a large sum of money for the reconstruction of the burned areas.

The earthquake of A.D. 526 did much greater damage. It
happened to occur on the evening of 29 May, the day before
Ascension Day, when the city was crowded with visitors who
had come to Antioch for the festival.[11] The shocks began at
a time when people were for the most part indoors, eating
their evening meal. As a result of these two coincidences, the
loss of life was much greater than it otherwise might have
been, and the figure of 250,000 dead, which is given in the
sources, is by no means impossible. The most distinguished
victim was the Patriarch Euphrasius.

The disaster destroyed practically the whole city, leaving
standing only the buildings along the slope of Mount Silpius.
As often happened on such occasions, the earth shocks started
fires, and people buried beneath the ruins were burned to
death, while sparks of fire filled the air. The foundations
of buildings, weakened by both the earthquake and the fire,
collapsed, and walls which had been left standing, later fell
and killed people.

[10] Malalas, p. 417, 9-19 (with the Church Slavonic version, p. 124);
Evagrius, *op.cit.*, IV, 5; Theophanes, p. 172, 1-11 ed. De Boor.

[11] Malalas was probably in Antioch when the earthquake occurred and
he describes it in detail, p. 419, 5ff., with further details in the Church
Slavonic version, pp. 125-131. See Vasiliev, *op.cit.*, pp. 345-350.

The Great Church stood alone for several days when everything else had fallen, and then caught fire and burned to the ground. The Church of the Archangel Michael built by the Emperor Zeno, as well as the Church of the Virgin Mary, likewise remained undamaged by the earthquake, but later burned. The Church of the Holy Prophets and the Church of St. Zacharias collapsed after remaining standing for some time.

Some of the survivors, fleeing from the city, were robbed by the country people, who killed any who refused to surrender their possessions. Thieves also entered the city and pillaged the ruins, finding chests of silver plate and gold and silver coins scattered about.[12] They also robbed the corpses, especially those of women who had been wearing jewelry.

Three days after the disaster, on Sunday, a vision of the Holy Cross appeared over the northern part of the city, and remained visible for an hour, while the people wept and prayed. As a result of this, the northern part of Mount Silpius, over which the vision had been seen, was renamed Mount Staurin ("Cross").

When he learned of the disaster, Justin was deeply grieved because he was familiar with Antioch, having been stationed there during his military career, before becoming emperor. He ordered the count Carinus to proceed to the city, with a large sum of gold, to begin excavating in a search for possible survivors, and clearing the site. Other officials were put in charge of the care of the survivors and of the rebuilding of the city. The bridges, the water system, and the baths

---

[12] It is a curious commentary on this part of Malalas' description that the archaeological excavations produced very large numbers of the coins of Justin and Justinian, the coins of the former being especially plentiful. Many of these coins of Justin were presumably lost in the earthquake, while those of Justinian were probably lost when the Persians captured and sacked the city in A.D. 540 (see below).

were to be restored as soon as possible, the baths being especially important for hygienic reasons.

The death of Euphrasius in the earthquake made it necessary to choose a new patriarch, and Justin and his nephew Justinian, the future emperor, who was his uncle's chief adviser, were eager to find a man who could oppose the Monophysites. The choice fell on a layman, Ephraemius, who had been Count of the East. At that time, laymen were sometimes chosen to occupy high ecclesiastical offices in which special administrative or political qualifications were necessary. Ephraemius was ordained and consecrated, and began a vigorous campaign against the Monophysites. In A.D. 531 the Monophysites in Antioch still had sufficient strength and leadership to riot and attack the patriarchate, throwing stones and shouting insults, when a particularly strong imperial edict, prescribing exile for heretics, reached the city.[13] The guards of the patriarchate, led by the Count of the East (who no doubt had been expecting trouble), made a sortie and drove off the mob and killed many of them. It is possible indeed that the popular reaction to the edict had been caused by the rigor with which Ephraemius had been carrying out his duties.

The seismic disturbance which had caused the great earthquake of A.D. 526 had not come to an end. The original earthquake was followed by a series of earth shocks for a year and a half, and these culminated in a second major disaster, on 29 November A.D. 528, early in the day.[14] The shocks lasted for an hour. The sources declare that the walls and all the buildings in the city fell. Damage extended to

[13] Malalas, p. 468, 1-9.

[14] The principal account of this earthquake is that of Theophanes, p. 177, 22ff ed. De Boor. The description preserved in the Oxford manuscript of Malalas (p. 442, 18ff) is much less detailed and is strikingly different from the full and vivid narration of the earthquake of A.D. 526. Malalas evidently left Antioch and went to live in Constantinople after the earlier disaster.

Laodicea and Seleucia Pieria. It was recorded that 4,870 people were killed. The leader of the people at this time was the Patriarch Ephraemius, who made the report of the disaster to the emperor.

Some of the survivors fled to other cities, or went to live in huts on the mountains around Antioch. To add to the distress, the winter that followed the earthquake was exceptionally severe and the people who remained in Antioch made constant supplication to God for pardon, weeping and throwing themselves headlong in the snow. Justinian (now sole emperor) and Theodora sent gifts for the rebuilding of the city, and as a propitiatory gesture the name of Antioch was changed to Theoupolis, "City of God."

Life in Antioch in these years was also very much concerned with the resumption of hostilities with the Persians, for the city was always a military headquarters and communications center of the first importance when campaigns were in progress on the eastern frontier. Fighting broke out again in A.D. 528, and in March of the following year the Arabs of al-Mundhir, the famous chief who was in the Persian service, made a swift raid that took them as far as the territory of Antioch. They burned property and killed numbers of people, and retreated with their captives and loot before the Roman troops could reach them.[15] The general Belisarius was appointed Master of the Soldiers, with headquarters in Antioch, to succeed Hypatius, who had not been able to deal with the raid; and in the middle of May the emperor's special envoy Hermogenes reached Antioch, en route to attempt negotiations (which eventually proved fruitless) with the Persians.[16]

[15] Malalas, p. 445, 1-7; John of Nikiu, *Chronicle*, xc, 79; Theophanes, p. 178, 7-15, ed. De Boor; Zachariah of Mitylene, *Chronicle*, viii, 5.

[16] Theophanes, p. 178, 15-22, ed. De Boor. A decree of Justinian (*Novella* 155), dated 1 February A.D. 533, which is addressed to the General Belisarius, shows that the general and the patriarch of Antioch, Ephraemius, were instructed to see that justice was done to a female minor of

The Persian war continued with annual campaigns, and in A.D. 531 a group of Christians who had been captured by the Arabs sent a message to the Patriarch Ephraemius begging him to raise money for their ransom. The captors allowed sixty days for the funds to be collected. When the petition was read in Antioch, the people, led by the patriarch, the clergy and the civil officials, took what they could of their own belongings to the treasuries of the various churches. Later there was a general public meeting and the people of the city placed their contributions on a carpet which had been spread on the ground. The ransom was dispatched and the captives were freed.[17]

One of the last major events in the history of Antioch is also, thanks to the historian Procopius' detailed and vivid account of it, one of the best known episodes in the city's life. The capture and sack of Antioch by the Persians in June, A.D. 540, was not only an almost unbelievable disaster in itself, but also one of the famous events of a reign that was notable for both its successes and its reverses.

In the spring of A.D. 540 large numbers of the troops stationed in Syria had been withdrawn and sent to Italy, which Belisarius was reconquering for the empire, and the Persians in their invasion of this year had an army large enough to overcome the very limited Roman defense forces that had been left. The Persian expedition, it was plain from its activities, was directed, not at the occupation of Syria or any part

---

the city, who had sent the emperor a complaint that her mother was not discharging properly her duties as a guardian, and was not rendering satisfactory accountings of her financial responsibilities. This document indicates that during the troubled period of the Persian wars the routine administration of justice had ceased to function normally in Antioch, and that it was necessary for the emperor to call upon such officials as the general and the patriarch for the redress of what seems to have been a serious wrong.

[17] Malalas, p. 460, 10ff.

of it, but at doing the maximum damage and collecting the maximum loot.[18]

When he learned of the initial Persian successes and realized that Antioch itself would be threatened, Justinian sent his relative Germanus to Antioch to inspect the fortifications and make sure that they were in order after the recent earthquakes. Justinian promised to send Germanus in time "a numerous army." Germanus found that the fortifications were not in perfect order, but the engineers claimed that it would not be possible to repair them before the Persians could be expected to arrive, and they pointed out that if the enemy did reach Antioch and found the repair work in progress, they would discover the weak points at once. As a consequence, nothing was done. Reports kept coming of the Persians' continued advance, and no Roman reinforcements arrived; evidently it was impossible to find them.

The people of Antioch, believing that the Persians would be able to capture the city if they tried, decided to attempt to save it by offering the Persians a ransom in cash—a device which could be expected to appeal to the Persians. The Patriarch Ephraemius was in favor of such an offer, and the popular support of the idea must have been great, for we do not hear that it was opposed by Germanus.

Megas, the bishop of Beroea, which was in the path of the Persians, had come to Antioch to seek aid and counsel; and he was chosen to go to King Chosroes to negotiate the ransom. After four days of continuous travel he found the Persian king and his troops not far from Hierapolis. Chosroes agreed to accept a large payment in gold, and Megas started to return with the news, while the Persians moved on Beroea.

[18] The principal source for this campaign is Procopius' account, *Wars*, II, 5-8. A detailed study of the military operations and of the negotiations, and of Procopius' use of his sources, has been made by G. Downey, "The Persian Campaign in Syria in A.D. 540," *Speculum*, XXVIII, 1953, pp. 340-348. The present account condenses part of this study, and also adds some new considerations.

Reaching Antioch ten days, or perhaps a little more, after he had left it, Megas found that the situation had changed. While he had been away, there had arrived in Antioch two envoys of the emperor, John and Julian, who had been dispatched by Justinian to negotiate with Chosroes. Evidently the emperor had realized that it would not be possible to find a force capable of stopping the Persians, and that it might be possible to save the people of Syria and their cities by the offer of a money settlement. As was proper in the circumstances, the ambassadors were instructed to forbid negotiation by the cities of individual ransoms, a process which would in the end be much more costly and would hamper future diplomatic dealings. In order to obtain the latest news of the situation, the ambassadors first visited Antioch, the military headquarters.

At the same time that the ambassadors were prepared to negotiate a general ransom with Chosroes, it was hoped that it would be possible to defend at least Antioch if that should prove necessary. Now that the direction and purpose of the Persian march were known, it would be possible to detach some of the Roman troops stationed along the southern part of the border, and an order was issued from Constantinople summoning six thousand troops from the Lebanon region to reinforce the garrison at Antioch. This was a sizeable force in those days, and one that could be expected to put up a real resistance in the fortifications of Antioch. There were mixed reactions within the city. There seems to have been a substantial party, represented by the Patriarch Ephraemius, which thought it would be better in the long run to purchase the city's immunity, and escape the horrors of a siege, by the payment of a ransom. Some people indeed began to flee from the city. A conference was held at which Megas was unable to persuade the men in command to go through with the agreement to pay the ransom. The patriarch held out for payment of a ransom, and was as a consequence charged with treason by the envoy Julian, who argued that a ransom would simply amount to turning over the city to the Persians, who on other occasions had accepted the ransom of a city and then had pillaged it and killed or enslaved the inhabitants. This had already been done, during the present campaign, at Sura. As a result of this conference, the patriarch found it necessary or prudent to leave Antioch, and went to Cilicia. Germanus departed not long after.

After he learned that the ransom he had negotiated would not be paid, Bishop Megas set out in haste to take this news to Chosroes—an action which required a good bit of courage, since the king might choose to make the bishop suffer for his disappointment. It was known in Antioch that Chosroes was now at Beroea, and more of the people of the city began to leave. There would have been a general exodus, the historian Procopius writes, if the six thousand troops from the Lebanon had not arrived.

The city waited. In due time the Persians came, and encamped along the Orontes. Chosroes sent his interpreter, the renegade Greek Paul, up to the walls, to announce the Persian demand for the ransom which had been agreed upon, though it seemed plain, Procopius writes, that Chosroes would have accepted less. Paul's appearance must have been especially distasteful to the people of Antioch, since he had been brought up in the city and had gone to school there.

Nothing resulted from Paul's message, and on the same day Justinian's ambassadors went to Chosroes and conferred with him, trying to arrange terms, but without result. On the following day, the people of Antioch mounted the battlements and shouted insults at Chosroes; and when the despised Paul appeared again and began to urge the people to pay a ransom, they shot at him with their arrows and nearly killed him. Upon this Chosroes decided to assault the wall.

The next day the attack was begun at several points along the river, and also on the top of the mountain. Mount Silpius was the vulnerable point since the ground outside the wall sloped away gently (not precipitously, as it did inside the city), and so made it possible for troops and siege engines to be brought into place relatively easily; and once a part of the wall could be occupied, the attackers would be in a commanding position and could shoot down into the city at their ease. It was on the top of the mountain that the Persians made their successful entry when they captured Antioch in the middle of the third century, as Chosroes doubtless knew.

At first the Romans met the Persians with equal strength, and the young men of the circus factions, who were trained and armed as a citizen militia, fought effectively alongside the soldiers. The Romans had brought a larger number of troops into action, and increased their fire power substantially, by constructing platforms of timbers and suspending them between the towers of the wall, so that an additional line of men could fight standing on the platforms as they hung over the heads of the troops stationed on the battlements.

As the fighting continued, it seemed on even terms, a sudden accident put an end of the Roman resistance. The ropes binding together the timbers of one of the platforms proved unable to bear the weight imposed on them, and broke. The platform fell to the ground with a great crash, followed by the confused cries of the soldiers who had fallen with it. The Roman troops who were out of sight of the accident, not knowing what had happened, supposed that the noise meant that the wall itself had been breached. The Roman lines immediately gave way and the men turned and fled down the side of the mountain into the city. Though the troops had given up, the young men of the circus factions stayed together in the streets and prepared to continue fighting. The regular soldiers did not stop but seized what horses they could find and rode off toward the city gates, which the Persians had refrained from attacking. The soldiers shouted that the Roman general Bouzes, with the mobile field force which thus far had avoided an engagement with the Persians, had arrived and was ready to join forces with the garrison, and they said they were going out to meet him. Seeing the soldiers in what looked like flight, the citizens began to rush toward the gates, where many of them were thrown to the ground in the crush and trampled by the mounted soldiers.

Meanwhile the Persians had been taking possession of the walls. They did not at first advance down the mountain, whether because they feared an ambush, or because Chosroes wished to give the Roman troops a chance to get out of the city so that he could occupy and pillage it more easily. Most of the Romans, with their commanders, were thus able to get away through the gate that led to Daphne, for the Persians had left this gate free while they seized the others. When the troops, and some of the populace, had left, the Persians descended into the city, but then they encountered the young men of the factions who were determined to continue resistance. Some of them were in heavy armor, though the majority were unarmed and could only use stones as missiles. The young men at first seemed to have the upper hand, and once even drove the Persians back. But Chosroes' troops brought up reinforcements and the Roman resistance was halted, whereupon the Persians began to kill everyone they encountered.

Chosroes then ordered his men to round up the survivors and hold them as captives, to be taken back to Persia as slaves. The pillaging of the city was begun,[19] and Chosroes, accompanied by the imperial ambassadors, went down into the city and made his way to the Great Church. Here he found the costly treasure of the church's gold and silver fittings and offerings, which had been left in place and not hidden or carried away. These made wonderful booty for the Persians, and Chosroes also had many of the ornamental

---

[19] See above, n. 12.

marbles removed from the church to be taken back to Persia. Chosroes then directed that after it had been pillaged, the whole city was to be burned. The Great Church was spared, at the instance of the imperial ambassadors, who pointed out that this church had furnished the Persians an abundance of loot.

The city (except for the church) was then burned systematically, though the southern quarter called the Kerateion escaped because there was an open space between it and the rest of the city. The Persians also burned the suburbs, except for the sanctuary of St. Julian and the dwellings attached to it, about three miles outside the city, where the imperial ambassadors had taken up their lodgings. The fortifications were left untouched, presumably because it would have taken the Persians too long to wreck them.

The consequences of the catastrophe at Antioch were many. In addition to being one of the greatest possible blows to the prestige of the empire, it added to the hostility toward the central government, which many people in Syria already felt as a result of the nationalistic movement. The material loss was very severe, for in addition to the waste of all the money that had been spent on reconstruction after the earthquakes of A.D. 526 and 528, Justinian felt obliged to spend a further large sum rebuilding the city; and the temporary halting of the city's commercial activities, coupled with what must have been a marked drop in the population, meant that there would be a real loss to the government in current revenue.

The reconstruction is described by Procopius, and from his account, and the independent witness of the archaeological evidence, we learn that the new Antioch which rose out of the devastation was much smaller than it had formerly been.[20] The new main street, for example, occupied only

[20] The description of the reconstruction of the city appears in Procopius' *Buildings*, II, 10, 2-25. An analysis of this account will be found in G.

the width of one of the sidewalks of the older colonnaded street.[21] Because of the recent loss of population, whole areas inside the lower part of the circuit wall were uninhabited, and the line of the wall was now reduced and straightened to make it more defensible. At the same time, better use was made of the Orontes as a defense by diverting the course of the river, so that it ran as near the wall as possible (Fig. 5).[22] Procopius' account also seems to suggest that at this time the island was abandoned as a part of the city.

Improvements were likewise made in the wall on Mount Silpius. The region within the fortifications on the top of the mountain was leveled and provided with better communications with the city. Baths and reservoirs were built inside the defenses, and a cistern for the storage of rain water was provided at each tower in the wall.

One feature of Justinian's work is still partly preserved, namely the Iron Gate, often called by its Arabic name, Bab el-Hadid (Fig. 9). This device was intended to control the winter torrent Parmenius whose flooding had been a problem since the city was founded, and Justinian now repaired or improved the dam fitted with sluice-gates which had been built in the circuit-wall to control the flow of the water. Part of the stream was diverted in a new channel, north of the main bed of the torrent.[23]

According to Procopius, the city had been so thoroughly burned and wrecked that nothing was left but mounds of

---

Downey, "Procopius on Antioch: A Study of Method in the *De aedificiis*," *Byzantion*, xiv, 1939, pp. 361-378. On the writing of the *Buildings* and its sources, see G. Downey, "The Composition of Procopius, *De aedificiis*," *T.A.P.A.*, lxxviii, 1947, pp. 171-183, and "Notes on Procopius, *De aedificiis*, Book I," *Studies Presented to D. M. Robinson on his Seventieth Birthday*, II, St. Louis, 1953, pp. 719-725.

[21] For the archaeological evidence see *Antioch-on-the-Orontes*, III, pp. 13f, 16.

[22] See *Antioch-on-the-Orontes*, III, p. 19.

[23] Evidence of this was found in the excavations; see *Antioch-on-the-Orontes*, III, p. 6.

ruins, and people were not even able to recognize the sites of their own houses. Forums, main streets, and side streets no longer existed. Justinian first had the whole city cleared of debris and then the streets, colonnades, and forums were freshly laid out. The water supply and the sewers were restored, and the necessary public buildings, including theaters and baths, were replaced. Laborers and craftsmen were brought to Antioch to help build the houses. The large Church of the Virgin was rebuilt and endowed with a generous income. There was also built a large Church of the Archangel Michael. The emperor likewise ordered the construction of hospitals for the sick poor, for men and women separately, and provided guest-houses for strangers who were visiting the city.[24]

Two years after the sack by the Persians, when the rebuilding of the city was still in progress, Antioch, along with the rest of the empire, suffered from a devastating visitation of the bubonic plague. Originating in Abyssinia, the plague spread through the empire from Egypt, reaching Antioch in A.D. 542 and Constantinople in the same year. In the capital it caused the death of two out of every four or five persons, and the normal activities of the city were completely disorganized. At Antioch, coming after so many other disasters, this must have seemed a final blow to the city's prosperity.

The effects of the arrival of the plague at Antioch and the symptoms it produced are described in a notable passage in the *Ecclesiastical History* of Evagrius, who had the plague himself as a boy in Antioch, but survived it.[25] There is also a

[24] Procopius notes early in the treatise on Justinian's buildings (I, 3, 1-2) that the emperor had a special interest in churches of the Virgin and built a number of them in all parts of the empire; and the frequency with which Procopius lists churches of the Archangel Michael built by Justinian indicates that the Archangel was another special object of the emperor's devotion.

[25] Evagrius, *Hist. eccl.*, IV, 29.

curious account of it in the biography of St. Symeon Stylites the Younger, who had taken the place of the elder Symeon as protector of Antioch. The younger Symeon was born at Antioch about A.D. 521, and had been named for the elder Stylite.[26] When he was a child, he lived in the quarter at the southern end of the city called the Cherubim, where the old gate stood on top of which Titus had placed some representations of cherubim as part of the spoils of the fall of Jerusalem. When the southern wall of the city was enlarged by Theodosius the Younger, the Gate of the Cherubim, as it had come to be known, was replaced by a new portal called the Daphne Gate; but the old gate, or part of it, remained standing, and in Symeon's childhood there were still to be seen traces of the old wall. The whole region of the Kerateion at this period was regarded as having special religious associations. It possessed an image of Christ which was an object of particular veneration, and on one occasion a holy man dreamed that Christ emerged from the image and spoke to him. Here, on the old city wall, while he was a child, Symeon had a vision of Christ accompanied by "the multitude of the just."

Symeon first mounted a column at the age of seven years. In time he became permanently established on his pillar on the Miraculous Mountain near the Orontes between Antioch and Seleucia Pieria; and here, through his holiness and his miracles, he came to exert a wide influence, especially at Antioch. He was frequently consulted by the people of the city, and he rendered aid in local crises. Pictures and medallions of Symeon were manufactured,[27] and the citizens, grateful for healing, set up images of the saint in their

[26] The *editio princeps* of the complete text of the biography of St. Symeon the Younger will be published by P. Van den Ven in *Subsidia Hagiographica*.

[27] For a study of one of these medallions, see P. Lesley, "An Echo of Early Christianity," *Art Quarterly*, II, 1939, pp. 215-232.

houses. There is a report of one of these which possessed miraculous powers.[28]

Symeon's biographer relates that when the plague was brought to Antioch by the devil, a throng of the people went to the Miraculous Mountain, as they would always do in such a calamity, to tell the saint of this new and great misfortune which had come to the "Gate of Syria," as one of the gates of the city is called here (this seems to have been the gate at the northern end of the city which led to Beroea and the greater part of Syria). The saint's mother, the blessed Martha, who dwelt at the foot of his pillar, bade her son pray that the place of his birth might be delivered from this manifestation of the divine anger. When Sunday dawned, the saint began to pray, and he then seemed to himself to be caught up by the Holy Spirit and borne to Antioch by a multitude of angels. When he reached the "Gate of Syria," he stood facing the east and prayed. It was granted to him in the dream to have his petition fulfilled for that part of the city only, and the mourning ceased in the region about that gate. The devil then took the plague to the gate at the southern end of the city, which led to Daphne, and there now arose a wailing in the Kerateion, which lay in that quarter, and the mourning extended from the Cherubim to the quarter called the Rhodion. When day came, Symeon recounted this vision to his mother Martha; and a multitude of people came to the saint and described to him their affliction.

As the plague continued, one of Symeon's disciples named Conon died of it, and was brought back to life through the prayers of the saint. The plague came to an end in a miraculous manner.[29] A monk named Thomas, member of a mon-

---

[28] See a passage from an unpublished life of Symeon printed by K. Holl, *Gesammelte Aufsätze zur Kirchengeschichte*, II: *Der Osten*, Tübingen, 1928, pp. 390f.

[29] The story of St. Thomas at Antioch is preserved in two versions which differ in some details; cf. Evagrius, *op.cit.*, IV, 35, and the *Pratum spirituale* of John Moschus, *P.G.* LXXXVII, pt. 3, col. 2945.

astery in the region of Apamea, came to Antioch on business of his community. While in Antioch he became ill of the plague, and died in Daphne—in the public hospital or in the Church of St. Euphemia, according to different accounts. His body was placed in the common grave outside Daphne, at the place called Elephanton, in which it was the custom to bury strangers who died in Daphne. When other burials in the common grave were made, it was noticed that Thomas' body always showed signs of supernatural power. This portentous phenomenon was reported to the patriarch of Antioch, and Thomas' remains were taken to Antioch in a festal procession and given suitable burial in the famous cemetery outside the Daphne Gate, where other distinguished religious figures had been buried. The presence of his body put an end to the plague in Antioch, and a small oratory was built over Thomas' tomb, and it became the custom of the people of Antioch to celebrate an annual festival in his honor.

We have a record of a prosecution in Constantinople, in A.D. 562, of a group of pagan priests, one of whom came from Athens, two from Antioch, and two from Hierapolis (Baalbek).[30] Justinian throughout his reign carried on a vigorous persecution of pagans and heretics, and the evidence for this late episode, preserved by chance, reminds us that earlier in Justinian's time there were many other trials for which we have no surviving records. It is characteristic of the history of the tenacity of paganism at this period to find the names of Antioch, Athens, and Hierapolis linked together.

The reign of Justinian's nephew Justin II (A.D. 565-578) opens what has been called "one of the most cheerless periods in Byzantine history," during which the state, weakened by the effort necessary for Justinian's ambitious undertakings, suffered from both political disorder and straitened means. This epoch, which lasted until the accession of Heraclius in

---

[30] Michael the Syrian, *Chronicle*, ii, p. 271, transl. Chabot.

A.D. 610, is a singularly obscure one in the history of Antioch, now declining in size and importance.

Hostilities with Persia, which had come to an end in A.D. 561, broke out again in A.D. 572, when Justin refused to pay the annual tribute which the empire had been engaged to send to Persia. The resumption of the war brought with it all the military activities that centered in Antioch during fighting with Persia. In A.D. 573 the Persian commander Adharmahan, with a force of mailed cavalry and Arab auxiliaries, made a raid into Syria, where the imperial forces were so weak that it seemed that the Persians would once more reach Antioch. We are told that the news of the Persians' approach produced disorders in the city. The walls were in ruins, not having been repaired after earthquakes that had occurred in A.D. 551 and 557, and there was only a weak garrison. The people must have been bitter against the government and the local authorities for leaving the city so badly protected. As the Persians continued to approach, many of the citizens fled, as did the Patriarch Gregory, taking with him the treasures of the churches. The Persians, when they came, did not in fact capture the city, but burned the suburbs, including the famous Church of St. Julian. They then went on to take Seleucia Pieria.[31]

Four years later, in A.D. 577, a severe earthquake destroyed the whole of Daphne though the damage at Antioch itself was not serious.[32]

At about this same time we have a record of an accusation of paganism in Antioch which not only furnishes another reminder of the persistence of the old cults in the city but shows what bitter feelings could be stirred up, and what false charges could be put about, when there was suspicion of pagan practice.

[31] Evagrius, *Hist. eccl.*, v, 9; Theophanes, p. 247, 8-10, ed. De Boor; John of Epiphania, frag. 4 (*F.H.G.*, IV, p. 275).
[32] Evagrius, *Hist. eccl.*, v, 17.

The story concerns both Gregory, the patriarch of Antioch, and Anatolius, the local representative of the praetorian prefect stationed in Edessa.[33] It is related that serious tension developed in Heliopolis, a strong center of paganism, between the pagans, who were in the majority in the city, and the Christians. When the pagans threatened to destroy them, the Christians appealed to the emperor, who dispatched a special commissioner, Theophilus, to deal with the unbelievers. He instituted an investigation, and the pagan leaders were arrested and examined. On being tortured, they named associates "in every district and city in their land, but especially at Antioch the Great." They described as high priest in Antioch one Rufinus. Theophilus sent an officer to arrest him. It was found that Rufinus had left Antioch to make a visit to Edessa. The imperial officials came upon him there while he was performing a sacrifice to Zeus, but—knowing the torture that awaited him—he succeeded in committing suicide on the spot. Some of the people present, on being questioned, named the official Anatolius as an associate. Taken to Antioch for examination, Anatolius and his secretary Theodore were driven to make confessions in which they accused Gregory, the patriarch of Antioch, and a priest named Eulogius (later patriarch of Alexandria) of having been present with them at the sacrifice of a boy, performed in Daphne. This report caused a commotion in the whole city and it is said that Gregory did not dare leave his residence. It was reported that Anatolius bribed the Count of the East, and was nearly acquitted, but that a mob prevented his release. Suspicion was worked up to such a point that the emperor ordered Anatolius and his companions to be brought to Constantinople and made to tell the truth about the patriarch. At this point, Anatolius' wickedness in accusing the patriarch was plainly demonstrated when an ikon of the

[33] Evagrius, *Hist. eccl.*, v, 18; John of Ephesus, III, 26-34, pp. 209-227, transl. R. Payne Smith.

Virgin, to which he had appealed in his prison, turned its face away from him. When this became known to the prison guards, it was taken as a sure sign of Anatolius' iniquity; and in addition the Mother of God appeared in a vision to some of the faithful and declared Anatolius' guilt.

When Anatolius was taken to Constantinople, the trial aroused great excitement, and when some of Anatolius' associates were condemned to exile, and not to death, a crowd seized them and killed them, and began to accuse the emperor and the Patriarch of Constantinople of betraying the faith. Finally Anatolius and his secretary were put to death, with barbarous cruelty. The Patriarch Gregory was acquitted after he had gone to Constantinople himself.

There is a report of one further event of great interest at Antioch at this time, namely the receipt in the city of a piece of the True Cross which had been preserved at Apamea. At the time of an earthquake at Constantinople, the emperor had been advised to send for this precious relic from Apamea, in the hope that it would protect the imperial city. The fragment was removed from Apamea—with some difficulty, for the people of the city were indignant at its loss. It was taken to Antioch where it was sawn in two lengthwise, so that one of the halves could be sent to the capital and the other returned to Apamea.[34]

We do not have a connected history of the city during the reign of Maurice (A.D. 582-602), but we do happen to possess a considerable amount of information about events in the years A.D. 588-589. The Patriarch Gregory once more is the leading figure. First we hear of a quarrel between the patriarch and the Count of the East, Asterius. Our source is the historian Evagrius, who was the patriarch's legal assist-

[34] This story is preserved by Michael the Syrian, *Chronicle*, ii, p. 285, transl. Chabot. Presumably Antioch was chosen for the partition of the relic because of the disorder which had been provoked at Apamea, and also because Antioch, as an apostolic foundation, was a suitable place for such an operation.

ant. Evagrius, as an admirer of the patriarch, does not mention what the origin of the unpleasantness was.[35] Given the religious and political circumstances of the time, this kind of dissension between the chief civil and religious dignitaries of the city cannot have been uncommon, and there must have been a number of similar episodes, involving other patriarchs, of which we do not hear; and so Evagrius' accounts of Gregory's involvements are valuable since they suggest a state of local feeling, and its developments, which must have been fairly typical. The structure of the government and of society in the Greek Christian state had become such that the bishop or patriarch was in effect the true leader of the people in both secular and religious matters, and in certain circumstances his prestige and influence were much greater than those of the local government officials. An inevitable result was that there was a natural state of rivalry between the secular authorities and the bishops.

On this occasion, Evagrius tells us, the whole city took the part of the Count of the East, and all kinds of insults against the patriarch were going about in the streets and in the theater, where the actors saw a good opportunity and joined with the townspeople. The clamor grew to such proportions that Asterius, as the official responsible for public order in Antioch, was removed from office, and his successor John was appointed with instructions to conduct an investigation of the disorders, though, Evagrius says, he was not in the least capable of carrying out such a commission.

When the investigation began, the whole city continued to be filled with uproar; and now a local money changer filed a written charge that the patriarch had had incestuous relations with his own sister, a married woman. From other similar sources came accusations that Gregory had caused disturbances of the public peace. The patriarch declared himself ready to answer all these charges, and on the accusation of

[35] Evagrius, *Hist. eccl.*, VI, 7.

incest he asked to be judged by the emperor and a civil and religious court. Taking Evagrius with him as his legal adviser, Gregory journeyed to Constantinople, where he was acquitted by a tribunal composed of the other patriarchs (or their representatives), a number of metropolitan bishops, and the Senate of Constantinople. His accuser was whipped in public and then paraded through the streets and sent into exile.

Gregory and Evagrius returned to Antioch at about the time when a mutiny of the imperial troops near Edessa was assuming serious proportions. This mutiny occurred when the new commander of the eastern front, Priscus, took up his duties at the fortress of Monokarton in Mesopotamia. Priscus, whose appointment had created considerable interest, and some dissatisfaction, had passed through Antioch en route to his new command.[36] He had the bad luck to be the bearer of an order which had the effect of reducing the troops' pay; and when he reached the camp, his arrogant behavior, combined with the loss of their wages, drove the troops to mutiny, on 21 April A.D. 588. The emperor was in time forced to remove Priscus and reappoint the former commander, Philippicus, but this still did not satisfy the troops, and the mutiny was continuing when Gregory returned to Antioch from Constantinople in June A.D. 588.[37]

The troops in the mean time had chosen a leader of their own, named Germanus, and were carrying on operations against the Persians during the summer; but they still refused to accept Philippicus as general.

When the autumn came, and the mutiny still continued, Antioch suffered from another severe earthquake.[38] This occurred at nine o'clock in the evening of the last day of October—which happened to be the day on which Evagrius

---

[36] Theophanes, p. 260, 4ff ed. De Boor; Theophylactus Simocatta, III, 1, p. 112, 13 Bonn ed.

[37] Evagrius, *Hist. eccl.*   [38] Evagrius, *Hist. eccl.*, VI, 8.

was being married. The whole city was shaken and many buildings were destroyed when their foundations were thrown up out of the ground. The whole of the Great Church was demolished, except for the dome, which the Patriarch Ephraemius had rebuilt with cypress wood from the grove at Daphne after the earthquake of A.D. 526. The dome had been tilted toward the north, Evagrius says, by the subsequent earthquakes (in A.D. 551, 557 and 577). It had remained in this position, braced with timbers, and then the shocks of A.D. 588 set it back in place.

Most of the quarter called Ostrakine, the Psephion, and the whole of the quarter called Byrsia, were destroyed. All the dependencies which surrounded the Church of the Virgin were thrown down, while, paradoxically, the colonnade of the courtyard around the church escaped. All the towers of the city wall surrounding the level part of the city were destroyed, though the walls themselves remained unharmed except for the battlements, which were in places tilted inward but did not fall. Other churches were destroyed, as well as the two public baths which were specially designed for use in the summer and in the winter. It was estimated, from the decline in the consumption of bread (the baking of which was officially supervised) that 60,000 persons were killed.

The Patriarch Gregory was saved, contrary to all expectation. His residence was totally destroyed, but the patriarch and those who happened to be with him were unhurt; and when another earth shock made an opening in the ruins, Gregory was let down to safety by a rope. The patriarch's enemy, the former Count of the East, Asterius, was killed. There was one divine dispensation, Evagrius notes, in that the earthquake produced no conflagration, although the city contained many fires in ordinary use, in hearths, public and private lamps, kitchens, ovens, baths and many other places.

As was customary on such occasions, the emperor made a

grant of money for relief work and restoration of the damage; but Evagrius does not add any details of the reconstruction.

The mutiny of the imperial troops in Syria which has been mentioned continued during the winter,[39] and while the soldiers obeyed Germanus, their own comrade whom they had chosen as leader, they still refused to receive the general Philippicus, whom the emperor had appointed to replace the unpopular Priscus. The Patriarch Gregory was now called upon by the authorities to try to bring the troops back to obedience.[40] Not only could he bring to bear upon the soldiers the tremendous prestige of his office, but he enjoyed great personal popularity because he often distributed gifts of money among the troops, and he had also been accustomed to supply recruits with money and food when they were on their way to join the service. Gregory undertook this mission, and sent out messengers summoning two thousand of the officers and most influential private soldiers to meet with him at Litarba, a road junction on the road between Antioch and Beroea. When the soldiers were assembled, during Holy Week, early in April A.D. 589, Gregory made a speech in which—according to the preserved report— he skillfully employed praise and flattery, and also made an official promise of full pardon for the mutiny. The soldiers were won over, and agreed to accept Philippicus for their commander; and to seal the reconciliation, the patriarch thereupon celebrated the holy communion in the open air. Gregory returned to Antioch the following day, and a messenger was sent for Philippicus, who was then at Tarsus on his way to Constantinople. He returned to Antioch and there met the soldiers, who had followed Gregory, and there was a ceremony at which the troops pledged their obedience and the general confirmed the amnesty.

[39] Theophylactus Simocatta, III, 4, p. 119, 18, Bonn ed.

[40] Evagrius, *Hist. eccl.*, VI, 11-13, describes the patriarch's mission, and its result, in detail, and gives the text of the address which he made to the soldiers.

In A.D. 602 the emperor Maurice was overthrown by a rebellion which began in the army, and the usurper Phocas (A.D. 602-610) got possession of the throne, murdering Maurice and his sons. Phocas' eight years in power were a reign of terror during which the empire grew steadily weaker. The government lost ground both in military strength and in the authority it exercised in its own cities and provinces. In addition, Syria and Egypt were weakened by the growing discontent of the Monophysites and their open opposition to the government, and there were continual factional disorders which were at least in part connected with the religious and political tensions. Naturally the Persians lost no opportunity to take advantage of what really amounted to a state of anarchy in the imperial territory.

The literary sources for this period are not extensive, and they have so much to report in the way of intrigue and violence throughout the empire that Antioch, among so many cities in the throes of disorder, is only seldom mentioned. In two successive years—ca. A.D. 606 and 607—Syria is said to have been "overrun" by the Persians, with large numbers of people led into captivity. Antioch is not mentioned by name in the tradition concerning these raids, but the presumption is that it would have been captured, or at least assaulted, in such large-scale operations as these raids seem to have been.[41]

In keeping with the history of the remainder of the empire at this epoch, the only specific picture of events at Antioch under Phocas is a meager but sensational record of a riot—or series of disorders—followed by repression which is described as being of the utmost brutality.

[41] The tradition of these raids is preserved in Theophanes, who places them in successive years (pp. 293, 23-26; 295, 14-16 ed. De Boor). The Armenian historian Sebeos (*Histoire d'Héraclius par l'évêque Sebêos, trad. de l'arménien par F. Macler*, Paris, 1904, ch. 23, p. 62) states that in one of these raids the people of Antioch submitted willingly to the Persians, hoping to escape the cruelties of Phocas.

This episode is dated in September, A.D. 610, the last month of Phocas' reign.[42] Two sources—one contemporary, the other written twenty years after the event—indicate that there were factional disorders, perhaps related to similar outbreaks elsewhere in the empire, and that the Patriarch Anastasius, who must now have been a very old man, was killed by troops.[43] How he was involved is not stated; the presumption is that he lost his life either by accident, or because he was leading some action which had to be opposed. The Count of the East, Bonosus, was given a force of soldiers and proceeded to punish the rioters in the most savage fashion. There is a report that the Jews took advantage of Bonosus' mission to attack the Christians under the pretext of helping to chastise the offending circus faction.

An even more sensational tradition, which appears in later sources and in somewhat greater detail, describes the original outbreak wholly in terms of fighting between Jews and Christians. The Jews, it is said, murdered the Patriarch

[42] Chronicon Paschale, p. 699, 16-18, Bonn ed.; Theophanes, p. 296, 17-25, ed. De Boor.

[43] The contemporary source is the Greek document called the *Doctrina Iacobi nuper baptizati*, ed. N. Bonwetsch, *Abhandlungen d. k. Gesellschaft d. Wissenschaften zu Göttingen, philol.-histor. Kl.*, N.F. xii, no. 3, 1910. This is a discussion of the Christian teaching, written by one of the Jews who were forcibly converted at Phocas' orders, and addressed to other newly baptized Jews. The author gives examples of his ignorance and hatred of Christianity before his conversion. In ch. 40, p. 39, 7-9, he tells how, when Bonosus was punishing the Greens in Antioch, he himself went to the city and, in the guise of a Blue and a friend of the emperor, pretended to take part in the punishment of the Greens, and in this way was able to inflict many sufferings on the Christians—which was his real object. This document has been shown to be valuable in other connections for the information it gives concerning the factional disorders under Phocas; cf. Y. Janssens, "Les Bleus et les Verts sous Maurice, Phocas et Héraclius," *Byzantion*, xi, 1936, pp. 520, 530. The other source for this period is the *Chronicon Paschale*, compiled soon after A.D. 629, by an author at Alexandria who might himself remember the events under Phocas. Here it is said that Anastasius was killed by troops, and that Bonosus inflicted the most severe punishment on the city (pp. 699, 16-18; 700, 4-6, Bonn ed.).

Anastasius, mutilated his body and dragged it along the main street and burned it, along with the bodies of many other people whom they killed. The Emperor Phocas sent the Count of the East and the general Kottanas to punish the guilty persons, and these officials collected troops in Cilicia, went to Antioch, and inflicted severe chastisement, which put an end to the disorders.[44] A background for this report is supplied by the texts which describe hostilities between the Jews and the Christians elsewhere in the empire under Phocas. It is said that the Jews in Syria and Mesopotamia had plotted to massacre the Christians and defile their churches; that the plot was discovered and that the Christians joined with the imperial authorities in punishing the Jews; and that the Emperor Phocas levied fines on the Jews in Antioch, Laodicea, and elsewhere.[45]

The reign of Heraclius (A.D. 610-641), which began shortly after the disorders in Antioch, marked a turning-point in the history of the empire, and a beginning in the revival of its strength; but it was too late to save Syria from the Moslem invasion, and the history of Antioch as a city of the ancient classical world comes to an end at this time.

The accession of Heraclius did not put an end to the Persians' attacks on Syria, and in a new invasion (May A.D. 611) Edessa, Apamea, and Antioch were captured, with great loss of life among the Romans.[46] This time the Persians remained in Antioch.[47] We hear no details of the history

[44] Theophanes, *loc.cit.* (above, n. 42).

[45] Agapius of Menbidj, *Patrologia Orientalis*, VIII, p. 449.

[46] Theophanes, p. 299, 14-18, ed. De Boor; Michael the Syrian, *Chronicle*, II, p. 400 transl. Chabot.

[47] The Persian occupation of Antioch is confirmed by the absence of any coins of Heraclius issued by the mint of Antioch. One coin type of Heraclius which has been assigned to Antioch, in the years A.D. 616-17, was in reality struck at Seleucia in Isauria; see P. Grierson, "The Isaurian Coins of Heraclius," *Numismatic Chronicle*, ser. 6, vol. XI, 1951, pp. 56-59. Grierson points out that the mint of Antioch does not seem to have been open at all during the reign of Heraclius and that there are no coins from this

of the city during their occupation. However, it is said of the Persian occupation of Syria in general that Chosroes collected the treasures of all the churches in the occupied territory, and that he forced all the Christians under his control to become Nestorians.[48]

The city remained in the hands of the Persians during all the campaigns through which Heraclius reestablished the Roman power and finally defeated the Persians. It is recorded that during Heraclius' operations of A.D. 622, he fought a battle with the Persians "under the walls of Antioch," but the imperial troops were defeated.[49] When Chosroes was overthrown, in A.D. 628, and his son hastened to make peace with the Romans, Antioch and the other occupied cities were evacuated and the Roman captives in Persia were released.[50]

During these last few years of its history, we hear very little of the city. It is mentioned in connection with the efforts which Heraclius had been making for some time to find a means of reconciling the Monophysites and reuniting them with the orthodox element in the empire. Heraclius understood very well the political effects of the monophysite position, which had always tended to alienate the indigenous elements in Syria and Egypt from the orthodox population and from the central government; and when Syria and Egypt were actually occupied by the Persians, whom the Monophysites welcomed as bringing relief from imperial persecution, Heraclius saw the pressing need for some formula which would supply a bond between the monophy-

---

mint even during the period of Heraclius' reign, October A.D. 610—summer A.D. 611, before the Persian invasion. There are likewise no coins of Heraclius from the mint of Antioch during the period between the Persian evacuation of the city, in A.D. 628, and the Arab conquest a few years later.

[48] Theophanes, p. 314, 23-26, ed. De Boor.
[49] Sebeos, ch. 24, p. 67 transl. Macler.
[50] Theophanes, p. 327, 10-16, ed. De Boor.

site Christians in the occupied lands and their orthodox brethren within the empire. However, the emperor was unsuccessful in his efforts to find a solution that would be agreeable to everyone.

The final loss of Antioch came very quickly. In the sweeping expansion of the Arabs, when so many cities and strongholds in Palestine and Syria were being occupied one after the other, we hear relatively little of Antioch. When the Moslems began their attack on this part of the imperial territory in A.D. 634, Heraclius made Antioch his headquarters; but when the overwhelming Arab victory at the battle of the Yarmuk (August A.D. 636) made it plain that it would not be possible to save Syria, the emperor left Antioch and retired to Constantinople.[51] In 16 a. H. (= February, A.D. 637—January, A.D. 638) the Moslem forces advanced on the main cities in northwestern Syria.[52] It was an easy conquest and the Monophysites were not altogether sorry to find themselves free from the orthodox government that had persecuted them. The Arabs offered the inhabitants the choice of leaving, or remaining and paying tribute. Planning a prompt occupation of the key cities, the Arabs moved on Kinnesrin (Chalcis), which was a military center. Here they met some resistance, though the city soon surrendered. A force of imperial troops managed to escape from Chalcis and reached Antioch. When the Arabs arrived, however, the city made little resistance, and was soon sur-

[51] See the Arab historian al-Balâdhuri, pp. 175f, 189, 210, transl. Hitti; Elias of Nisibis, *Chronicle*, ad ann. 15, p. 64 transl. Brooks (*Corpus Scr. Christ. Orient., Scr. Syri*, ser. 3, tome VII); Theophanes, p. 337, 8-10, ed. De Boor. See P. K. Hitti, *History of the Arabs*, 6 ed., London and New York, 1956, pp. 152f. The sources for this part of the Arab advance, and the capture of Antioch, are translated and evaluated by L. Caetani, *Annali dell'Islam*, III, Milan, 1910, pp. 794f, 800, 816-818; cf. the same scholar's *Chronographia Islamica*, I, Paris, 1912, pp. 180, 191.

[52] The account of al-Balâdhuri, p. 211, transl. Hitti, of the way in which the Christians and Jews in Syria welcomed Moslem rule is not entirely an exaggeration.

rendered on the terms which the Arabs were offering everywhere; and some of the inhabitants left.[53] The Arab sources make it plain that the conquerors regarded the possession of Antioch as a matter of the first importance, and a strong garrison was stationed in it.[54] We have a report that Antioch, like some others of the newly occupied cities, very soon rebelled against the new masters and had to be subdued by force, but the details of this tradition do not seem to be entirely trustworthy.[55]

This brings to an end the history of Antioch as a city of the Graeco-Roman world. There was a notable exodus of refugees from Antioch and Syria at this time. A number went to the western part of the empire. At Milan, for example, one finds the cults of St. Babylas and St. Romanus, who were specifically Antiochene saints, and the plan of the Church of San Lorenzo clearly reflects that of the great shrine at Seleucia Pieria which was recovered in the excavations. Since St. Babylas and St. Romanus were not commemorated elsewhere in Italy, it seems plain that it must have been refugees from Antioch and Seleucia who introduced into Milan these memorials of their homeland.[56]

The history of Antioch under the Arabs, the Crusaders and the Turks, which lies beyond the scope of this book, has already been written.[57] The life of the city at this period is

---

[53] Theophanes, p. 340, 12, ed. De Boor; Patriarch Nicephorus, *Historia Syntomos*, p. 23, 3f, ed. De Boor; Michael the Syrian, II, p. 421, transl. Chabot; al-Balâdhuri, *loc.cit.*; cf. Caetani, *locc.citt.*, and M. J. De Goeje, *Mémoire sur la conquête de la Syrie*, Leyden, 1900, p. 111.

[54] See al-Balâdhuri, p. 227, transl. Hitti.

[55] See al-Balâdhuri, pp. 213f, 227, 246, transl. Hitti. On the criticism of the sources, see Caetani, *Annali* (above, n. 51), III, pp. 817f.

[56] See U. Monneret de Villard, "Antiochia e Milano nel VI° secolo," *Orientalia Christiana Periodica*, XII, 1946, pp. 374-380.

[57] See for example Hitti, *History of the Arabs* (above, n. 51), and the monograph of C. Cahen, *La Syrie du Nord à l'époque des Croisades et la principauté franque d'Antioche*, Paris, 1940; also M. Gaudefroy-Demom-

well known, and we have several Arabic descriptions of Antioch. We also learn, from the intellectual history of both the Arab and the Byzantine states, something of the share of Antioch in the transmission of the scientific and philosophical legacy of the Greeks to Islam.

After more than three centuries of Arab rule, Antioch was recaptured by the Byzantine army of Nicephorus II Phocas in A.D. 969, and served as an outpost of the Byzantine Empire for more than a century, until in A.D. 1084 it was taken by the Seljuk Turks. In A.D. 1098, after a long and famous siege, the city was captured by the Crusaders under Bohemond and the Frankish principality of Antioch was founded. This lasted until A.D. 1268, when the city was taken by the Mamelukes under Bibars. It then remained under the Egyptian sultans until it passed into the control of the Ottoman Turks in A.D. 1517.

---

bynes, *La Syrie à l'époque des Mamelouks d'après les auteurs arabes*, Paris, 1923.

EPILOGUE:

THE LEGACY OF ANTIOCH

IN FULFILLING their functions as centers of civilization, Greek cities provided the environment for the growth of society and the formation, custody, and transmission of culture. Sometimes like Antioch, the city itself eventually disappeared, but left a heritage that had the power to survive the city's physical existence.

What of the legacy of Antioch? Although much of the ancient city is still buried, its creative role has become a part of the history of civilization. In the works of its artists, its theologians, its men of letters and historians, Antioch has made its characteristic and unique contribution to the civilization of our own day, mediated through Byzantium, and still present and active everywhere in the heritage absorbed into modern European culture, its elements rediscovered and analyzed by the scholars of our time. The material *testimonia* of the civilization of Antioch—the domestic and liturgical silver, jewelry, mosaics, sculpture, glassware—are to be seen in the museums of America and Europe, as well as in the museum built in Antakiya itself to house the local share of the archaeological finds. The writings of the Antiochene authors are better known than ever.

What is the significance of this legacy? Antioch had a mission not quite like the mission of any other city in the Graeco-Roman world. Founded as an outpost of Greek civilization in Semitic lands, it was destined from the beginning to bring together and amalgamate diverse threads of religion and culture.

Although it could not claim the antiquity of Athens or of the other great cities of the old Greek world, in its foundation and history Antioch possessed a living link with the great age of Greece, and this link only grew stronger as time went by. Not only in blood did Antioch think of itself as an off-shoot of Athens, but all the religious and intellectual activity of the city was a continuation and reaffirmation of the achievement of classical Greece. In its worship of the old gods, in its study of classical literature, history, and philosophy, in its rich artistic activity, in its local counterpart of the famous Olympic Games of Greece, Antioch could justly and proudly claim that it endeavored to live in the great tradition of ancient Hellas. In Antioch, the tradition had been transplanted into a barbarian land, but it lived all the more strongly for that.

Even when Antioch was changed from a Hellenistic royal capital to a Graeco-Roman metropolis, capital of one of the most important and most powerful provinces of the Roman Empire, it remained, in its culture and its social life, more Greek than Roman.

For the essential role of Antioch in the history of civilization, the significance of the Roman regime in the city was that the Roman power, by bringing commercial prosperity and by preserving the city with little real interference with its cultural life, ensured the continuation of the Greek Hellenistic social and cultural tradition.

Not Rome but Christianity was the rival to the old tradition in Antioch, and a struggle seemed clearly marked out when Christianity built one of its strongest centers here. In the world of the New Testament, the philosophy and learning of the Greeks were looked upon as vain deceit. The Christian could have nothing to do with a civilization as sensual and immoral as Hellenism. Tertullian was only echoing the thoughts of many Christians with his famous question, "What has Athens to do with Jerusalem?"

But not all Christian thinkers were willing to discard utterly the intellectual tradition of the world about them. There was much in the ancient writings—notably in the thought of Plato—that could be not only pleasing but profitable for a Christian. Hellenic literature, studied within the framework of the Christian tradition, and leaving to one side its grosser aspects, could make a valuable contribution to the education of Christians. Moreover, it was a part of the ancient national heritage of the Greek-speaking Christian, and to abandon or repudiate it would be to disown the intellectual achievement that distinguished the Greek from the barbarian. A Christian could still be proud of being a Greek.

It is here that we can see one of the spheres in which Antioch made its most significant contribution to the development of our civilization. In the fourth century of our era, the conversion of Constantine the Great and the emancipation of the Church gave a new direction to history. In both politics and society the world was changed—though the change, to be sure, was not effected all at once—and it was inevitable that the new society of the growing Christian Roman Empire should look for a new intellectual expression of its outlook on the world to replace the pagan tradition which had supported the old Roman Empire founded by Augustus. The Christian imperial regime had new political roots, and the Christian people, their religious life rooted in the Scriptures, had to consider their position vis-à-vis what had been the classical intellectual heritage of the state. Once more Christianity had turned the world upside down.

The change was as great for the pagans as for the Christians. If the pagans thought they were living through the end of one world, not all the Christians realized the shape that the new Christian world was taking; but it was in cities such as Antioch and Alexandria in the century of Constantine the Great, Julian, and Theodosius—the "new-old" fourth century, as a modern scholar has called it—that a new civilization was being built out of the living substance of the old.

Inevitably such a development took time. But by the time of Theodosius the Great at the close of the fourth century the work of the Cappadocian Fathers of the Church, notably

St. Basil the Great, had assured the acceptance of the best parts of Hellenism within Christianity, and while not all Christians would ever be prepared to follow the Hellenic tradition in their own educations, the Greek tradition was no longer in an equivocal position.

The distinction of Antioch, and the reason for its individual significance in the development of the new synthesis, was that in this single city both elements, Hellenic and Christian, lived with a special intensity and strength. They were confronted in the devotion and the energy and the faith of a Libanius and a St. John Chrysostom. When the Christians decided that they might take over and subsume the Hellenic tradition, they absorbed a certain element of strength that was to play a creative role in the Greek Christian world of the future. Thus Christianity was enriched as the work of the great masters of classical antiquity came to a new fruition. This process of harmonization passed through many hands in many places and Antioch shared the labor with other cities, notably Alexandria and Gaza. Alexandria in its own sphere played a similar role to that of Antioch.

Antioch, acting as custodian and transmitter, never fully realized the arrival of the new Athens which came to take its place along with the new Jerusalem. Instead, Antioch handed on its tradition in art and literature to Constantinople, where at the court of Justinian the Great (A.D. 527-565) the Greek Christian culture came to its full realization. It was Justinian who completed the integration of church, state, and culture which had been begun by Constantine and further developed by Theodosius the Great. By this time, the great days of Antioch were past. From this time on, in Antioch, paganism remained strong and intellectual life declined, until the city fell before the Moslem invaders. But Antioch had served its role. It had played its part as a *polis* even if another *polis*, Constantinople, brought the new synthesis to its ultimate development. Founded in an alien land, and living throughout its career in the midst of a Semitic people whom it could not wholly Hellenize, Antioch as a *polis* always had a special self-consciousness. It was the virtue of the Greek tradition that it could create this self-consciousness and give it its compelling strength.

When the vitality of the Greek intellectual achievement was joined to the power of Christianity, the resulting spiritual and intellectual force gave to Byzantine civilization an integrity and an inner strength that made Constantinople for over a thousand years the spiritual, intellectual and artistic center of the empire which had been founded by Augustus. It was this Greek Christian heritage that formed the backbone of the strength of the Byzantine Empire and enabled it to resist the assaults of so many enemies for so many centuries. The Greek people of Byzantium continually renewed their strength and courage from the two strands, Christian and classical, of their inheritance, and church and learning combined to give the empire and its people a life force they could not otherwise have had. Byzantine education, continuing the ancient and proven tradition of Athens, Antioch, and Alexandria, preserved the Greek classics for transmission to the West. Here Antioch was a vital link in the continuity between ancient Greece and the present.

Such was the energy that radiated from the city that long lay virtually unknown beneath a not very important town in the northwestern corner of Syria, cut off from contact with the western world whose civilization it had helped to shape. The course of recent scholarship in the study of Antioch and its antiquities has shown us how the progress of study only begets further progress, and how our investigation of the ancient and mediaeval world can never become a closed and finite thing, but must inevitably enlarge itself and create new insights and bring new rewards. We have only to compare our knowledge of Antioch a hundred years ago, fifty years ago, or even thirty years ago, with what we know today to understand the truth of this. We cannot expect to recover the whole of the past, and what we do possess sometimes only makes us aware how much has been lost. But we have also been learning—increasingly in recent years—how much there is that we can still hope to recover; and if we can now feel that we have reached a new prospect in our view of the ancient and mediaeval world—including Antioch—we can also know that much more lies ahead of us.

Our enlargement comes in many forms and from many sides. In the history of Antioch, we can study an epoch, a form of art or literature, or an individual figure. In any such special studies we would find both the particular and the general, the specific topic leading to the overall picture. The larger picture would be essentially the same, that of Antioch, with its people and their works, as a center for the collection, preservation, transmutation, and transmission of a tradition. And it was this that was always the real function of the classical and mediaeval city, that is, the city—the *polis*—as the natural center, in the world of those times, of every kind of activity—social, political, commercial, intellectual, and artistic. The modern city has naturally retained this function to some extent, but with the multiplication of great cities in the modern world and the diffusion of culture outside the cities, the situation is no longer quite the same. It was by virtue of its foundation as a *polis* that Antioch took up its destined role, and it was through the various stages of its development as a city that Antioch achieved its characteristic stamp and made its own special contribution to the history of civilization.

LIST OF ABBREVIATIONS

A.J.A. *American Journal of Archaeology*

Antioch-on-the-Orontes, I-IV *Antioch-on-the-Orontes (Publications of the Committee for the Excavation of Antioch and Its Vicinity)*, I: *The Excavations of 1932*, ed. by G. W. Elderkin, Princeton, 1934; *Antioch-on-the-Orontes*, II: *The Excavations, 1933-1936*, ed. by R. Stillwell, Princeton, 1938; *Antioch-on-the-Orontes*, III: *The Excavations, 1937-1939*, ed. by R. Stillwell, Princeton, 1941; *Antioch-on-the-Orontes*, IV, pt. 1: *Ceramics and Islamic Coins*, ed. by F. O. Waage, Princeton, 1948; *Antioch-on-the-Orontes*, IV, pt. 2: *Greek Roman, Byzantine and Crusaders' Coins*, by Dorothy B. Waage, Princeton, 1952.

B.C.H. *Bulletin de Correspondance Hellénique*

BMC Galatia etc. *British Museum, Catalogue of the Greek Coins of Galatia, Cappadocia and Syria*, by Warwick Wroth, London, 1899.

BMC Seleucid Kings of Syria British Museum, Catalogue of Greek Coins, Seleucid Kings of Syria, by Percy Gardner, London, 1878.

Cod. Iust. Code of Justinian

Cod. Theod. Code of Theodosius, transl. Clyde Pharr, Princeton, 1952.

F.H.G. *Fragmenta Historicorum Graecorum*, ed. C. Müller.

Förster, "Antiochia" R. Förster, "Antiochia am Orontes," *Jahrbuch des k. deutschen Archäologischen Instituts*, XII, 1897, pp. 103-149.

Guidi, "Descrizione araba" I. Guidi, "Una descrizione araba di Antiochia," *Rendiconti della R. Accademia dei Lincei, Classe di Scienze Morali, Storiche e Filologiche*, ser. 5, vol. VI, 1897, pp. 137-161.

I.G.L.S. *Inscriptions grecques et latines de la Syrie*, ed. by L. Jalabert and R. Mouterde, Paris, 1929—(in progress)

J.H.S. *Journal of Hellenic Studies*

Kraeling, "*Jewish Community*" C. H. Kraeling, "The Jewish Community at Antioch," *Journal of Biblical Literature*, LI, 1932, pp. 130-160.

279

Levi, *Antioch Mosaic Pavements*   Doro Levi, *Antioch Mosaic Pavements*, Princeton, 1947.

P.G.   Migne, *Patrologia Graeca*

P.L.   Migne, *Patrologia Latina*

R.E.   Pauly-Wissowa-Kroll, *Realencyclopädie der klassischen Altertumswissenschaft*

Sauvaget, *Alep*   J. Sauvaget, *Alep*, Paris, 1941

T.A.P.A.   Transactions of the American Philological Association

Welles, *Royal Correspondence*   C. B. Welles, *Royal Correspondence in the Hellenistic Period*, New Haven, 1934

SELECTED BIBLIOGRAPHY

(See also the works entered in the List of Abbreviations)

Bellinger, A. R., "The End of the Seleucids," *Transactions of the Connecticut Academy of Arts and Sciences*, xxxviii, 1949, pp. 51-102.

Bevan, E. R., *The House of Seleucus*, London, 1902.

Bikerman, E., *Institutions des Séleucides*, Paris, 1938.

Bouché-Leclerq, A., *Histoire des Séleucides*, Paris, 1913-1914.

Devreesse, R., *Le Patriarcat d'Antioche*, Paris, 1945.

Diehl, C., "L'École artistique d'Antioche et les Trésors d'Argenterie Syrienne," *Syria*, ii, 1921, pp. 81-95.

Dohrn, T., *Die Tyche von Antiochia*, Berlin, 1960.

Downey, G., *A History of Antioch in Syria from Seleucus to the Arab Conquest*, Princeton, 1961 (with detailed bibliography).

———, "Libanius' Oration in Praise of Antioch (Oration xi), translated with introduction and commentary," *Proceedings of the American Philosophical Society*, ciii, 1959, pp. 652-686.

———, *Antioch in the Reign of Theodosius the Great*, Norman, Oklahoma, 1962 (Centers of Civilization Series).

———, *Constantinople in the Age of Justinian*, Norman, Oklahoma, 1960 (Centers of Civilization Series).

Haddad, G., *Aspects of Social Life in Antioch in the Hellenistic-Roman Period*, Diss., Chicago; New York, 1949.

Honigmann, E., "Syria," *R.E.*, iv A (1932), cols. 1549-1727.

Jacquot, P., *Antioche, centre de tourisme*, Antioch, 1931.

Malalas. Books i-viii and xiii-xviii are cited from the Bonn edition of L. Dindorf (1831). Books ix-xii are cited from the text of A. Schenk von Stauffenberg, *Die römische Kaisergeschichte bei Malalas*, Stuttgart, 1931. "Church Slavonic Version" refers to *Chronicle of John Malalas, Books VIII-XVIII, translated from the Church Slavonic by Matthew Spinka in collaboration with Glanville Downey*, Chicago, 1940.

Morey, C. R., *Early Christian Art*, 2d ed., Princeton, 1953.

———, *The Mosaics of Antioch*, New York, 1938.

Müller, C. O., *Antiquitates Antiochenae*, Göttingen, 1839.

Pack, R. A., *Studies in Libanius and Antiochene Society under Theodosius*, Diss., Michigan, 1935.

Petit, P., *Les Étudiants de Libanius: Un Professeur de Faculté et ses Élèves au Bas Empire*, Paris, 1956.

———, *Libanius et la Vie Municipale à Antioche au IVᵉ siècle après J.-C.*, Paris, 1955.

Rorimer, J. J., "The Authenticity of the Chalice of Antioch," *Studies in Art and Literature for Belle Da Costa Greene*, Princeton, 1954, pp. 161-168.

Ross, M. C., "A Small Byzantine Treasure Found at Antioch-on-the-Orontes," *Archaeology*, v, 1952, pp. 30-32.

———, "A Silver Treasure from Daphne-Harbie," *ibid.*, vi, 1953, pp. 39-41.

Sellers, R. V., *Two Ancient Christologies: A Study in the Christological Thought of the Schools of Alexandria and Antioch in the Early History of Christian Doctrine*, London, 1940.

Stinespring, W. F., *The Description of Antioch in Codex Vaticanus Arabicus 286*, Diss., Yale, 1932, unpublished.

Weulersse, J., "Antioche, Essai de Géographie Urbaine," *Bulletin d'Études Orientales* (*Institut Français de Damas*), iv, 1934, pp. 27-79.

———, *L'Oronte: Étude de Fleuve*, Tours, 1940.

CHRONOLOGY

333 B.C. Alexander the Great passes through Syria

323 B.C. Death of Alexander the Great

300 B.C. (April) Foundation of Seleucia Pieria
(May) Foundation of Antioch

281 B.C. Death of Seleucus Nicator, founder of Antioch

246-244 B.C. Occupation of Antioch by the Egyptians

83-69 B.C. Occupation of Syria by Tigranes, King of Armenia

69-64 B.C. The last of the Seleucid rulers

64 B.C. Occupation of Syria by the Romans under Pompey

47 B.C. Julius Caesar visits Antioch

40-39 B.C. Occupation of Antioch by the Parthians

31 B.C.-A.D. 14 Reign of Augustus; public buildings of Augustus and Tiberius

ca. A.D. 34 or 36 Beginning of Christian mission at Antioch

ca. A.D. 47 Beginning of missionary journeys of St. Paul based on Antioch

A.D. 41-54 Foundation of the Olympic Games of Antioch under Claudius

A.D. 115 Great earthquake under Trajan

A.D. 235-260 Anarchy and invasion; Antioch captured by Sapor I

A.D. 261-272 Antioch dominated by the rulers of Palmyra

A.D. 284-305 Public buildings and economic revival under Diocletian

A.D. 306-337 Reign of Constantine the Great; Constantine's conversion to Christianity and the emancipation of the Christian Church

A.D. 361-363 Pagan reaction under the Emperor Julian

A.D. 387 Insurrection and destruction of the imperial statues

A.D. 458 Great earthquake under Leo I

A.D. 484 Antioch serves as headquarters for the rebellion of Illus and Leontius

A.D. 525-526 Fire and earthquake

A.D. 528 Great earthquake

A.D. 540 Antioch captured and sacked by the Persians

A.D. 542 Epidemic of the plague

A.D. 573 Suburbs of Antioch burned by the Persians

A.D. 611-628   Antioch occupied by the Persians

A.D. 637 or 638   Antioch captured by the Arabs

A.D. 969   The Byzantine Emperor Nicephorus II Phocas recaptures Antioch from the Arabs

A.D. 1084   Antioch taken by the Seljuk Turks

A.D. 1098   Antioch captured by Crusaders under Bohemond

A.D. 1098-1268   Frankish Principality of Antioch

A.D. 1268   Antioch captured by Mamelukes under Bibars

A.D. 1517   Ottoman Turks capture Antioch

INDEX

ILLUSTRATIONS

1. PANORAMA OF ANTIOCH FROM ACROSS THE ORONTES.
View of the modern city (1934) from across the Orontes river (1). The
Frankish citadel (2) crowns the top of the mountain. The ancient walls and
towers follow the top of the mountain (Fig. 8), and the remains of the
southern wall of the city (3) descend the mountain to the right of the
citadel. The road to Daphne (4) runs south, to the right of the picture.
The "Iron Gate" (5, and Fig. 9) spans the cleft of the mountain.

2. PANORAMA OF ANTIOCH FROM THE TOP OF MT. SILPIUS.
View of the modern city (1934) looking west. The Orontes river appears in
the middle ground, flowing south, towards the left of the photograph. Modern
Antakiya occupies only the southern portion of the ancient site; the remainder of the city lay in the area at the right, now covered with orchards
and fields. The dotted line shows the position of the ancient island, although
the island may not have extended as far to the right as this line indicates.
The arm of the river, which in antiquity separated the island from the
mainland part of the city, was gradually filled in during the Middle Ages
and is now represented by a depression in the ground; the ancient left bank
of the river along the mainland, opposite the island, is shown by a dotted line.
    At the left, the road to Daphne (1) follows the line of the ancient road
at this point. At the left of the road is the rectangular enclosure containing
the modern barracks (2). Trial excavations have indicated that the Christian
cemetery lies beneath this area. The barracks stand just outside the ancient
southern wall of the city (Fig. 7), which extended along the nearer side
of the watercourse seen between the barracks and the modern city (3). The
Daphne Gate (4) stood at the southern end of the main colonnaded street.
    The original Seleucid settlement lay in the southern part of the site, be-
tween the main street and the river (5). In the pre-Roman period, the street
that later became the main colonnaded street ran along the outer side of
the wall of the Seleucid city (6). Later in the Seleucid period the island
was settled, and the city also expanded up the slope of the mountain.
    Near the center of the panorama the bridge across the Orontes (7, and
Fig. 6) leads to the road to Seleucia Pieria, which runs south along the
right bank of the river (8), and to the road to Alexandretta and Cilicia,
which runs west across the plain (9). In antiquity, the plain across the river
from the city served as a Campus Martius.
    The gridiron plan of the ancient streets has been preserved in many places
in the modern city (see Figs. 4-5).
    The remains of the hippodrome may be seen on the outer side of the
island (10). The palace and the octagonal Great Church of Constantine
the Great lay near this.

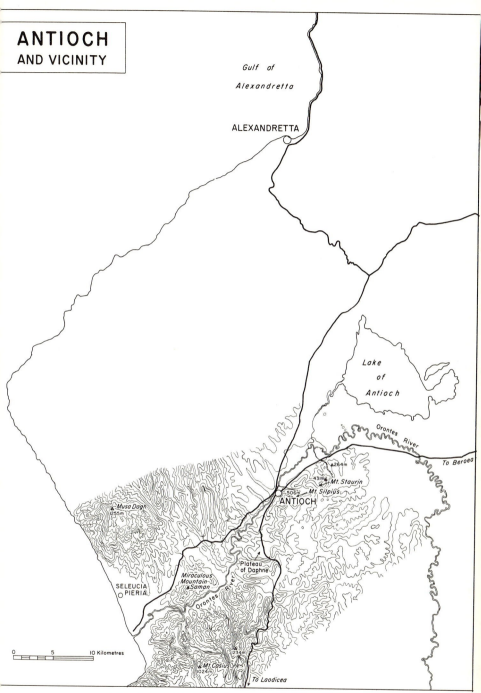

ANTIOCH AND VICINITY

Gulf of Alexandretta

ALEXANDRETTA

Lake of Antioch

Orontes River

To Beroea

▲264m

43Im▲ ▲Mt. Staurin

▲506m ▲Mt. Silpius

ANTIOCH

▲Musa Dagh
1255m

Plateau of Daphne

Miraculous Mountain
▲Saman

SELEUCIA PIERIA

Orontes River

▲234m

▲Mt.Casius
1024m

To Laodicea

0   5   10 Kilometres

3. TOPOGRAPHICAL MAP OF THE REGION OF ANTIOCH.
Contours are at intervals of 100 meters; heights are in meters above sea level.

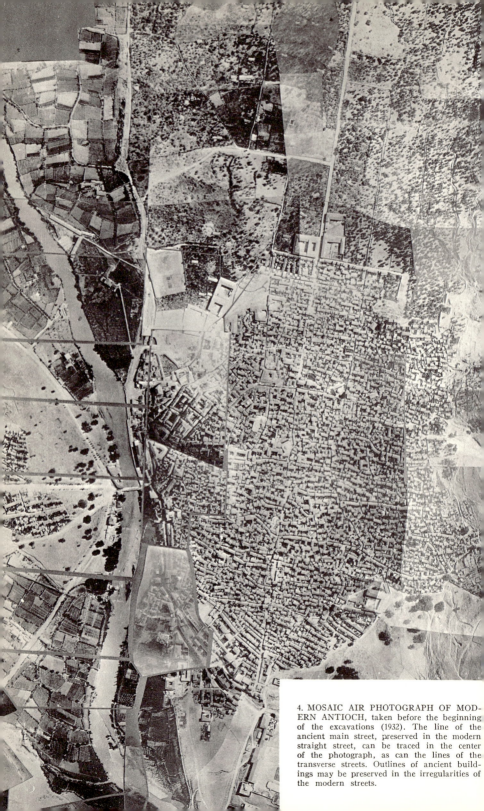

4. MOSAIC AIR PHOTOGRAPH OF MODERN ANTIOCH, taken before the beginning of the excavations (1932). The line of the ancient main street, preserved in the modern straight street, can be traced in the center of the photograph, as can the lines of the transverse streets. Outlines of ancient buildings may be preserved in the irregularities of the modern streets.

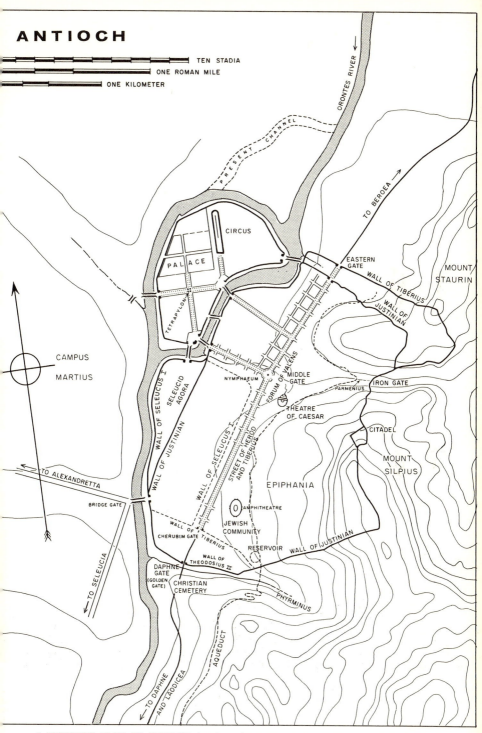

ANTIOCH

TEN STADIA
ONE ROMAN MILE
ONE KILOMETER

ORONTES RIVER

PRESENT CHANNEL

TO BEROEA

CIRCUS

PALACE

EASTERN GATE

WALL OF TIBERIUS

MOUNT STAURIN

WALL OF JUSTINIAN

TETRAPYLON

MIDDLE GATE

FORUM OF VALENS

NYMPHAEUM

PARMENIUS

IRON GATE

CAMPUS MARTIUS

SELEUCID AGORA

WALL OF SELEUCUS I

THEATRE OF CAESAR

CITADEL

WALL OF JUSTINIAN

WALL OF SELEUCUS I

STREET OF HEROD AND TIBERIUS

MOUNT SILPIUS

TO ALEXANDRETTA

EPIPHANIA

BRIDGE GATE

AMPHITHEATRE

JEWISH COMMUNITY

WALL OF TIBERIUS

CHERUBIM GATE

RESERVOIR

WALL OF JUSTINIAN

TO SELEUCIA

WALL OF THEODOSIUS II

DAPHNE GATE (GOLDEN GATE)

CHRISTIAN CEMETERY

PHYRMINUS

TO DAPHNE AND LAODICEA

AQUEDUCT

5. RESTORED PLAN OF ANTIOCH, based on the literary texts and the results of the excavations, shows monuments and topographical features that actually exist or can be traced on the terrain, and indicates the principal buildings and topographical data known from literary texts and from the excavations.

6. VIEW OF ANTIOCH FROM ACROSS THE ORONTES.
Engraving by the French artist Louis-François Cassas,
who visited the city between 1784 and 1787.

7. REMAINS OF THE SOUTHERN WALL OF THE CITY,
by Cassas. The masonry of the towers is characteristic of the period of
Justinian (A.D. 527-565).

8. VIEW OF THE WALLS ALONG THE TOP OF MOUNT SILPIUS, by Cassas.

9. THE "IRON GATE," by Cassas.
It was constructed in the city wall in the time of Justinian
to control the flow of the winter-torrent Parmenius and prevent it from
flooding the city. The ruins are in essentially the same condition today.

10. RUINS OF THE CITY WALL AND GATE, by Cassas.
The road to Beroea (Aleppo), seen from outside the city.

11. THE SAME, SEEN FROM INSIDE THE CITY.
Some of the massive paving blocks of this road were still in place and in use in 1932.

12. THE TYCHE OF ANTIOCH, Roman copy of the statue by Eutychides, now in the Vatican Museum. The goddess is seated on a rock which symbolizes Mount Silpius, and wears a turreted crown representing the city wall. The wheat in her hand symbolizes fertility and prosperity. At her feet a young swimmer represents the Orontes.

13. THE CHARONION. At the right shoulder of the bust of the Charonion stands a smaller figure. View looking east, taken after the excavation of the area below the figures in 1932.

14. (Above) SILVER COIN OF TIGRANES OF AR-
MENIA, king of Syria 83-69 B.C., struck at the mint of
Antioch, showing the head of the king and the Tyche
of Antioch (cf. Fig. 12). British Museum.

15. (Right) BRONZE COIN OF SELEUCUS I NICATOR
(d. 281/0 B.C.), struck at the mint of Antioch, showing
the head of Apollo and the statue of Athene at Antioch. American Numismatic Society.

16. (Below) SILVER TETRADRACHM OF DEMETRI-
US I SOTER (162-150 B.C.), struck at the mint of Antioch, showing the head of Demetrius and the statue of
the Tyche of Antioch holding a cornucopia. American
Numismatic Society.

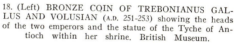

17. (Above) SILVER TETRADRACHM OF ANTIOCHUS IV (175-163 B.C.), struck at the mint of Antioch, showing the head of Apollo and the statue of Apollo which stood in the temple at Daphne. The god, dressed in a long robe, holds his lyre in his left hand and with his right hand is pouring a libation. American Numismatic Society.

18. (Left) BRONZE COIN OF TREBONIANUS GALLUS AND VOLUSIAN (A.D. 251-253) showing the heads of the two emperors and the statue of the Tyche of Antioch within her shrine. British Museum.

19. (Below) SILVER TETRADRACHM OF SELEUCUS I NICATOR (d. 281/0 B.C.), struck at the mint of Antioch, showing the statue of the youthful Herakles wearing the lion's skin, and the statue of Zeus at Antioch. Zeus, seated on his throne, holds in his hand the figure of Victory. American Numismatic Society.

20. BEARDED MALE HEAD,
marble, about 8 1/2 inches high, found in the excavation of a sculptor's shop
which seems to have specialized in statuettes.
End of first century B.C. or early part of first century A.D.

21. BRONZE GROUP, about 7 1/2 inches high, found at Antioch, interpreted as showing Hermes as the teacher of wrestling and other gymnastic sports. The wings and lotus leaf springing from Hermes' head are traditional attributes of the god. The group is thought to date from the end of the Seleucid period. Istanbul, Archaeological Museum.

22. EXCAVATION OF THE "HOUSE OF MENANDER" at Daphne, so called by the excavators because it contained the mosaic of Menander and Glykera (cf. Fig. 25). One of the largest houses explored in Antioch and Daphne, this was occupied from the first half of the second century A.D. to the fourth century.

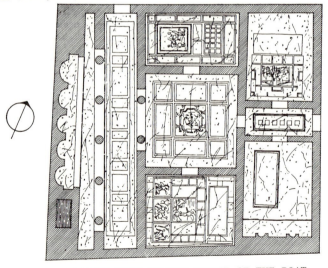

23. RESTORED PLAN OF THE "HOUSE OF THE BOAT OF PSYCHES" at Daphne, named by the excavators for a mosaic found in it. This is a typical suburban villa of the second and third centuries A.D. One entered a colonnade flanked on the right by five ornamental niches containing pools of water lined with mosaics. From the middle of the colonnade one entered the square *triclinium* or dining room. Three of the other rooms were similarly decorated with mosaics.

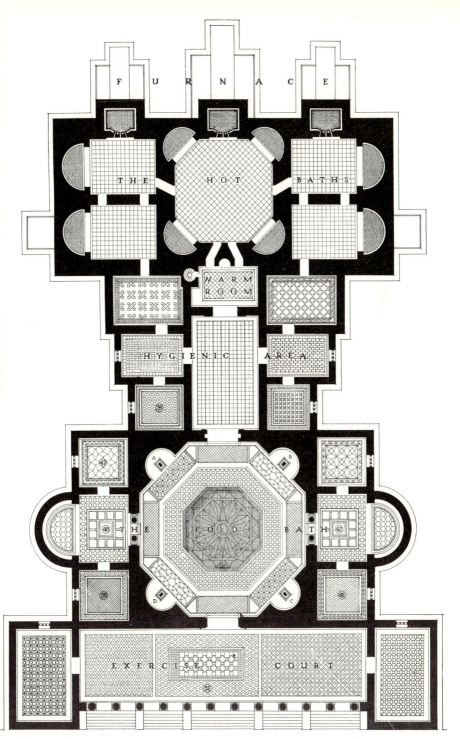

24. RESTORED PLAN OF THE LARGE PUBLIC BATH on the island in the Orontes called "Bath C" by the excavators. A typical thermal establishment, this was built in the first century A.D., destroyed in the earthquake under Trajan (A.D. 115), and rebuilt in the second half of the fourth century A.D.

25. MOSAIC OF THE COMIC POET ME-NANDER with his mistress Glykera and a personification of Comedy holding an actor's mask, while another mask rests upon the *scrinium* or case for keeping books. Found in a house at Daphne (cf. Fig. 22). Princeton University Art Museum.

26. A SCENE FROM EURIPIDES' *HIP-POLYTUS*, showing (l. to r.) Phaedra, the nurse, and Hippolytus, with a statue of Aphrodite on a pedestal at the left. On the ground lies the letter delivered to Hippolytus by the nurse. Found in a house in Daphne of the first part of the second century A.D. Antioch, Museum.

27. A SCENE FROM EURIPIDES' *IPHIGENEIA IN AULIS*,
showing (l. to r.) Iphigeneia, Clytemnestra, Agamemnon, found in a house in Antioch
of the late second or early third century A.D. Antioch, Museum.

28. MOSAIC OF THE JUDGMENT OF PARIS, found in a house of the first century A.D. on the island in the Orontes. One of five sumptuous mosaics in the *triclinium* or dining room, this shows the judgment of the three goddesses, which local tradition claimed took place at Daphne. The shepherd Paris is seated on a rock with Hermes behind him. Hera sits between Athene (on her right) and Aphrodite, all three holding long scepters. In the background a winged Psyche faces an Eros. Paris, Louvre.

29. PERSONIFICATION OF *GE*, "EARTH,"
from a house at Daphne of the middle of the fifth century A.D.
This medallion occupied the center of a floor, at the four corners of which were personifications of the four seasons. Princeton University.

30. BUST OF DIONYSUS, from the villa at Daphne of the period of Constantine the Great. Providence, Rhode Island School of Design.

31. DAPHNE AND APOLLO. The maiden Daphne is being transformed into a laurel tree to save her from Apollo. From a house at Daphne of the third century A.D. in which the mosaic of Menander and Glykera was found (cf. Fig. 22). Princeton, Committee for the Excavation of Antioch and its Vicinity.

32. DETAIL OF A MOSAIC FLOOR (42 x 34 feet), probably the pavement of an open court, showing the Phoenix, surrounded by a border of heraldic rams' heads. Fifth century A.D. Paris, Louvre.

33. BERIBBONED LION. This panel was the central figure of a mosaic floor (34 x 27 feet) which probably covered an open courtyard. Found in a house of the late fourth or fifth century A.D. at Daphne. Antioch, Museum.

34. EROTES FISHING, from the "House of Menander" (cf. Figs. 22, 25). The accurate rendition of the fish, which is typical of other mosaics at Antioch, enables them to be identified as varieties known in the Mediterranean. Washington, Dumbarton Oaks.

35. EROS RIDING A DOLPHIN, from a villa in Daphne (cf. Fig. 23). The theme is a favorite one at Antioch. Princeton University Art Museum.

36. HUNTING SCENES. MOSAIC
FLOOR (23 x 20 feet) found in a
house of ca. A.D. 500 at Daphne.
Worcester Art Museum.

37. MOSAIC SHOWING A BUFFET SUP-
PER ready to be served on a semicircular
table, with a panel depicting Ganymede giving water to the eagle of Zeus. Found in a
house of the late second or early third century at Daphne. The courses of the meal are
laid out in order, beginning at the spectator's
right. For details, see Figs. 38-40. Antioch,
Museum.

38. THE HORS D'OEUVRES—artichokes, pig's feet, and boiled eggs in cups—
served on a silver dish (detail of Fig. 37).

39. A FISH SERVED ON A SILVER PLATTER, with two round loaves of bread in the foreground (detail of Fig. 37).

40. A JOINT OF HAM SERVED ON A SILVER DISH, with a round loaf of bread in the foreground (detail of Fig. 37).

41. ENTERTAINERS, from the vestibule of a large public bath ("Bath E") on the island, near the hippodrome, dating from the early fourth century A.D. The man on the left holds a monkey resting on his left arm. The man in the center carries bagpipes near his left shoulder. The third man, bearded, carries a skin or a net hanging down over his left shoulder. From his right hand hang clappers or castanets. Antioch, Museum.

42. MAN IN A CARRIAGE, from a mosaic found in the house at Daphne which contained also the mosaics of Menander and Glykera (Fig. 25) and of Daphne and Apollo (Fig. 31). First half of the third century A.D. Antioch, Museum.

43. ORNAMENTAL PATTERNS, part of a large mosaic floor from an inn at Antioch of the sixth century A.D. The inscription illustrated in Fig. 44 is from the same inn. Antioch, Museum.

44. INSCRIPTION OF WELCOME TO AN INN at Antioch of the sixth century A.D. (cf. Fig. 43). The text opens with a phrase from I Samuel 16:4 "Thy coming is peaceful, you who behold this. Joy and blessing to those who dwell here. The paving with mosaic of the *triclinium* [dining-room] took place in the time of Megas and John and Anthusa, keepers of the inn, in the month of Gorpiaios, in the fifth indiction." Antioch, Museum.

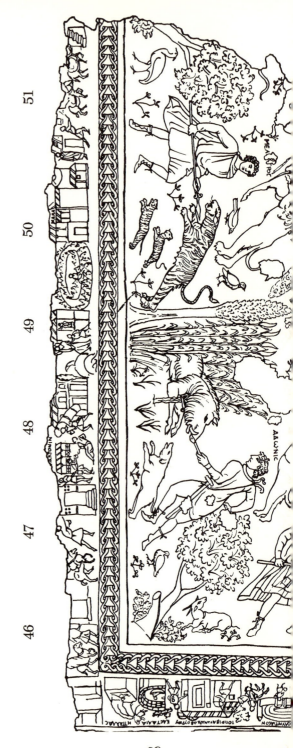

45. Mosaic floor of a large room in a villa at Daphne of the latter part of the fifth century A.D. (from a drawing). The central medallion is a personification of *Megalopsychia*, "Greatness of Soul." The names of the huntsmen are inscribed (reading counter-clockwise): Hippolytus, Meleager, Adonis, Narcissus, Tiresias, Acteon. The scenes of buildings and people around the border illustrate an imaginary tour of Antioch and Daphne beginning at the lower left corner and proceeding clockwise. Marginal numbers refer to Figs. 46 to 59, which illustrate details of the border. Antioch, Museum.

1	2	3

46. The city gate (see Fig. 10), on the road from Beroea, modern Aleppo, indicates the opening of the tour of the city (1). A man (2) leads a horse, on which a woman is riding, past a massive structure (3), which is probably a public building.

7	8	9	10	11

48. Beyond the entrance to a house (7), with grilled windows on either side of the door, a servant (8) steadies a bundle balanced on his head. In his left hand he carries a basket. In front of a two-storied café (9) with an open porch on the upper floor, a reclining patron accepts refreshment offered by servant. A porter (10) carries a rolled carpet or bundle of wood from the direction of a two-storied building (11) with a colonnade across the lower story.

MOSAIC BORDER DEPICTING A TOUR OF ANTIOCH AND DAPHNE

4   5   6

47. An official or important personage rides along the main colonnaded street, preceded by a servant clearing the way (4-6). The colonnade can be seen in the background, the dark cubes indicating the shade under the roof of the portico.

12   13   14

49. A bridge across the Orontes (12) indicates that we are passing over to the island (Fig. 5). A woman (13) leading a child approaches the bridge. From a two-storied building (14), a figure looks through a window or door of the upper story and perhaps waves farewell to the departing woman and child.

15 16 17 18

50. A rider (15) exercises his mount on a track lined with evergreen trees, probably the emperor's private track in the imperial palace. The palace (16), on the island in the Orontes, carries a colonnade on its upper story. Before it stands a column (17) bearing a statue. The octagonal Great Church of Constantine the Great (18) is surrounded by a colonnade. At the right is a figure in the attitude of prayer.

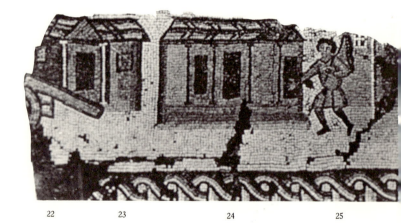

22 23 24 25

52. A portion of a cart (22) carrying a large timber disappears to the left of buildings with colonnaded fronts (23-24). A traveler (25) carries a bundle on a stick across his shoulder.

MOSAIC BORDER DEPICTING A TOUR OF ANTIOCH AND DAPHNE

19   20   21

51. A man driving two donkeys (19) approaches a set of steps (20) leading to the entrance to a building. The Orontes river or a bridge (21) indicates that the tour returns to the mainland. At this point there is a break in the sequence (see Fig. 45).

26   27

53. A man on horseback (26) is followed at a distance by a figure on foot (27).

28	29	30	31	32	33

54. The colonnades of a principal street (28) show tie-rods between the columns. Beyond imperial statues on pedestals (29, 31, 32) and the winter-torrent Parmenius (30), two men play a game (33) before a large building with a colonnaded upper story.

37	38	39	40	41

56. The trees (38) symbolize the road from Antioch to Daphne. The inclusion at this point of three villas bearing the names of their masters suggests that the owner of the mosaic instructed the artist to include the residences of three special friends. The first villa (39), either in Daphne or on the road to it, belongs to Maieourinos (Latin Majorinus). A man with a small boy (40) stands before it, possibly Maieourinos and his son. The villa of Heliades (41) and

MOSAIC BORDER DEPICTING A TOUR OF ANTIOCH AND DAPHNE

34   35   36

55. To the right of a figure (34) standing on the steps of a building, meat is prepared and sold on three-legged portable chopping blocks (35), and a man purchases a round loaf of bread from a vendor with a portable table (36). Here the Tour turns the corner of the Border where, as seen below, a vendor (shown vertically) has his wares spread out on a table (37).

42   43   44   45   46

57. . . . the villa of Leontios (42) are shown next with a servant (43), his status indicated by the short tunic, carrying parcels. A figure in front of "The Public Bath" (44) may represent an honorific statue of the donor. A man (45) sells refreshments from a table outside "The Covered Walk" (46), a public place of recreation, which affords among other things an opportunity for a game resembling dominoes or checkers (also shown in No. 33).

47 48 49

58. In front of the "Workshops of the Martyrion" (47), where souvenirs were made for pilgrims to the shrine of St. Babylas, reclines the manager of the establishment, Markellinos (Latin Marcellinus), accompanied by his dog. At the left, a servant, Chalkomas, offers refreshment to his master. A group (48) composed of a man, an elderly woman, and a young woman seem to pause to the left of "The Olympic Stadium" (49), which has a tower and a monumental entrance gate. A servant carries a basket, and beyond him a rider approaches a private bath, an establishment that, as distinct from a public bath, charges an entrance fee.

60. Scene from the topographical border (Fig. 54, No. 33) compared with a snapshot opposite taken at Antioch immediately after the mosaic had been discovered.

MOSAIC BORDER DEPICTING A TOUR OF ANTIOCH AND DAPHNE

50   51   52

59. This "Private Bath of Ardabourios" (50), with two domes, has a garden symbolized by foliage at the left. A servant on foot clears the way before the rider. On the right, a servant carries a bundle toward the entrance to the bath. The spring "Kastalia" (51) is represented by a tree and the colonnaded semicircular reservoir in which the water of the spring was received. Another spring called "Pallas" (52) flows into a reservoir in which a swimming figure symbolizes the deity of the spring.

61-63. SCENES FROM THE HOUSE OF THE EVIL EYE (first century A.D.). Herakles as an infant strangles two serpents (Fig. 61), foreshadowing his later "labors." Magic and superstition, a common feature of life in the ancient Mediterranean world, are illustrated in "The Lucky Hunchback" (Fig. 62) and "The Evil Eye" (Fig. 63). In the former, the Lucky Hunchback bears pointed objects turned against the Evil One. In the latter, the Evil Eye is attacked by popular talismans: raven, trident, sword, scorpion, serpent, dog, centipede, panther.

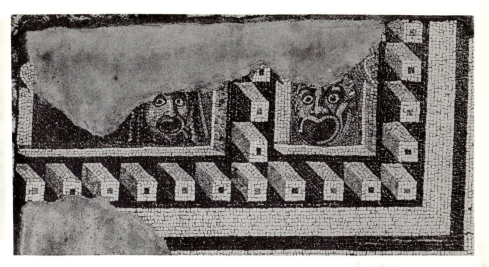

64-65. INTEREST IN *TROMPE-L'OEIL* EFFECTS is demonstrated in a border framing a tragic and a comic mask (Fig. 64) from the "House of the Mysteries of Isis" (early third century A.D.); and a geometric decoration (Fig. 65) from the "House of Menander" imitates a coffered ceiling reflected in the waters of a pool (third century A.D.; cf. Figs. 22, 25, 31, 34, 42).

66-67. Realistic genre scenes like this one from the "Constantinian Villa," in which a dog watches expectantly as his master ties on his hunting boots, are in sharp contrast to the delicate decorative effect of a border from the same villa in which a rounded classic face is framed in leaves.

68-69. A carefully-reproduced architectural frieze from the "House of Dionysus and Ariadne" (early third century A.D.) contrasts with a graceful floral border of a floor from the "House of the Buffet Supper," in which spring flowers accent a more elaborate continuous design (late second or early third century A.D.; cf. Figs. 37-40).

70. THE ANTIOCH CHALICE, detail.
Metropolitan Museum of Art,
The Cloisters.

71. INSCRIBED SILVER ALTAR CROSS of the sixth century A.D., found at Hama. "Kyriakos, having made a vow, presented (this cross) to St. Sergius." Walters Art Gallery.

72. INSCRIBED SILVER CHALICE used in the eucharist, dated in the sixth century A.D., found at Hama. On the sides are representations of four saints. Walters Art Gallery.

73. SILVER CANDLESTICK of the early seventh century, found in the excavations at Antioch. Dumbarton Oaks.

74. SILVER VASE of the fourth century A.D., found in Syria. Cleveland Museum of Art.

75. SILVER SPOONS (sixth century A.D.) used in the administration of the eucharist, found at Hama. The spoon on the left is inscribed "From Thomas and John, sons of Theophilus." The spoon on the right is inscribed "In fulfilment of the vow of Heliodorus." Walters Art Gallery.

76. SILVER SAUCE BOAT of the fourth century A.D., found in Syria. Cleveland Museum of Art.

77. SILVER BOWL of the fourth century A.D.,
found in Syria. Cleveland Museum of Art.

78. SILVER EUCHARISTIC PATEN of the sixth century A.D., found at Hama.
"(Property) of (the church of) St.' Sergius, in memory of Baradatus, son of
Heliodorus." Walters Art Gallery.

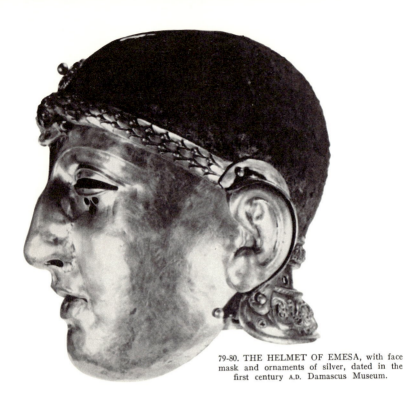

79-80. THE HELMET OF EMESA, with face mask and ornaments of silver, dated in the first century A.D. Damascus Museum.